SOCIAL HOUSING

SOCIAL HOUSING: AN INTRODUCTION

STEPHEN HARRIOTT AND LESLEY MATTHEWS
(with Paul Grainger)

 LONGMAN

Addison Wesley Longman Limited
Edinburgh Gate, Harlow
Essex CM20 2JE, England
and Associated Companies throughout the world

First published 1998

ISBN 0-582-28534-8

British Library Cataloguing in Publication Data

A catalogue record for this book is
available from the British Library

Set by 30 in Baskerville
Produced through Longman Malaysia, ACM.

CONTENTS

ABOUT THE AUTHORS

Stephen Harriott is Managing Director of English Churches Housing Group. He has experience of housing management at all levels in a variety of different social housing organisations, including local authorities. He has also lectured on a range of professional housing courses in higher education and has contributed to many staff development and training initiatives. He is a former Branch Education and Training Officer and Chair of the Northern Region Branch of the Chartered Institute of Housing.

Lesley Matthews is a Principal Lecturer and Programme Director in the Division of Housing Studies, University of Northumbria at Newcastle, which is designated as the Northern Regional Centre for Housing Education by the Chartered Institute of Housing. She has lectured to students with an interest in housing for many years and contributed to the development of a full range of Chartered Institute of Housing approved professional housing courses at the university. She is currently responsible for all academic issues relating to housing courses at the University of Northumbria, and teaches a wide range of both full-time and part-time students of housing.

ACKNOWLEDGEMENTS

We gratefully acknowledge the contributions of:

Paul Grainger, who wrote large parts of Chapter 2 of the book, sections for Chapter 7, read initial drafts and offered valuable comments on other sections. He is an experienced housing manager who has held a number of senior positions in local authority housing departments. He is currently a lecturer in Housing Studies at the University of Northumbria at Newcastle whilst awaiting the call to play in midfield for Middlesbrough Football Club. Having reached the age of 36 Paul suspects that the call is never going to come!

Paul Crompton, who provided invaluable help in assisting us to clarify our initial ideas for the book and to define its focus and structure. He is Head of the Division of Housing Studies at the University of Northumbria at Newcastle, with substantial experience as a principal lecturer in housing studies. He initiated and led the development of a full range of professional housing courses at the University.

Many other people have contributed, both intentionally and unintentionally, to the development of this book, not least the students on the various professional housing courses at the University of Northumbria at Newcastle as well as our colleagues in housing throughout the North East of England and elsewhere. Our respective families are also owed a debt of gratitude for readily accepting our many absences from family life during the writing of this book.

Our thanks are offered also to those who have so generously given permission to publish their work, especially to Edwin Trotter of Edwin Trotter Associates for permission to use his design drawings of Turnbull Street and other material; George Kennedy of G.R. Kennedy, Chartered Architects of Dunoon, Scotland, for so kindly supplying a range of materials relating to the redevelopment of Commercial Buildings; Newcastle City Council, which gave permission to reproduce their Tenants Repairs Receipt; the Policy Press for Figure 5.2, the Vacancy Matrix, taken from Smith and Merrett (1988) *The Challenge of Empty Housing;* and Tees Valley Housing Association which kindly allowed use of their Repairs satisfaction survey card. Thanks are offered also to Dianne Mulcaster for word processing parts of the text; to Jonathon Smurthwaite for help with the index; and to Rosemary Whalton (University of Northumbria), Alison Thain, Barrie Westbrook, Carol Middleton, Mick Glew and Alison Behan for commenting on various early drafts of the text.

Any opinions expressed in the text are, of course, entirely our own, and we remain responsible for these as well as any unintended errors.

This book was completed in the spring of 1997 and the election of the Labour government in May 1997 will almost certainly have an impact on key housing policies, such as Compulsory Competitive Tendering and the use of capital receipts from council house sales. Chapter 7 includes a small section on recent developments to September 1997 but readers should keep abreast of developments through the housing press, in particular by reading *Inside Housing, Housing Today, Housing Magazine, Housing Review, Agenda* and *Roof.*

LIST OF ABBREVIATIONS

ACG Annual capital guide guideline. The government's limit for each local authority's capital spending programme.

ADB Approved development body. Welsh housing associations who were approved by Tai Cymru to obtain capital allocations. No longer applies since the introduction of rent bidding in 1995.

ADP Approved development programme. This is the Housing Corporation's total capital programme in any one year. It is normally broken down into rented housing, shared ownership and other home ownership initiatives.

AI Architect's instruction. This is an instruction to a contractor in relation to a building contract.

BCA Basic credit approval. A limit set by the government annually on the borrowing each local authority can undertake for all capital projects.

BES Business expansion scheme. A scheme (no longer available) which allowed investors to invest money in the private rented sector and obtain significant tax benefits.

CCT Compulsory competitive tendering. A government initiative which requires local authorities to submit the delivery of parts of their services to competitive tendering. Introduced into housing management services from 1995.

CDM Construction, Design and Management Regulations. Introduced by the Health and Safety Executive placing obligations on clients in relation to health and safety. In particular they require most construction projects to have a planning supervisor appointed.

CIH Chartered Institute of Housing. This is the professional body for housing managers.

CIS Cash incentive scheme. This offers a cash giant like TIS but is operated by local authorities with government support. The cash grant assists tenants to buy a property in the open market. The amounts vary between local authorities.

CTB Council tax benefit. A subsidy paid to low income households to reduce their council tax liability.

DIYSO Do-it-yourself shared ownership. This is a housing association scheme where applicants can ask a housing association to buy a private property and the applicant part buys and part rents the property from the association. They can increase their share of the property by staircasing up;

	eventually to outright ownership. The scheme is only open to council or housing association tenants and the resulting vacancy must be let to an applicant in priority need.
DoE	Department of the Environment.
ERCF	Estates renewal challenge fund. A government initiative introduction in 1996 to offer grants to local authorities to transfer their stock to new landlords who would be able to carry out refurbishment works. The grant was necessary to enable transfer to take place as most had a negative market value.
EU	European Union.
GNI	General needs index. A government compiled index of need used as a factor to allocate resources to local authorities.
GNP	Gross national product. The annual value of output of the United Kingdom economy.
GRF	Grant redemption fund. Established in the 1980 Housing Act to recoup revenue surpluses generated in housing association accounts from fair rent increases. Abolished in the 1988 Housing Act and partly replaced by the Rent Surplus Fund (RSF).
HAG	Housing association grant. A capital grant from the Housing Corporation/Scottish Homes/Tai Cymru to registered housing associations for capital works. Now renamed social housing grant in England and Wales as a result of the 1996 Housing Act.
HAMA	Housing associations as managing agents. An initiative promoted in the mid-1990s where housing associations would manage empty properties on behalf of private owners and landlords and rent out the properties.
HAT	Housing action trust. Set up under the 1988 Housing Act to undertake large scale refurbishment of council housing stock. At the end of the trust's life the tenants will have the option of returning to local authority or to new landlords.
HB	Housing benefit; the main means tested benefit towards meeting the rented housing costs of low income households.
HC	Housing Corporation.
HIP	Housing investment programme. Refers to the local authority's annual bid for capital resources from the government.
HMP	Housing market package. A one-off initiative in 1992/93 which allocated HAG to housing associations to purchase properties in the private sector in an effort to kick-start the housing market.
HNI	Housing needs index. A housing corporation index of housing need used in resource allocations decisions.
HRA	Housing revenue account. This is the revenue account which all housing authorities have to establish for their council housing activities. Since the 1989 Local Government and Housing Act this account has been ring-fenced and must balance.
JCT	Joint Contracts Tribunal. A professional body which issues draft building contracts reflecting the needs of client and contractors.
LA HAG	Local authority housing association grant. This is similar to HAG except the grant comes from the local authority itself rather than through the Housing Corporation/Scottish Homes/Tai Cymru.

LHC	Local housing company. This is a new form of registered social landlord created under the 1996 Housing Act. These bodies will be set up by local authorities and associations and will be controlled by a board with typically councillors, tenants and independent members in equal proportions.
LSE	Leasehold schemes for the elderly. A form of shared ownership where a housing association develops a scheme for the elderly which is sold at 75 per cent of the market value.
LSVT	Large-scale voluntary transfer. This refers to the transfer of council owned stock to a housing association, normally one which has been set up specifically to receive the council housing stock. The resulting associations have become known as LSVT associations.
MIRAS	Mortgage interest tax relief at source. An Inland Revenue scheme which enables tax relief to be deducted from the mortgage interest payments due rather than via individual's own tax code.
MITR	Mortgage interest tax relief. Mortgage interest currently attracts tax relief at 15 per cent on the interest of the first £30,000 of a mortgage.
NFHA	The National Federation of Housing Associations. This represents the interest and concerns of housing associations in England. Following the 1996 Housing Act which introduced the concept of registered social landlords the NFHA changed its name to the National Housing Federation to enable non-housing associations, such as local housing companies, to join.
NHBC	National House Builders Council. The trade body for house builders. Offers ten-year building guarantees and undertakes building inspectors' work.
NHF	National Housing Federation. See NFHA.
NIHE	Northern Ireland Housing Executive. The NIHE provides 'council' housing in Northern Ireland, rather than the local authorities.
PES	Public expenditure survey. Undertaken by the Treasury on an annual basis.
PFI	Private finance initiative. A government scheme designed to encourage private finance into public sector capital projects.
PPBS	Planning, Programming Budgeting Systems. A method of budget setting which focuses on objectives and alternative ways of meeting them.
PRS	Private rented sector.
PSBR	Public sector borrowing requirement. This is the annual amount which the public sector needs to borrow to meet its expenditure plans.
PSL	Private sector leasing. Similar to HAMA where associations and local authorities lease privately owned properties usually to house homeless households.
QS	Quantity surveyor.
RCCOs	Revenue contributions to capital outlays. These are amounts of money set aside in the housing revenue account to pay for capital improvements to council housing out of rental revenue income.
RSF	Rent surplus fund. Set up after the 1988 Housing Act to set aside part of the surpluses of housing associations as a result of fair rent increases to provide for major repairs to their stock.
RSL	Registered social landlord. A new term introduced into the 1996

Housing Act which refers to organisations registered with the Housing Corporation and Tai Cymru. These could be housing associations or local companies.

RSG   Revenue support grant. The annual sum of money made available by the government to subsidise a local authority's revenue spending.

RTB   Right to buy. Introduced in the 1980 Housing Act which enables qualifying tenants to buy their property at a discount.

RTIAs   Receipts taken into account. These are the projected capital receipts from sales which the government takes into account when deciding on capital borrowing allocations to local authorities.

SCA   Supplementary credit approvals. These are additional borrowing approvals granted to local authorities by government (in addition to the BCA) for specific projects.

SCG   Specified capital grant. Allowances in the ACG for specific private sector grants such as improvement grants.

SH   Scottish Homes.

SHG   Social housing grants. The new name for HAG as a result of the 1996 Housing Act. The name had to be changed as SHG is now payable to registered social landlords other than housing associations; such as local housing companies.

SO   Shared ownership. This is where associations develop schemes and sell them on a part buy part rent basis, with owners taking a 25 per cent, 50 per cent or 100 per cent share. The remaining equity is owned by the association which charges a rent for this. In later years shared owners can increase their equity stake and eventually staircase to full ownership.

SOE   Shared ownership for the elderly. This is like LSE although under SOE properties can be sold at 50 per cent of the value, with applicants renting the remaining share to 75 per cent of the value.

SOOTS   Shared ownership off the shelf. A Scottish Homes scheme similar to DIYSO.

SRB   Single regeneration budget. Operates in England and includes the budgets of many government departments concerned with regeneration. Since 1995 local authorities have been able to bid for SRB funds in a series of bidding rounds. The successful bids receive funding over a seven-year period from the government to implement these bids. The bids include partnerships between the private and public sectors.

SSA   Standard spending assessment. A government assessment of necessary revenue expenditure by each local authority on individual services. It is used in the determination of the revenue support grant.

TCI   Total cost indicators. These are costs which the Housing Corporation and Tai Cymru publish annually which show maximum allowable costs for new developments to be funded by SHG.

THFC   The Housing Finance Corporation. A body set up to obtain private loans for a number of smaller housing associations who might find it difficult or more expensive to arrange loans on their own behalf.

TIC   Total indicative cost. Allowable capital costs for housing association schemes published by Scottish Homes. Similar to TCI.

TIS   Tenants incentive scheme. This is a housing association scheme which gives existing tenants a cash grant to assist them in buying a property in the open market. The amounts vary between local authorities. The resulting vacancy must be let to an applicant in priority need.

TMV   Tenanted market value. The assumed market value of an estate which takes account of the predicted net income of the stock.

TPAS   Tenants Participation Advisory Service. A consultancy set up to promote tenant participation. Used extensively by local authorities and housing associations.

UBR   Uniform business rate. Business rates, once set by individual local authorities, are now set nationally by the government.

Chapter 1

AN INTRODUCTION TO SOCIAL HOUSING

1.1 Introduction

This text is primarily directed at students of housing studies who wish to learn about the nature of *social* housing in the United Kingdom, the key features of its management, and its place in the United Kingdom housing system. It has been written specifically for those pursuing (or interested in) a career in social housing management, and for individuals new to the profession, since it reflects the requirements of Part One of the Chartered Institute of Housing's (CIH) Professional Qualification. It is, therefore, particularly suited to courses of study such as the BTEC Higher National Certificate in Housing Studies and the Graduate Foundation Course of the CIH, as well as undergraduate degrees in Housing Studies. However, this text will also be useful to anyone with an interest in social housing or social housing management, such as those taking a wide range of courses in social policy, public administration, estate management, building management, housing development or surveying.

This first chapter introduces the concept of *social housing*, initially by considering what is meant by social housing in the context of the United Kingdom and then tracing its historical development and the reasons for (and nature of) the involvement of the public sector in housing provision. It then identifies the types of organisations which provide social housing in the United Kingdom today, and considers how they vary in size and location. Finally, there is a brief examination of what is involved in the *management* of social housing provision by these organisations, which is the primary focus for much of the rest of the text.

Chapter 2 considers the wider context within which social housing is provided by housing organisations, examining the place of social housing in the United Kingdom housing system. Most housing in the United Kingdom is provided within a market system, which basically means that it is allocated according to the ability to pay. Social housing is different in this key respect. This chapter explores the significance of these different *tenures*, each distinguished by differing legal rights and obligations attached to occupation. Tenures exhibit many differences, in terms of influences on their provision, their changing size and importance, the types of households they attract, the types of property they contain and the condition of those properties. These differences are explored in some detail, as well as the ways in which different tenures interact with each other. Tenure is not static, in that properties may transfer between tenures. The main movement during this century has been from the private rented sector to owner occupation, as private landlords sold their properties to private buyers. However, since 1980, there has also been a significant switch from local authority tenure to owner occupation, mainly as a result of government policies permitting local authority tenants to purchase their homes with substantial discounts – the *right to buy* policy. The effects of these changes are also considered.

Chapter 3 resumes the examination of the management of social housing, with an exploration of the financial framework within which social housing providers operate. Since this is the first, essential step to achieving a social housing scheme, it considers the significant influence of the *economic context* for public housing finance, as well as the specific financial frameworks which govern the provision of finance to social housing organisations. This is examined not just in the context of differences applicable to different social tenures, but also in the context of increasing government emphasis on the *targeting* of financial subsidy to those most in need, via means-tested housing benefit payments. It also examines other ways in which public finance for housing has been redirected in recent years, and the reasons for these changed priorities.

As the next step in the achievement of a social housing scheme, Chapter 4 turns to the *process* by which social housing is *developed* in the United Kingdom, with a detailed examination of the steps which are essential to achieving a social housing development or refurbishment. It identifies the roles of different professionals in the development process, and considers the requirements of the various stages in development, from a management perspective. It identifies key aspects which will influence the likely success of the constructed scheme, both for its occupiers and for those who must manage it.

The development of a new social housing scheme having been dealt with, Chapter 5 examines the tasks which are conventionally viewed as 'housing management' tasks, in that it identifies the key roles of social housing managers in allocating social housing, setting and collecting the rents, and ensuring that the stock is adequately maintained. These are the 'front-line' tasks of housing managers, the activities which will most directly affect tenants and hence their satisfaction with the service provided. Approaches to these key tasks are explored in some detail, and issues of 'best practice' identified.

Chapter 6 moves on to consider the delivery of the social housing service in more detail, by examining different possible approaches to *organising the housing service*. It considers the different ways in which the delivery of the key tasks can be structured in social housing organisations, and the reasons for this. In recent years, there have been a number of important influences on service delivery which have resulted in many different approaches. These include the growth of different forms of *tenant participation* in the management process, the *decentralisation* (and recentralisation) of some key management tasks, and the introduction of *compulsory competitive tendering* (CCT) for the management of council housing.

Finally, Chapter 7 explores the *changing face of social housing*, drawing together and reflecting on some of the issues identified in the other chapters. Over recent years, the nature of social housing provision and social housing organisations has undergone substantial change. This results primarily from the housing policies of the Conservative governments since 1979, which focused on private sector provision and a considerably reduced role for the public sector. The increased role for local authorities as *enablers* has resulted in new partnership approaches with other providers. However, there are also concerns that social housing tenants comprise, increasingly, only the most disadvantaged households in the United Kingdom, with wider implications arising from this form of social exclusion. This chapter explores the possible future direction for social housing, in the light of these recent developments and the election in May 1997 of a new Labour Government.

1.2 What is social housing?

The use of the term *social housing* is relatively recent in the United Kingdom. It is generally understood to refer to housing provided and managed by local authorities – commonly called *council housing* – and (more recently) by housing associations and other organisations which together form *the voluntary housing movement*. These organisations are 'voluntary' in the sense that, unlike local authorities, they have no statutory obligation – an obligation imposed by a *statute* (a law passed by Parliament) – to provide housing. In general, however, the essential characteristic of social housing is that it is provided by organisations which do not seek to make a profit.

Social housing organisations generally provide homes for those households which find it difficult to obtain a home of an appropriate size or quality in private housing markets. This may result from low incomes, which means that private rents and prices are not affordable, or there may be other reasons why access to suitable housing is difficult, for example, for some households or individuals with special needs. The involvement of the public sector in the provision of housing was intended to help to meet these housing needs, to ensure that every household (regardless of income) could attain a decent home.

Since social housing providers exist to ensure that homes are available to households in housing need, the process of obtaining access to social housing is very different to the private tenures. In the private rented sector, or in owner-occupied markets, the ability to obtain a home depends very heavily on the *ability to pay* for it. In general (unless there is discrimination), if households have sufficient income they can obtain a property of the type they want. Their *demand* for housing – the desire for housing backed by the ability to pay for it – will ultimately be met by a private housing provider.

In contrast, in the social tenures the ability to pay is *not* a criterion. In the absence of any *supply constraints* – a shortage of available properties to let – social housing organisations could permit anyone who wanted a home to occupy, and pay rent for, one of their properties. However, there *are* shortages in the supply of social housing. In most areas of the United Kingdom, there are insufficient homes in the social housing sector to meet the requirements of everyone who might want properties. For this reason, social housing organisations must identify (and publish) the criteria by which they will determine which households gain access and which do not. These are known as *allocations policies*, which are examined in detail in Chapter 5.

In addition to providing homes, local authorities are also an important vehicle through which the government provides various types of financial subsidy to the housing costs of individual households, including those in social housing. For example, most households with low incomes may obtain *housing benefit*, which pays some or all of the property's rental costs. Indeed, a very large (and increasing) proportion of social housing tenants are in receipt of housing benefit, and this is examined in detail in Chapter 3.

The nature of the housing provided by local authorities and housing associations varies considerably, in part reflecting differences in the housing needs which different organisations attempt to meet. A number of housing associations exist primarily to provide housing for one particular type of housing need, such as for the elderly, so their properties will reflect this specialism. Until recently, local authorities were more likely to provide homes for general, family needs, so they tend to have higher proportions of houses than housing associations. However, some local authorities, particularly large urban authorities, have considerable numbers of flats in tower blocks. In Glasgow, for example, the local authority has over 20,000 flats in tower blocks (Hansard, 19/3/96). The largest estates have been built by local authorities, some of them extremely large and typically located on the outskirts of big cities. In contrast, housing association estates tend to be small, and may only consist of a single building, such as a hostel, or two or three properties on a small rural development. Hence, there is no *typical* profile for the housing stock of different providers. Social housing is provided in all varieties of building and in a huge range of locations.

1.3 How has social housing evolved in the United Kingdom?

Prior to the advent of social housing provision in the United Kingdom, households with low incomes were unable to afford the private, market rents which were demanded for decent housing. They were forced to make do with whatever they could afford, which meant either renting substandard, *slum* housing and/or living in very cramped, overcrowded conditions. By the mid-nineteenth century, these problems had become particularly acute in the rapidly expanding urban areas of the United Kingdom. It was concerns about the impact of these overcrowded conditions on public health and the environment which first led to government involvement in housing issues.

Regulation: nineteenth- and early twentieth-century public intervention

In 1846, the first Nuisances Removal Act permitted local authorities to take action to deal with acute public health problems, such as the *middens* which provided working-class sanitary facilities. The Public Health Act of 1848 permitted the setting up of local

Health Boards, intended to address problems of sanitation and reduce the incidence of epidemics of cholera and typhoid, which regularly swept through the overcrowded dwellings in urban areas. Later, the Torrens Act of 1868 permitted local authorities to demolish properties which were *unfit for human habitation*, and an attempt was made to address the problems of poor quality building standards with the 1875 Public Health Act, which encouraged local 'by-laws' for minimum standards of construction. Shortly after, the Cross Act (Artisans' and Labourers' Dwellings Improvement Act) of 1875 extended the powers of *clearance* – demolition – to entire slum areas.

These Acts marked the beginning of attempts to *regulate* the private provision of housing, but the view of most politicians at that time was that housing provision, and its finance, were private sector concerns. In general, the Acts gave *enabling powers* to local authorities rather than statutory *duties*, and since local authorities' incomes were raised from their local populations, local voters were reluctant to take on any unnecessary obligations which would raise their taxes. These voters were also likely to be the landlords of the overcrowded properties. The result was that, when the Shaftesbury Acts (the Labouring Classes' Lodging Houses Act and the Common Lodging Houses Act) were passed in 1851, local authorities largely ignored their new powers to build housing.

The Housing of the Working Classes Act of 1890, which largely consolidated and amended earlier Acts, again permitted local authorities to provide council housing; but since no government subsidy was available and the finance had to be found by the local authorities themselves, for reasons identified above, few councils engaged in housing provision or slum clearance.

Around this time, however, a number of private benefactors, appalled by the housing conditions in which many households lived, set up charitable trusts to provide private finance for decent rented housing – individuals such as Peabody, Guinness and Rothschild – but the scope of the problem was such that they made little impact; and, due to the quality of the dwellings provided, the rents were relatively high, affordable only by skilled workers.

Octavia Hill, viewed by some as the founder of modern housing management, took a somewhat different approach, focusing on the improved management of existing properties *and their tenants*. She effectively combined improved housing management with social work, and '...was able to show that, by an authoritarian, labour-intensive system of management, using trained middle-class women managers and rent collectors, it was possible to make profits out of housing the poor in decent conditions' (Malpass and Murie, 1994, p. 36).

The extent to which social housing management should reflect a 'social work' dimension remains, to this day, a topic for debate amongst social housing managers, and is explored in the final chapter. Malpass and Murie argue that the later municipalisation of working-class housing resulted in the redefinition of housing management as 'a bureaucratic-administrative activity done by men' (p. 37), with few elements of the Octavia Hill approach.

In the early twentieth century, the government first intervened more directly in housing markets with the introduction of *rent controls* in 1915, in response to rapidly rising rents at the start of the First World War. This fixed private rents at pre-war levels, effectively forcing private landlords to subsidise the housing costs of their tenants. Some form of rent control – latterly known as 'fair rents' – largely existed from then until their abolition (for new tenancies) in the 1988 Housing Act. By reducing the returns available to private landlords, rent controls undoubtedly contributed to the decline of the private rented sector in the United Kingdom since the First World War.

Twentieth century: the emergence of council provision in the inter-war years

The first significant involvement of the public sector in the *provision* of housing followed the end of the First World War. There were chronic housing shortages, and council house building was viewed as the best and quickest way to respond effectively to the situation. With the Housing and Planning Act (the Addison Act) of 1919, the government encouraged councils to build new homes by, for the first time, offering significant subsidies. The Tudor Walters Report of 1918 changed perceptions about house design, so that the preferred home changed from the tightly packed, 'high density' form of nineteenth century terraced housing for the working classes to more spacious environments of homes with a garden and inside amenities (baths and WCs). Many council homes were built with a 'garden village' approach in the 1920s when the quality of council housing was high but rents were beyond the reach of the poorest. The later Wheatley Act (Housing (Financial Provisions) Act) of 1924 improved the subsidy arrangements, so that by 1939 over a million council homes had been produced, representing around 10 per cent of the total housing stock (Malpass and Murie, 1994).

In 1930, the Greenwood Act changed the emphasis of housing policy from simply expanding housing supply to *slum clearance*, encouraging councils to demolish sub-standard dwellings and provide new council homes for their occupiers. This was intended to supplement the provisions of the Wheatley Act, but by the early thirties, the government was under pressure to reduce public spending. As a result, the Housing (Financial Provisions) Act of 1933 repealed the Wheatley Act, so that subsidy was now available *only* to build new housing for households from slum clearance areas. Local authorities did succeed in rehousing large numbers of households – over a quarter of a million homes were demolished between 1931 and 1939 – but the quality of new council homes declined during this period, and councils now had new problems, with large numbers of much poorer tenants from the demolished slums.

Until 1935, the financial accounts of new council estates were effectively separated, depending on the Act (the subsidy system) under which they had been provided. This meant that tenants in properties built with lower subsidies had to pay higher rents. Partly as a way of helping councils to introduce *rebates* on rents for poor tenants, a new unified Housing Revenue Account was introduced by the 1935 Housing Act, so that subsidies could be transferred between schemes. Much later, this would permit councils to cross-subsidise newer schemes from the rents of older schemes. The more recent evolution of local authority housing revenue accounts is examined in Chapter 3, while rent setting is examined in Chapter 5.

Expansion of council housing and owner occupation following the Second World War

The Second World War created new and acute housing shortages. During the war, there was very little construction or repair, and, in contrast to the First World War, around 400,000 homes were destroyed by bombing. Public sector attention was, therefore, directed once again to expanding the supply of housing, and for a time, slum clearance virtually ceased. The Housing (Financial and Miscellaneous Provisions) Act of 1946 introduced new subsidies, and in response to shortages, a system of building licences ensured that construction activity was undertaken largely by councils. This was also the period in which new, *system-built* techniques of construction were first introduced, employing factory produced components in an attempt to reduce the need for skilled labour.

By the early 1950s there was a new Conservative government that wished to encourage greater private sector provision. Building licences were phased out, and as council house building declined (except for slum clearance), there was a boom in the construction of properties for owner occupation. As subsidies were progressively reduced during the fifties and early sixties, councils were encouraged to build high- density developments, including high-rise and medium-rise blocks of flats (which attracted higher levels of subsidy from 1956 to 1967). Many of the system-built developments proved to be particularly problematic in management terms, due both to poor design and poor standards of construction, and a number have since been demolished.

The 1957 Rent Act removed rent controls from better quality private rented properties, with decontrol of the remainder as they became vacant. This was intended to revive the private rented sector, but probably had the reverse effect, by permitting landlords to sell their newly decontrolled dwellings for owner occupation. A further boost to owner occupation was provided in 1963, when the government abolished Schedule A income taxation – a tax on the *imputed* rent income which owner occupiers chose to forego. In effect, owner occupiers were choosing to take this income 'in kind', by occupying the property themselves, instead of renting it out. (This is similar to being taxed on the value of services received from, say, a company car: it is a benefit in kind, which nevertheless has value to the recipient and so is effectively another source of income.) The abolition of Schedule A taxation therefore represented a significant tax advantage to owner occupiers.

The Housing Act of 1961 provided the first significant public funding for housing associations, with £25 million available as loans from the National Federation of Housing Societies to provide homes at *cost-rents*. The 1964 Housing Act set up the Housing Corporation to regulate and finance housing associations, extending their interests into co-ownership schemes. However, at this time, two thirds of any finance had to be raised from the private sector – usually building societies – which is similar to the present system of housing association finance, examined in Chapter 3.

The new Labour government of 1964 promised a huge expansion of council house building, with a target of half a million homes a year. Rent controls were reintroduced for the private sector with the 1965 Rent Act, known as *Fair Rents*, and assessed by a Rent Officer (employed by the Civil Service). The 1967 Housing

Subsidies Act increased the subsidies available to local authorities, and new minimum (and very generous) space standards were introduced as a result of the Parker Morris Report. Few new homes built today by housing associations meet these standards, an issue which is taken up in Chapter 4.

Policies for social housing in the 1970s

By the late sixties, general economic problems caused a reduction in council house building and slum clearance, and instead, there was a new policy emphasis on the rehabilitation of the existing, private sector stock. The 1969 Housing Act introduced *general improvement areas*, followed in the 1974 Housing Act by *housing action areas*. These encouraged local authorities to identify areas for systematic improvement, and more generous improvement grants were made available to private owners.

By the early 1970s, issues of housing *finance* became key policy issues. The 1972 Housing Finance Act introduced, for the first time, a *mandatory* (compulsory) rent rebate scheme for council tenants. This was necessary because rent controls – *fair rents* – were also introduced for council tenants, with the intention of increasing council rents to private sector levels and removing their connection with the cost of provision. As a result, the housing revenue account – the rent income account – could now generate a surplus; rents could be higher than the amount required to repay debt interest and the costs of management and maintenance. Fair rents were later abandoned (for council housing) by the 1975 Housing Rents and Subsidies Act, because this was widely perceived as unfair to council tenants.

The 1974 Housing Act also extended the role of the Housing Corporation, by introducing housing association grant for housing associations. This was a very generous grant system, no longer requiring that associations obtain private finance. This marked the beginning of the considerable, recent expansion of housing association provision of social housing, albeit on a very small scale in comparison with local authorities.

The Cullingworth Report of 1969 reflected a growing view that local authorities took too narrow a view of their responsibilities for housing. It recommended that all restrictions on the allocation of local authority housing should be lifted, and in particular, that local authorities should look after the most vulnerable households in their area. (Allocations policies are examined in detail in Chapter 5.) A new requirement in the 1970s, that local authorities produce *housing strategies* for their areas (see Chapter 3), was intended to force authorities to adopt a wider role in housing. However, it was not until 1977 that for the first time local authorities were given a statutory duty to provide housing for some categories of homeless households, by the Housing (Homeless Persons) Act.

Housing policy since 1979

The election of the Conservative government in 1979, under Margaret Thatcher, marked a turning point in the provision of social housing in the United Kingdom. In pursuit of a 'property-owning democracy', the expansion of owner occupation now became the central goal of housing policy. The Housing Act and Housing (Tenants' Rights, etc.) Scotland Act in 1980 introduced the right of most council tenants to purchase their council home at a discount – the *right to buy* policy – as well as new public sector tenancies with new rights. The later Building Societies Act of 1986 deregulated the provision of housing finance for owner occupation, bringing 'high street' banks into the market, so that a great deal more finance was available, and many more households became eligible for mortgages.

As part of a substantial policy shift in favour of individual subsidies, the rent rebate system was reformed in 1982 to provide a new *housing benefit*. The results of this new policy shift were to influence housing in the United Kingdom throughout the 1980s, with policies which would continue to affect social housing provision throughout the 1990s. The details and implications of these policies are examined throughout the remainder of the book, in particular, in relation to the 1988 Housing Act which changed perceptions of social housing for the next decade and beyond.

1.4 Who provides social housing in the United Kingdom?

In Great Britain the two key providers of social housing are local housing authorities and housing associations. Northern Ireland has the Northern Ireland Housing Executive, with roles and responsibilities in relation to social housing which are similar to local authorities in the rest of the United Kingdom.

Local authorities

Although in recent years the government has attempted to reduce the role of local authorities as social housing landlords they nonetheless still remain the main provider of social housing in Britain. However, not all local authorities have the key housing responsibilities. Shire county councils in England only play a minor role in the provision of housing services.

For housing authorities in England and Wales most of their legal duties are set out in the 1985 Housing Act, which was a consolidating piece of legislation, bringing together a plethora of housing legislation contained in earlier acts of Parliament. In Scotland the responsibilities of housing authorities are laid down in the Housing (Scotland) Act 1987. The 1996 Housing Act has changed the responsibilities of local authorities in England and Wales significantly in relation to issues of the letting of homes and dealing with homelessness.

The key responsibilities of local housing authorities include:

- the assessment of housing needs in the area and the development of plans to meet those needs;
- the provision of rented accommodation and the management of that housing stock, including the allocation of dwellings, rent collection, arrears recovery and the enforcement of tenancy conditions;

- assisting housing associations and private developers to provide housing within their area: the *enabling* role;
- the provision of accommodation and other services to the homeless;
- exercising powers to tackle disrepair in private sector housing and in relation to houses in multiple occupation;
- the provision of housing advice services;
- the administration of housing benefits for both private and public sector tenants.

It is apparent that the responsibilities of housing authorities for housing in their area is much more extensive than simply the management of their own housing stock; indeed there is no requirement in the legislation for housing authorities to manage their own housing.

In the development of their *housing plans* – annual plans for housing in their area, required as part of their bid for resources (and examined in Chapter 3) – housing authorities are required to take a wide-ranging *strategic* view of the housing needs in their area, including the provision of both rented and owner-occupied housing. This view of the local authority as having a wide-ranging responsibility for housing in the area is reflected in a general desire of government to see housing authorities undertaking an enabling role – assisting other providers to achieve housing development – rather than providing new housing themselves.

The changing role of local authorities

The new role for local authorities was spelt out very clearly in the 1987 Government White Paper, *Housing; the Government's Proposals*, which identified four aims of its housing policy:

- to reverse the decline for rented housing;
- to give tenants the right to transfer to other landlords;
- to target money more accurately on the most acute problems;
- to encourage further the growth of home ownership.

In the White Paper the government set out its view that the landlord role of the local authority should decrease and that:

> 'local authorities should increasingly see themselves as enablers to ensure that everyone in their area is adequately housed; but not necessarily by them. The future role of local authorities would essentially be a strategic one identifying housing needs and demands, encouraging innovative methods of provision by other bodies to meet such needs, maximising use of private finance, and encouraging the new interest in the revival of the private rented sector.' (Government White Paper, 1987.)

This strategic role clearly echoes the wide range of responsibilities set down in the 1985 Housing Act. However, the White Paper went further in that it argued very strongly that the local authorities' role should not be that of providing houses themselves.

This was reinforced in the 1995 Government White Paper on Housing, *Our Future Homes*, which said that local authorities should:

- take a strategic approach to housing needs and act as enablers;
- reduce their landlord role.

As a result of the 1987 White Paper and subsequent legislation, the role of local authorities as providers of social housing has been changing. There have been significant reductions in the amount of money available to local housing authorities to provide new housing directly, which is examined further in Chapter 3. This has encouraged authorities to pursue their 'enabling' role more actively, working more closely with local housing associations and private sector developers to achieve some of their goals in relation to the provision of affordable housing.

Financial constraints have also stimulated some local authorities to engage in the *large-scale voluntary transfer* of their stock to a new housing association, since associations face fewer constraints on their ability to obtain finance for spending to refurbish housing stock.

More recently, the introduction of compulsory competitive tendering, requiring local housing authorities to put a significant part of their housing management function out to competitive tender, has generated a need for local authorities to examine critically the range and detail of their service provision. The service provision, together with service standards, must be carefully specified, so that tenderers know exactly what they are bidding to provide. Many local authorities have now separated the 'client' (*purchaser* of services) role from the 'contractor' (*provider* of services) roles, so that monitoring requirements for contracts can be made more explicit. However, this also affects many relationships within the local authority housing department, and the long-term effects of such developments on the service have yet to be assessed.

However, in spite of these pressures, local housing authorities still remain significant landlords in their own right, as well as having the strategic and enabling role which the Government has advocated.

Local housing authorities in Great Britain from April 1996

From the 1st April 1996 a new system of local government was introduced in Scotland and Wales (and also in some parts of England). The main result of this change has been to reduce the number of local authorities in Great Britain mainly through the abolition of the Welsh county councils, the Scottish regional councils and in England the abolition of some shire county councils and the amalgamation of other district councils. (Council housing in Northern Ireland is still provided by the Northern Ireland Housing Executive, with funding from the Department of the Environment.)

Housing authorities in Great Britain from April 1996

England:

- metropolitan district councils
- non-metropolitan district councils
- London borough councils (and the City of London)
- new unitary district councils

Wales:

- new unitary councils

Scotland:

- new unitary councils

Housing authorities in England

English metropolitan district councils

Following the Local Government Act of 1972' thirty-six metropolitan district councils were established in England in the main urban conurbations in Merseyside, Greater Manchester, South Yorkshire, West Yorkshire, the West Midlands and Tyne and Wear. These metropolitan district councils are now responsible for housing functions in their areas.

Following the abolition in the mid-1980s of the metropolitan county councils these district councils became all-purpose unitary authorities, responsible for all local government activities in their area. The metropolitan district councils vary significantly both in terms of population size and the housing stock managed; the largest is Birmingham City Council with a stock of 98,000 homes and the smallest is Bury Metropolitan District Council with a stock of 10,000 dwellings.

English non-metropolitan district councils

Prior to April 1986 there were a total of 334 non-metropolitan district councils in England and Wales but following a review of local government initiated in the mid-1990s the Local Government Commission has reviewed the structure of local government in England. This review has led to a number of significant changes being proposed for local government in England. In some cases shire county councils have been abolished and their functions transferred to new all-purpose district councils, whilst in other areas the shire county council lost part of its geographical area to a new unitary authority.

Where new unitary district councils have been established these have responsibility for housing. In the shire areas where the two-tier system remains the county councils have a responsibility for key services such as education and social services whilst district councils take on responsibility for more 'local' services, such as housing, planning, leisure services and refuse collection.

London borough councils

Within London there are 32 borough councils who together with the City of London operate as unitary authorities and have responsibility for all local government matters, including housing, in their area. Each of these councils has a landlord function with the housing stock ranging from 2,250 homes in the City of London to 54,500 dwellings in the London Borough of Tower Hamlets.

Housing authorities in Wales

In Wales, a review of local government was conducted in the mid-1990s by the Welsh Office and this review has led to the abolition of all of the previous eight county councils and the 37 Welsh district councils. In their place a new structure of local government was introduced consisting of 24 new unitary all-purpose councils, all of which have a responsibility for their housing.

Housing authorities in Scotland

Prior to April 1986 mainland Scotland had nine regional councils and 53 district councils. In addition, there were three separate islands authorities for Western Isles, Shetland and Orkney. In Scotland the housing function had been carried out by the district councils and the islands' authorities. Following the review of local government for Scotland conducted by the Scottish Office, local government for Scotland was reorganised in April 1986 with the creation of 32 new unitary authorities and the abolition of the regional councils, though the three authorities for the Scottish islands remain.

In the new structure, all of the unitary authorities including the islands' councils have responsibilities for all local government services including housing. The smallest authority is Orkney with a population of 20,000 and the largest is Glasgow City Council with a population of 624,000.

Housing associations

The local authorities remain the most important provider of social housing in Great Britain. The other important provider of social housing, and the sector with the key role now in providing new 'social housing' is the housing association sector. Under the 1985 Housing Associations Act a housing association is defined as:

> 'a Society, body of trustees or company:
>
> (a) which is established for the purpose of, or amongst whose objects or powers are included those of, providing constructing improving or managing, or facilitating or encouraging the construction of, housing accommodation and which
>
> (b) does not trade for profit....'

Housing Associations are essentially non-profit seeking organisations which exist to provide housing for people in need. They are independent bodies controlled by unpaid voluntary committee members, although in the larger housing associations the committee of management may employ staff to carry out the day-to-day work of managing the association on their behalf. Most housing associations will have received public subsidy in the form of grants from the Housing Corporation (or Scottish Homes/Tai Cymru) and are subject to scrutiny by these government agencies in respect of their activities.

Types of housing associations – England

There are a number of different categories of housing association which usually reflect the type of housing they provide or the particular housing need that the association wishes to meet. The majority of housing associations are general needs associations. This means that the association has been established to meet a range of needs and will provide housing for families, couples, single people and the elderly. However, there are a number of specialist housing associations as set out below.

Abbeyfields

These are smaller housing associations, usually only owning a handful of properties, which specialise in providing shared housing for the elderly. The usual model is for three or four elderly people to share a house, with a housekeeper being employed to offer care and support to the residents.

Almshouses

These are perhaps the earliest form of sheltered housing, with some having their roots back to the 12th century. They provide sheltered housing for the elderly and are found throughout the United Kingdom, often owning a handful of properties.

Hostels

Many housing associations will provide hostel accommodation. Hostels will normally provide shared accommodation with each household having their own bedroom facilities but with cooking and bathrooms usually being shared. Another feature of hostel accommodation is that the housing association will normally provide support workers, usually with specialist skills in meeting the needs of hostel residents. These needs will vary, and hostels are provided to help, amongst others, women fleeing domestic violence, the homeless, the mentally ill, people with physical disabilities and young people who have left the care of the local authority.

Cooperatives and co-ownerships

Cooperatives are a form of housing association in which the accommodation is collectively owned and managed by the people who live in it, although the members' only stake in the equity (value) of the properties is their £1 membership share.

Co-ownerships are a very different form of co-operative housing, in that when a member leaves this rented accommodation they are entitled to a share of some of any increase in the value of the property, depending on how long they have lived there and paid rent.

Sale/leasehold associations

Recently a number of specialist housing associations have been set up which have concentrated on providing housing for low cost home ownership, rather than for rent. This can take the form of shared ownership housing where residents will part-buy their home on a mortgage and rent the remainder from the housing association, with the option of increasing their share (*staircasing*) to full ownership when their resources allow. Some specialist *leasehold schemes for the elderly* (now called shared ownership for the elderly) have been set up where elderly persons can buy a property at 75 per cent of its market value, the housing association retaining ownership of the remaining equity in the property. Many general needs associations now operate low-cost home ownership schemes alongside their rented provision, although in some cases they have set up specialist associations to deal with this particular type of provision.

Table 1.1 gives details of housing associations registered with the Housing Corporation in England at March 1996.

Table 1.1 English housing associations at 31 March 1996

Category	Number
General needs	791
Abbeyfields	353
Other hostels	107
Almshouses	610
Cooperatives	255
Co-ownerships	58
Sale/leasehold	58
Total	2,232

Source: authors' correspondence with Housing Corporation (1997)

At 31 March 1996 English housing associations registered with the Housing Corporation owned 796,000 homes and 21,900 bedspaces of shared/hostel accommodation.

Types of housing associations – Scotland

The range of Scottish housing associations is similar to England, although in Scotland, Scottish Homes (which was formed as a result of the amalgamation of the earlier Scottish Special Housing Association and the Housing Corporation in Scotland) retains a large landlord role.

A particular feature of the Scottish housing association movement is the development of cooperative and community-based housing associations. These have been particularly encouraged by Scottish Homes through the transfer of its own stock to new associations.

Table 1.2 gives details on the number of Scottish housing associations. Between them they own almost 94,000 homes.

Table 1.2 Numbers of Scottish housing associations at 31 March 1996

Category	Number
General needs	70
Abbeyfields	62
Charitable	55
Cooperatives	44
Community based	39
Co-ownerships	3
Total	273

Source: Scottish Homes (1995/96)

Types of housing associations – Wales

In Wales registered housing associations are regulated and funded by Tai Cymru (Housing for Wales). At 31 March 1996 there were 97 housing associations registered with Tai Cymru owning a total of 49,534 homes.

As with England and Scotland the majority of housing associations in Wales own only a handful of homes, with 50 of the 97 associations owning 25 homes or less, and only 15 associations owning more than a 1,000 homes. Indeed these 15 Welsh associations own over 74.3 per cent of the total stock.

Table 1.3 gives details of the numbers of housing associations in Wales.

Table 1.3 Housing associations in Wales at 31 March 1996

Category	Number
General needs	53
Abbeyfields	34
Almshouses	9
Co-ownerships	1
Total	97

Source: Tai Cymru (1996)

The size of housing associations

The housing association movement is a diverse one with a large number of associations owning a handful of properties, and a small number of associations owning in excess of 10,000 properties. For example, in England at 31 March 1994, 31 per cent of associations owned fewer than six homes and only eleven associations owned more than 10,000 properties. Table 1.4 shows the six largest associations in England at 31 March 1996.

Table 1.4 Largest housing associations in England at 31 March 1996

Name	Units
North British HA	38 453
Anchor Trust	30 134
Home HA	25 876
London & Quadrant HT	24 280
Orbit HA	22 071
Sanctuary	21 557

Source: adapted from NHF Directory of Members, (1997)

Table 1.5 shows quite clearly the diversity in stock sizes.

Table 1.5 Homes managed by housing associations in England at 31 March 1996 (NHF members only)

Number of units	Number of HAs
499	1078
500–2499	74
2500–4999	175
5000+	61

Source: adapted from NHF Directory of Members, (1997)

In Wales, as Table 1.6 shows, a similar picture emerges of a relatively small number of associations owning most of the stock.

Table 1.6 Distribution of Welsh housing association stock by size of association at 31 March 1996

Size of HA (homes)	Number of HAs	Percentage of HAs	Total stock owned
0–5	9	9.3	17
6–25	41	42.3	405
26–100	12	12.4	578
101–250	4	4.1	761
251–500	5	5.1	1915
501–1000	11	11.3	9041
1000+	15	15.5	36 817
Total	97	100	49 534

Source: Tai Cymru (1996)

Scottish housing associations own almost 94,000 homes but most of the properties are owned by the largest associations, as shown in Table 1.7.

Table 1.7 Stock owned by Scottish housing associations at 31 March 1996

Units owned	No of HA's	Total units
0–25	41	223
26–100	23	1548
101–500	90	22 354
501–1000	29	20 938
1001–2500	25	36 276
2501+	4	12 407
Total	212	93 746

Source: Scottish Homes (1995/96)
[a] In addition the 62 Abbeyfields own 904 bedspaces of accommodation for the elderly.

1.5 The management of social housing organisations

The provision and management of social housing demands a wide range of knowledge and expertise. As shown in the previous section, most of the social housing stock is provided by relatively large organisations, though there are some which are exceedingly small. The task of managing them is a complex one, just as it is for any private sector organisation with a wide variety of functions. The main difference is that, since social housing organisations do not exist to make a profit, there is no simple measure of 'success' as there is for a private firm. As for all parts of the public sector, the social housing organisation cannot examine its profitability to see how well it has performed. For this reason, performance is gauged from a series of *performance indicators*, which relate to some of the key tasks undertaken by housing managers. What are these tasks?

Firstly, if properties are to be built or refurbished, the key requirement is that *finance* is obtained. In general, this will be from a combination of grants from the central government, borrowing from the private sector and from income generated from rents. Obtaining and managing this finance has become increasingly important for many social housing organisations. In addition, housing organisations must ensure that the income received from rents is managed wisely, to ensure that funds are available to provide an appropriate range and quality of services to the tenants on a week-to-week basis.

In those organisations where some or all of their services are decentralised, so that services are provided from a number of different locations, each manager may have control of a *budget* to pay some or all of the costs of management activities. These resources must be carefully managed to ensure that they are spent in an appropriate and timely manner. Indeed, in the light of increasing restraints on the resources available to social housing over recent years, managing the organisation's financial resources well has become a key issue.

A few, usually small, associations undertake no new housing development and very few local authorities now have sufficient resources to build new homes. However, *all* social housing providers will need, at some stage, to refurbish ageing properties, and most medium to large housing associations still undertake new development. This demands the ability to undertake a range of development tasks, ranging from identifying suitable sites, to managing the design of the planned development and arranging for its construction. Hence, the management of social housing may also require a knowledge of the process of development, the roles of the key professionals and the ways in which a high quality of development can best be achieved.

Once the properties have been built, new occupiers, the *tenants*, must be allocated to them, and suitable arrangements must be made to collect rent and minimise arrears, to manage the letting of vacant properties and to arrange for their repair and maintenance. These latter tasks are perhaps conventionally thought of as the key tasks of social housing managers, and they are certainly the tasks which have the most immediate and direct impact on the tenants. Increasingly, however, as explored above, some knowledge of finance and development issues is also required for effective management.

Since the managers of social housing have an obligation to ensure that their properties are allocated to households in housing need, identifying and defining needs is also an important task. The aim is to identify all of those *needs* which are unlikely to be met by the private sector, usually because the households lack the ability to pay. As identified above, local authorities have an obligation to identify housing need in their area, and to plan an annual housing strategy which addresses these needs. Chapter 2 considers the nature of the housing needs which are generally met by social housing organisations, while Chapter 3 examines the role of the *Housing Plan* in bidding for public finance.

Unlike private sector firms, the people responsible for strategic management issues in social housing organisations form an *unpaid, voluntary committee*. In local authorities, these are the *elected members*, the councillors who sit on a committee such as the housing committee. Housing associations have management committees, and, as in local authorities, these committees take key decisions, with advice from the senior management team. Senior managers need, therefore, to be fully conversant with committee procedures and it is their job to 'operationalise' the decisions taken in committee – to turn the policies into reality in the organisation. However, these are high level management tasks, beyond the scope of an introductory text.

As might be anticipated from the wide variation in the numbers of properties controlled by different housing organisations, the numbers of staff employed to undertake the management of the stock varies considerably. In very small associations it is likely that almost all of the work involved in running the association will be carried out on a voluntary basis by committee members. For example, 943 housing associations in England at 31 March 1994 employed no staff at all, though these associations only accounted for 3 per cent of the stock. It is only when the association is larger that the committee will be able to afford to employ paid staff to run the association on a day-to-day basis. However, this applies to most of the properties owned by housing associations in England; 557 associations with more than five staff own 95 per cent of the stock.

In contrast, in Wales at 31 March 1996, 60 of the 97 associations employed no staff and carried out their work on a voluntary basis. Most of these associations will be Abbeyfields but others will be those associations which employ a larger association to manage the day-to-day affairs of the association on its behalf under a *management agreement*. Only nine Welsh associations employ more than 40 staff and these nine associations accounted for 58 per cent of the total Welsh housing association stock.

The situation is quite different for local authorities, all of which employ some staff to undertake housing management. However, as will be seen in Chapter 6, there are huge variations in the location of some of these tasks in the organisation, so some important management tasks may be undertaken by departments other than the housing department; for example, it is quite common for housing benefit payments to be administered by the treasurer's department. In addition, local authorities have a much broader range of responsibilities for housing than associations, as identified earlier in this chapter. Hence, in a local authority, housing management potentially embraces an even wider range of tasks.

This text, primarily, sets out to explore the nature of the management roles and responsibilities which are undertaken by social housing organisations, and most of the remainder of the book is directed to that objective. However, before doing so, the next chapter examines the *context* within which social housing operates and its place in the housing system of the United Kingdom.

Further reading

Balchin, P. (1990) *Housing Policy: an Introduction*, Routledge, London.

Burnett, J. (1978) *A Social History of Housing, 1815–1970*, David and Charles, Newton Abbot, Devon.

Grant, C. (1992) *Built to Last? Reflections on British Housing Policy*, Shelter, London.

Malpass, P. and Means, R. (1993) *Implementing Housing Policy*, Oxford University Press, Oxford.

Merrett, S. (1979) *State Housing in Britain*, Routledge & Kegan Paul, London.

Power, A. (1993) *Hovels to High Rise: State Housing in Europe since 1850*, Routledge, London.

Chapter 2

SOCIAL HOUSING IN CONTEXT

2.1 Introduction

The need for shelter is a fundamental human requirement and the quality and availability of housing affects all of us. However, 'housing' is not a single entity; it is a heterogeneous item, available in many different locations, in different sizes and styles, of variable quality, and in a number of distinct tenures. This chapter considers the various ways in which households in the United Kingdom might satisfy their need for housing, through a discussion of the United Kingdom housing system and the different ways in which housing is made available to households. It explores the context in which the social housing sector operates in order to set the scene for the issues considered throughout the subsequent chapters of this book.

The chapter begins by examining key concepts relating to the requirement for housing, such as housing *desire, need,* and *demand.* It also identifies the main tenures, which have implications for the rights and responsibilities of the dwelling's occupants. It examines influences on the demand for housing, and the ways in which this can vary over time and between tenures. It considers the problems arising from the fact that private housing markets can only respond to the desire for housing when it is accompanied by an ability to pay. The inability of households to pay has resulted in the concept of housing 'need', as distinct from housing demand, and the provision of *social* housing to meet housing needs. It also explores the ways in which housing need has been defined by both governments and social housing providers and why this concept changes over time.

The factors affecting the supply of housing to each of the tenures are also considered, together with the implications of the choice of housing tenure for the quality of the housing occupied by households.

2.2 Housing desire, demand and need

Housing desire

This can be conceived as a household's *preferences* for housing. It will include not only preferences for the size of the accommodation, its physical attributes and qualitative standards, but also preferences for tenure type and location. This means that all households, or potential households, will have particular desires in relation to their homes.

Housing need

The assessment of housing need – is considered in more detail later – involves the identification of the minimum housing standards which are required by particular households, and the measurement of whether households achieve those standards. It involves a qualitative judgement about the requirements of different households, and as a result, perceptions of housing need can change over time. Different societies may also have quite different perceptions of housing need.

The concept of housing need is a crucial element in the allocation of social housing. In general, only those households considered to be in *housing need* will be offered a social housing dwelling, which may, or may not, meet with their desires or aspirations. This is in contrast to private sector housing provision, which is allocated largely in response to demand.

Housing demand

The term *demand* (or, more accurately, 'effective demand') is used here as an economic term to describe the situation in which housing 'consumers' have a desire for particular accommodation *and* have the financial resources to pay it. In this precise economic definition, therefore, 'effective demand' only exists if individuals' desires or needs coincide with an ability to pay the market price (or rent) for that accommodation. The desire for housing, or the need for it, does not, in itself, permit the household to demand it.

2.3 Tenure

Within the United Kingdom at any one time, housing may be located in any one of four main tenure types. The key determining factor of which tenure type a particular dwelling is in will be the ownership of the accommodation. The four main tenures are owner occupation, local authority (council) housing, housing association, and private rented accommodation.

Owner occupied dwellings are owned by the occupants, either outright or purchased with the assistance of loans – usually mortgages, for which the home will act as security for the loan. Within the United Kingdom this is the far largest tenure type with around 70 per cent of the population living in such accommodation. The other three tenures consist of accommodation which is owned by someone other than the occupier, who pays rent to the owner.

Local authority housing is the stock of dwellings owned by local councils; as the owner occupied sector has continued to expand in recent years there has been a corresponding reduction in the stock of council housing. The reasons for these changes are considered later in the section on housing supply. This tenure type is currently occupied by around 18 per cent of the population.

Housing associations are non-profit seeking organisations which exist both to provide (through new building and renovation) and manage good quality housing for letting at 'affordable' rents. The issue of affordability is an important one, and is explored in the last chapter. This is the smallest tenure type with around 4 per cent of the total housing stock in the United Kingdom.

The private rented sector consists of those dwellings owned by private individuals and companies, and let for rent usually with a view to making a profit. From a situation at the end of the First World War in which over 90 per cent of the United Kingdom housing stock was within this tenure type, this sector has reduced to around 8 per cent of the total stock.

2.4 Demand and supply in private housing markets

A market is any arrangement which permits the exchange of goods or services, whether for money or other consideration. In the case of housing, this refers to the arrangements by which dwellings are bought and sold, or let. Traditionally, economists have focused on the operation of markets, and the way in which markets are assumed to reach an 'equilibrium', when they achieve a balance between supply and demand. In the long term, the supply of housing should equal its demand, because price will provide the 'equilibrating mechanism' linking the two. The Cambridge economist Alfred Marshall suggested that the equilibrium price of any particular commodity would be determined through market forces where the number of articles demanded was exactly equal to the number supplied.

In very simple terms, the process by which a market reaches equilibrium is as follows:

As demand for a product increases the price will rise, because the lack of supply will result in consumers 'bidding up' the price; they will be competing for a scarce product, which always results in a higher price.

As the price increases, manufacturers (or, builders and sellers, in the case of houses) will be encouraged to produce (or sell) more of the item.

As more become available, the price will stop increasing and a new equilibrium will be found where the number of articles (houses) demanded is equal to the number being supplied.

The price remains steady until levels of demand or supply alter again.

If supply expands so that it exceeds demand, or if demand falls, the price will soon start to fall. There will be insufficient buyers to take up the supply. Falling prices will eventually result in a contraction in the supply, as builders put off new developments and owners delay selling their homes. Eventually, equilibrium is restored, and prices become steady again.

While the theory of supply and demand and price equilibrium may be particularly accurate in describing the market for many products, such as shoes or loaves of bread, the supply of housing is rather 'inelastic', in that an increase in demand with an associated increase in price cannot quickly be followed by an increase in supply. Housing supply – the 'flow' of houses into the market, those offered for sale or rent at any one time – responds only slowly to changing prices. This is because of the long lead-in times involved in the production of new houses compared to shoes or loaves of bread.

The supply of housing within tenures is further complicated by factors which are, largely, outside the control of either the potential buyer or the seller (or the potential renter and landlord). These include:

- the mobility rates of existing occupiers, which affect how often dwellings become available to rent or buy;
- the attractiveness of renting as a profitable activity for landlords, in comparison with other investment opportunities;
- the significance of government policies affecting housing.

This means that the operation of housing markets is particularly complex. The complexity of factors affecting both the demand for and supply of housing, and the ways in which these differ between each tenure, are now considered in greater detail.

The factors influencing the overall demand for housing

The overall demand for housing is affected by a number of factors. These include the following:

Demographic factors

The demand for housing will be affected by a range of demographic (population) factors. Self-evidently, the size of the population will have an impact on the numbers of people requiring accommodation, and therefore on the level of demand. The United Kingdom population has undergone a fairly steady increase over the past four decades, rising from 50.25 million in 1951, to 57 million at the time of the 1991 Census. However, the rate of growth has been reducing over this period, and future projections suggest that by the year 2031 the total population level will have begun to decrease (OPCS, 1994; Registrar General's Mid-Year Estimates and Projections, 1995).

Such changes in the total population will clearly have an influence on the number of people requiring accommodation, but this in itself will only be one factor affecting the numbers of homes required. A further influencing factor is the composition of the population, which means the numbers of people in different age groups, as well as the way in which it is structured – the relative size of each age grouping.

Census data show that there has been a significant increase over the past 40 years in the proportion of the population which is over 65 years of age; and this is most marked in the group aged 75 years and over. In addition, future projections suggest that this trend is likely to continue through the next 40 years (OPCS, 1994; Registrar General's Mid-Year Estimates and Projections, 1995).

This pattern can be expected to have implications not only for the level of demand for accommodation, but also for the demand for housing of designs which are appropriate to the needs of older people. As such the changing age profile can be expected to have an impact on both the level of demand and the types of accommodation being required.

Another demographic factor which will have an impact on levels of demand for accommodation is the extent of migration among the population. At a national level, the relative rates of outward migration (emigration) and inward migration (immigration) will affect the size of the population. However, levels of internal migration may also be significant. For example, during the 1980s and early 1990s rising levels of unemployment elsewhere in the country resulted in net migration of people into the South East of England with an associated impact on the levels of demand for accommodation in that region.

Clearly demand can be influenced by issues related to the labour market. The requirement to move for employment purposes is, however, only one of a range of ways in which mobility impacts on housing demand. It will also be affected by the age of individuals, with young single people traditionally being the most mobile group within the United Kingdom population. As such, the numbers of this group in the overall population will impact on the overall level of demand.

Family life cycles also have an influence on the levels of demand and the type of accommodation required. As the number of children in a family increases, larger accommodation is usually required. As the children of the family grow, and begin to form new independent households, there is a demand for more accommodation to house this increased number of household units.

The rate at which new households form will therefore affect demand levels. So far the consideration has mainly been around demographic factors in terms of total numbers or proportions of the whole population. As has also been suggested, however, the level of demand for housing will be more specifically affected by the number of households requiring accommodation. The Government Statistical Office, in the 1995 edition of *Social Trends*, defined a household as:

'...either people living alone or groups of people living together as a unit. Most households consist of one family, but sometimes two or more families live together in a single household (for example, grandparents, mother and daughter living together would be one household but two families) and sometimes people live together who are not related, such as in student households.'

One definition would suggest, then, that a household could constitute any number of individuals who choose or are caused to live together in shared accommodation. It would be usual for people living in such circumstances to share some of the functions of housekeeping. The reasons for new households forming can be many and varied and could include, for example, a young person attaining an age at which they choose to leave the parental home to become more independent, or two new households forming as the result of a breakdown of a marriage or other family relationship.

The rate at which this new household formation occurs will in turn be affected by income levels and a range of social factors, for example rates of marriage and divorce, and changing expectations of independence among young adults.

Census data show an expectation that the number of separate households in the United Kingdom will continue to increase throughout the 1990s. In 1991 there were 19,215,000 households. Projections suggest that by 2001 there will be 21,046,000, an increase of 1,831,000 households (OPCS, 1994; Registrar General's Mid-Year Estimates and Projections, 1995).

The data also show that the largest anticipated increase is among single person households, from 5,116,000 in 1991 to 6,509,000 in 2001 – an increase of 1,393,000 (OPCS, 1994; Registrar General's Mid-Year Estimates and Projections, 1995).

As discussed above the total numbers in the population are expected to continue to increase throughout the same period. This increase, together with the increasing numbers of the population who are expected to live in single person households, is likely to result in a significant increase in demand for accommodation and an increased emphasis on single persons' dwellings.

A further demographic factor which affects the level of demand is the size of individual households. This can also be expected to affect not only the number of dwellings required but also the size of those dwellings. Household size can also affect levels of demand resulting from households sub-dividing if existing accommodation is not sufficient to meet existing needs. For example, an older child of a family which is overcrowded in their present accommodation might be influenced to leave the family home and form a single person household earlier than would have otherwise occurred in order to ease the overcrowding situation.

Throughout the past four decades, as the number of households has steadily increased, the mean average of people within each household has steadily reduced as smaller family sizes, single person households and divorce have become more commonplace. Census data indicates that the proportion of the population living in single person households increased from 14 per cent in 1961 to 27 per cent in 1991. At the same time the proportion of the population living in households of four or more people reduced from 34 per cent in 1961, to 22 per cent in 1991 (Government Statistical Officer, 1995). Clearly such demographic and social changes affect the level of demand for accommodation with more households requiring dwellings, and with a need for smaller individual units of accommodation.

Income

Levels of income, and the distribution of income throughout the population influences demand. The level of a household's income will affect its ability to express its housing desires through the market. For example, a young person living with relatives who aspires to independence will need to achieve sufficient income to fund the independent accommodation they seek.

Similarly, if a household aspires to move into larger accommodation, or to a dwelling in a more desirable area, it is likely that their ability to achieve this wish will be linked to their level of income. As the level of this household's income rises, they are more likely to be able to afford their desired accommodation.

The *distribution* of income throughout the population will also be important. Increasing levels of income among greater numbers within the population will multiply the above effect with more households being in a position to afford their desired accommodation.

A further relevant factor is, however, the perceived permanence of the income. A temporary increase in income is unlikely to result in a household expressing a different housing preference, for instance by moving from rented into owner-occupied accommodation, as any such change would be unlikely to be sustainable in the long term. A subsequent fall in income could have serious implications for the household.

Price

The price of accommodation, whether the cost of buying or the level of rents, is also an influence on demand. As the effective demand for accommodation will be a function of the ability of potential occupants to pay for accommodation, it follows that when the price for particular accommodation is lower, the level of demand will be affected by this situation and will increase. Conversely, price increases can have an influence on reducing demand.

As the price of accommodation fluctuates this will affect the rates at which new households form, with lower prices allowing more new households – or those 'concealed' households previously living in with relatives – to be in a position where they are able to afford to pay for independent accommodation. Similarly as prices rise fewer of these households will be able to realise their independent ambitions and will continue to live in multi-household situations. At the same time some households who were living in independent accommodation can find themselves unable to continue meeting their housing costs at times of rising prices and may be forced to enter into multi-household arrangements, moving to live with relatives or friends until such a time as they can once again afford independent accommodation.

Perceived availability

The availability of accommodation, or the perception among households of its availability, will have an impact on levels of demand. If there is a perception that dwellings are not available, those new households who might be about to form and to seek independent housing will be discouraged from doing so. The perception of availability will often be linked to issues of household income and the price of accommodation. More of the factors affecting availability are considered in greater detail later.

Factors influencing the demand for different tenure types

The factors considered above as having an influence on the *overall* level of demand for accommodation will have an influence on the levels and types of demand for accommodation within the different tenures in different ways.

Familiarity

Research suggests that many new households choose their parents' tenure type, possibly because it is the tenure with which they are most familiar. An Office of Population Censuses and Surveys (OPCS) *Survey into Recently Moved Households* in 1984 looked at the 'housing pathways' followed by different households – that is, the history of the different tenures and types of accommodation occupied by a sample of those who had recently moved house. The survey identified that newly forming households were likely to move directly from parental homes into owner occupation (33 per cent of those surveyed) and furnished renting (35 per cent). A further 15 per cent moved directly into local authority rented accommodation. Whilst this balance is not equivalent to the proportions of the stock in each of the different tenures, there are limitations on access to social rented housing and owner occupation, and therefore these tenures might be underrepresented among those taking the first step to independence. The survey showed, however, that a significant proportion of the population follow their parents' tenure choice, or would choose to if finance and availability allowed.

Social class or socio-economic group

In addition, there is significant evidence to suggest that social class, or 'socio-economic group' will influence tenure choice (see Figure 2.1).

The main trends which emerge from the statistics are the decreasing use of rented accommodation when moving from 'lower' to 'higher' socio-economic groups. At the same time there is an increase in the proportion of owner occupiers when moving from 'unskilled manual workers' to 'professionals'. Such statistics support the contention that most of the population aspire toward owner occupation, as those in the 'higher' socio-economic groups are more likely to be in a financial position, with secure employment or continuing expectations of a sustained level of income, to take on the financial responsibilities associated with home ownership.

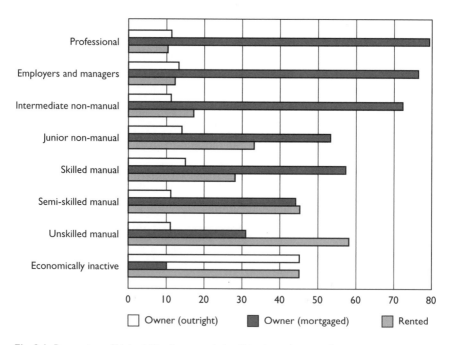

Fig. 2.1 Proportion of United Kingdom population living in each tenure by socio-economic group
Source: Adapted from Social Trends (1995)

This also means that at the local – or regional – level the occupational distribution can have important implications for the demand for particular tenures. The extent to which the local economy of any particular area is dependent on industries with a preponderance of workers from a particular socio-economic grouping will influence local demand for those tenures which are traditionally available to these groups. For example, in a local area in which there is a preponderance of industries in which there is a high concentration of unskilled manual workers, we would expect to see a high demand for rented accommodation, particularly social housing. In another area in which there was a high proportion of professional groups, for instance in a commuter belt, there is likely to be a higher demand for owner occupation and a lower level of demand for rented dwellings.

Migration

Levels of migration will also have a tenure specific impact. Traditionally in the United Kingdom young single people have always been the most mobile group within the population. In addition to the influence this will have on total demand for accommodation, there will be a disproportionate demand for particular tenures. The relatively long time taken to enter and exit from owner occupation through selling and moving elsewhere, as well as the high costs of this process (so-called 'transactions' costs'), will tend to discourage highly mobile groups from choosing this type of accommodation. Access to local authority and housing association dwellings have traditionally been lengthy processes due to high levels of demand and the bureaucratic rationing mechanisms adopted by many through their allocations and lettings policies as a way of dealing with that excess demand. As a result the private rented sector has tended to allow the quickest and easiest entry and exit for the highly mobile within the population, and as a result, young single people are the largest group represented among tenants of private rented dwellings.

Income

There is a marked difference between the incomes of households in owner occupation and those in council renting. The General Household Survey, conducted in 1991 (Office of Population Census and Surveys, 1993), found that the mean average weekly income of households in owner-occupied dwellings was £402, whereas the average for council tenants was £158. Housing association tenants were seen to have similarly low incomes, with an average of £148; private rented tenants fell in between the two extremes with an average of £197 for those in unfurnished tenancies, and £276 for those in furnished tenancies.

It can be concluded from these figures that as income increases households are more likely to move from social rented accommodation to home ownership. It can also be concluded that the first choice tenure for many of the United Kingdom population is owner occupation. When this accommodation is not available the option of renting will be considered. In most cases it could be anticipated that renting with the 'social' landlords – local authorities and housing associations – will be preferred due to the emphasis on affordable rents. For higher income groups, however, for whom owner occupation might not be an option due to, for example, the need for job related mobility, higher quality private rented accommodation might be a preferred option.

In general, however, rising incomes will generally lead to an increase in demand for owner-occupied housing. In the United Kingdom, although not necessarily elsewhere in Europe, the demand for rented accommodation tends to fall as incomes rise. Among households with lower income levels, however, the effect of rising income may be a qualitative one, stimulating demand for better quality rented accommodation if the costs of home ownership are still prohibitive.

Wealth

Wealth and the way in which it is distributed is another key factor affecting the demand for accommodation. In the United Kingdom today most assets are held in the form of housing. The ownership of residential property is seen as socially desirable, a situation which has been encouraged by the policies of successive United Kingdom governments to promote owner occupation as the 'natural' tenure choice. Increasing levels of relative wealth, bringing home ownership within the reach of more households has been assisted through policies to encourage home ownership, such as the provision of tax relief on mortgage interest.

Another conclusion which might be drawn is that some of the increase in demand for this type of tenure is due to those households who can afford it deciding on owner occupation in order not to be 'left behind' by rising house prices which might exclude them from a future option to purchase their own accommodation. Households who, given other circumstances, might prefer to take advantage of the more flexible rented sectors as they experience life changes may decide to buy earlier than would otherwise have been the case fearing that house price inflation will take the option of home ownership beyond their financial reach.

Price

The factors which will be considered to contribute to the 'price' of accommodation within different tenures will vary but many of the impacts of changes in price will be the same. There are a number of elements making up the price of owner-occupied accommodation. The purchase price of the dwelling is the main element. If purchase takes place with the aid of a mortgage the interest payments due in respect of the loan, together with any capital or endowment policy payments, will be part of the 'price' of the accommodation. A further element of the price will be the costs of insurance and maintenance costs for which the owner occupier is responsible.

The main element of the 'price' of rented accommodation will be the rent due to the landlord. The attraction for many who choose to rent is the payment of a one-off rent to cover all of the different elements to be met by those who own their accommodation. The price of accommodation within any tenure will have an impact on demand. Expectations of future price levels are also crucial, particularly in relation to owner-occupied property. As was suggested earlier, there is a tradition, particularly in the United Kingdom, for owner occupation to be seen as an investment in addition to a means of satisfying an individual's housing need. As a result of this convention the impact of house price increases is to stimulate a corresponding increase in the numbers of properties available for sale as prices reach a level at which owners will decide to cash in on their investment. One result of this phenomenon, as seen during the house price boom of the late 1980s, is the increase in demand for more expensive properties as long-standing owners within different property value bands 'trade up' to take account of the increase in equity caused by price rises. Equally, owners who hold residential property as an investment will choose to sell once they feel that house prices have reached a plateau, or if they feel that a fall in prices is imminent, in order to maximise the profit from their investment.

The impact of expectations of future price changes is less in the rented sectors because of the existence of housing benefit. Whilst high levels of state subsidy are available to owner occupiers through tax relief on their mortgage interest payments, it is in the rented sectors that government intervention is more clearly seen. A tenant of a private landlord who is entitled to housing benefit will see any increases in rent met by increased benefit payments, so long as the increase is considered to be within reasonable limits in terms of the rent officer's assessment and the *local reference rents* for the area. (This is examined further in Chapter 3.) A prospective tenant will not be dissuaded from taking up a tenancy which may have a relatively high rent if she/he will be entitled to housing benefit, and the rent levels are such that the rent will be paid. As such the impact of an increasing 'price' – in this case rent – for the accommodation will have less impact in affecting demand levels than the fluctuating price of owner-occupied dwellings.

Similarly, those tenants of social landlords who receive housing benefit will find the impact of any rent increases tempered by the benefits system. As such the impact of rising rents on the demand for rented accommodation has been, to date, fairly limited.

As discussed earlier, rented accommodation, mainly in the private sector, has traditionally been used as a starting point, or stepping stone, by new households setting up home for the first time and looking in the longer term to move into other types of accommodation. One likely impact of rising rents is therefore to discourage new household formation if this 'first step' is out of the reach of some who would otherwise seek to use it.

In addition to discouraging new household formation, an increase in rent levels could also be expected to encourage multiple occupation with more than one household sharing accommodation, and 'concealed' households living in with others due to the lack of financial ability to obtain the desired independent accommodation.

Increases in rent can also have an impact in reducing the differential cost between renting and owner-occupation (during periods when the cost of owner occupied housing is static or reducing), and as such can be expected to encourage the decision to enter owner-occupation among some tenants who might not otherwise have chosen this step. Similarly, those who see owner occupation as a long-term aim may make the move earlier than planned if rent levels increase and the difference between the costs of the two types of tenure appears less prohibitive.

The price of accommodation, whilst influencing overall demand for accommodation in all types of tenure, as discussed earlier, can specifically affect the demand for owner-occupied housing in different ways. In relation to first-time buyers, rising prices may have two opposing effects. As prices rise, the quality of dwellings which can be afforded will be lower. In addition fewer first-time buyers will be in a position to enter the housing market. If, however, prices are expected to continue to rise, this may stimulate additional demand in the short run, as new buyers choose to enter the market earlier in an effort to 'beat' the increases. At the same time existing owners might be stimulated, by price rises, to 'trade up', selling their existing properties to release equity which can be used to buy more desirable and more expensive properties.

Interest charges add to the 'price' of owner-occupied housing. Any owner with a mortgage has to meet the cost of interest payments in relation to the loan. The level of interest rates at any given time will be a cost to the owner and will influence their economic decisions about continuing in their present accommodation, or whether it is possible or necessary to 'trade' up or down. Increases in interest rates may depress demand, as was seen in the house price crash in the late 1980s. During that period the government, faced with inflation in the housing market, used interest rate policy as the main tool for controlling inflationary pressures. The rise in interest rates reduced the amounts that individual lenders could afford to borrow – and therefore the amount they could afford to pay when moving house – with the net result that house prices fell dramatically in some areas.

The availability of finance

The returns available from substitute investments may affect demand, both from owner occupiers and from landlords. Potential purchasers of dwellings may choose to invest any additional income or wealth elsewhere, if this gives better returns than they would anticipate from the ownership of residential property. Existing private landlords might also decide under certain economic conditions that investment in other markets is more attractive and decide to move out of private landlordism. Any such decisions will reduce levels of demand for housing purchases among this group.

Growing wealth among the population will generally increase the demand for owner-occupied housing. As most wealth in the United Kingdom is held in housing, it follows that the greater the proportion of owner occupiers in total demand, the greater will be the level of quality adjusted demand. This situation will occur as the increased demand leads to increasing house prices, which in turn leads to existing long-standing owners 'trading up' into more expensive properties, and thus the demand for higher quality dwellings will increase.

The availability of credit will also affect the demand for owner occupation. During the 1980s the expansion in the availability of housing finance undoubtedly contributed to the explosion in demand, which generated huge price rises in many areas. During 1980 the average advance loaned by United Kingdom building societies was equivalent to 73.8 per cent of the full cost of the property being purchased. At the same time societies were loaning on average an amount equivalent to 2.26 times the annual income of borrowing households. By 1988 the average advance was 84.8 per cent of the purchase price, and 2.66 times the annual income of borrowers. Such relaxation of the restrictions on lending both contributed to, and were a response to, the increase in house prices which occurred during this period.

Perceived availability of dwellings

As discussed earlier, the demand for all tenures will be influenced by availability. However, if a particular type of tenure is perceived as unavailable, then those demanding accommodation will be forced to transfer to alternative tenures. For example, in areas where the local authority has a lettings policy which precludes single people under a certain age from joining the waiting list, or has very little single person's accommodation among its housing stock, young single people will have to look to other types of tenure, typically the private rented sector, to meet their housing need. Traditionally in the United Kingdom the private rented sector has often provided an essential first stage for young people leaving home, including students and those saving a deposit to buy their own home. It also serves as a complement to the social rented sector to meet demand for accommodation from those people on low incomes, and those who prefer to rent rather than to buy.

The impact of government policies

Government policies will clearly have an enormous influence on demand for particular tenures. For example, rent controls and increased security of tenure following the 1977 Rent Act encouraged the demand for private rented accommodation, though this was increasingly unavailable due to the impact of these restrictions on the attractiveness of rented accommodation as an investment opportunity for private landlords, and much of the demand switched to public rented housing.

Successive governments of different political hues have promoted home ownership through a range of policies. Tax concessions to owner occupiers have greatly stimulated the demand for this tenure. In addition, the right to buy provisions introduced in the 1980 Housing Act have contributed greatly to the increase in owner occupation over the past two decades. Since the implementation of the right to buy for tenants of local authorities and many housing associations, the levels of discount available on the sale price have periodically increased, thus reducing the cost of purchasing for many tenants. At the same time, changes in the financial regimes for both local authorities and housing associations have forced rent increases, in turn lessening the differential between the cost of renting and purchasing as part of a government policy of encouraging owner occupation as widely as possible.

Summary

The overall level of demand for housing is influenced by a range of factors, including demographic issues such as the total numbers in the population, and the age profile of its members. The number of households and the rate at which household formation occurs will also have an impact. Levels of income and the distribution of income throughout the population affect demand, as do the price and availability of accommodation.

The levels of demand for housing *within* the different tenures are affected by a broad range of factors. Many of the factors affecting demand for particular tenures are related to affordability – the price for particular accommodation being at a level for which the income of the particular household is sufficient. It follows, therefore, that the existence of a housing need will not necessarily automatically result in the satisfaction of that need. Indeed, within a private market the ability to translate a 'want' or desire for housing into 'effective demand' depends on the ability to pay.

Increased mobility will raise the demand for privately rented accommodation, since this is the only tenure which permits fairly rapid entry and exit. This may of course be related to the age profile of the population, as well as migration, since young people are generally more mobile. Since the public sector tends to apply residence criteria in its selection processes, and has generally more security of tenure and lower turnover, this tenure is generally least suited to highly mobile sections of the population.

Table 2.1 summarises the main influences on demand for accommodation in different types of housing tenures.

Table 2.1 Examples of specific influences on demand for different tenure types

Influence on demand	Owner-occupied/bought	Rent – public/private
Increased income	Increased demand and increased qualitative demand	Increased demand at low income levels Decreased demand at higher income levels
Increased mobility	Decreased demand, due to high transaction costs and relatively long entry and exit times.	Increased demand for private renting Decreased demand for public renting due to waiting lists, and allocations criteria
Increased wealth	Increased demand and increased qualitative demand	Decreased demand
Increased price of owner-occupied accommodation	May be some decreased demand (diverted to renting); but demand may also increase if future price rises expected 'trading up' occurs	Demand may increase if renting seen as a more affordable alternative to buying
Increased rent levels	May be some increased demand if cost of renting is rising to a level which is close to the cost of buying	Demand may reduce if rate of household formation falls, and levels of multi-occupation rise. Some may direct to buy.
Increased availability	Reflected in reduction in price. If credit is available demand will increase	In public sector depends on government policy. May be increased demand for private renting as new households form
'Higher' social class	Increased demand and increased demand for accomodation at 'higher quality' end of the market	Reduced demand (except for high quality private rented accommodation

2.5 The supply of housing

Throughout the 1980s and early 1990s there has been a continuing increase in levels of owner occupation. At the end of 1995 around 70 per cent of the total housing stock of the United Kingdom was within this tenure, with 18 per cent in local authority ownership, 8 per cent rented privately and 4 per cent within the housing association sector. A fuller picture can be gained by looking at the age and type of dwellings available within each tenure (Table 2.2).

Table 2.2 Age and type of accommodation in each type of tenure England (per cent)

	Owner occupied	Private rented	Local authority	Housing association
Houses				
Pre-1919	22	30	2	11
1919–1944	18	10	17	6
1945–1964	14	5	21	5
Post 1964	25	7	12	10
Flats				
Pre 1919	5	29	2	19
1919–1944	1	4	3	4
Post 1945	5	10	35	41
Bungalows	10	5	8	4
Totals	100	100	100	100

Source: adapted from English House Condition Survey, 1991 (1993)

It is clear from Table 2.2 that there are marked differences between types of tenure in the age of accommodation. Within the private rented sector 73 per cent of properties were built prior to 1945. Of the dwellings owned by housing associations and owner occupiers 40 per cent and 46 per cent respectively are of this older stock. Local authority dwellings are of more recent construction with only 24 per cent being more than 50 years old.

It can also be seen that there are some differences in the types of accommodation between tenures. Within the owner-occupied sector 79 per cent of the housing stock consists of houses, with only 11 per cent of dwellings being flats and 10 per cent bungalows. In contrast within the housing association sector 64 per cent of dwellings are flats, and only 32 per cent are houses with the remaining 4 per cent being bungalows. Whilst the total numbers of dwellings in each tenure indicate that the housing association sector is by far the smallest tenure, the preponderance of flats within this sector is significant in terms of the types of developments traditionally undertaken and the ethos behind much of the voluntary housing movement in catering for other than 'traditional' general needs family housing. The table also shows that 40 per cent of local authority dwellings consist of houses built prior to 1964, with only 12 per cent of the stock being houses built since 1964, reflecting the large-scale local authority house building which took place following the First World War and a particular boom during the 1950s. It is also notable that only 5 per cent of local authority dwellings are flats built prior to 1945, reflecting the emphasis on building houses in the first half of the century. The immediate post-Second World War policy of building as many new homes as possible, together with a commitment from governments of both political hues to clear slums and replace with large-scale family housing, is reflected in the table which shows that 35 per cent of the total local authority stock consists of flats built since 1945.

It will be useful to now look at some of the factors which will have an impact on the supply of housing within the existing housing stock within all of the types of tenure.

Patterns of household life cycles will have an impact on the availability of housing. As the numbers of households increase, causing an expansion in demand, so there will be an associated impact in reducing the supply as available accommodation is taken up in increasing numbers.

If there are rising proportions of young households, levels of mobility among the population will increase; this will cause increased supply in the private rented sector, which is used most by these mobile groups. Clearly, high levels of mobility will result in high levels of turnover and thus increased availability of accommodation.

Conversely if there are rising proportions of families, family housing within the public sector, for which there are usually long waiting times to gain access and greater security of tenure than in the private sector, will tend to have comparatively lower levels of turnover. The net outcome will be less supply of available accommodation within existing stock in this sector.

The supply of privately rented housing

The rate at which new privately rented accommodation becomes available is affected by economic investment decisions reached by existing and would-be private landlords. The return on investments in private rented accommodation – chiefly the income from renting – is a major factor determining whether new housing stock will enter the tenure. The level of returns realised by landlords will be influenced by other factors, such as government regulation through rent controls or the restriction of housing benefit levels, and the existence of tax concessions through schemes such as the business expansion scheme (BES).

The upturn in the numbers of privately rented dwellings from the 1989 low point followed a number of government policy initiatives which had the stated aim of stimulating growth in the tenure. Assured tenancies, which had been a small scale and rarely used initiative within the 1980 Housing Act, were redefined and extended by the 1988 Housing Act to cover all new lettings within the 'independent rented sector', a newly defined tenure grouping including both private renting and housing associations – in what can be seen as an attempt to separate the voluntary sector from the local authority sector with which it had previously been strongly associated. The new 'assured tenancy' offered less security of tenure than the previous 'secure tenancy' by extending the mandatory grounds for a landlord to obtain possession.

In tandem with reduced security of tenure the 1988 Act also deregulated rents on all new lettings in the independent rented sector, defining a new role for the rent officer. Instead of setting a 'fair rent' as the case would be for a secure tenancy, the rent

officer's role in relation to assured tenancies is to determine 'reasonable' levels of housing benefit payable. The aim of this change in role was to 'free up' the private rented
sector so that rent levels would be more sensitive to market forces, and therefore more
attractive to potential landlords. In practice this policy was only a partial success as it
resulted in rapid increases in expenditure from Department of Social Security budgets
in respect of housing benefit as payments increased with spiralling rent levels.

The business expansion scheme (BES) was originally introduced to stimulate
investment in industry, and in 1988 was extended to encourage companies to invest
in dwellings for the private rented sector. Under the scheme investors were eligible
for tax relief on investments up to £40,000 per year. In addition, an investor who
had held shares in a business expansion scheme company for five years could sell
their shares without being liable for capital gains tax. Research by the Joseph
Rowntree Trust found that 8,200 dwellings for rent had been provided as a result of
the BES in the first two years. The long-term effects were limited, however, as the
scheme was abolished in 1994 and therefore the tax incentives to new investors
ceased. Between 1988 and 1993 the scheme is estimated to have attracted £3.3 billion of investment in about 80,000 homes. Since 1 April 1996, under provisions in
the Finance Act 1996, investers have been able to set up Housing Investment
Trusts – companies established to own residential properties for rent – with exemption from capital gains tax and a reduced rate of corporation tax.

Many landlords, particularly in the United Kingdom, hold housing as a capital
investment – seeking future capital gains from an anticipated increase in value, in addition to the revenue returns from renting. As house prices rise the attraction of housing as
a longer term capital investment increases, and properties purchased for their long-term
investment value are likely to find their way into the private rented sector until the price
reaches a level at which the landlord chooses to realise the capital tied up in the property. Asset values will be affected by a range of market factors, among them the security
of tenure enjoyed by tenants. The deregulation of tenancies through the Housing Act
1988 was an attempt by central government to make private renting more attractive to
potential landlords with decreased security of tenure enabling landlords to obtain vacant
possession more easily and therefore liquefy their assets more quickly.

In addition to rent controls and security of tenure for private tenants, government policies in relation to taxation and planning regulations will also have an
impact on the supply of housing as will the availability of finance. Lending to private
landlords is in turn affected by the perceptions of financial institutions about likely
available rental income and long-term asset value, and thus whether private renting is
seen as a good investment. The availability of private finance is also of key importance
to both the refurbishment of dwellings and the development of new stock by housing
associations, as the reduction of grant levels from central government pushes them to
rely increasingly on the money markets to raise funds.

The attractiveness to both lenders and landlords of investment alternatives influences the availability of finance to fund new private rented stock. If revenue and
capital returns from residential property are expected to yield less than other investment opportunities, there will be less finance available to fund the purchase of
housing stock for private renting purposes.

A further factor is the mobility of existing tenants. Traditionally in the United
Kingdom the private rented sector has been seen as having the advantage of flexibil-

ity for tenants due to its being relatively easy to gain access quickly, subject to having the ability to pay, when compared to social rented housing or owner occupation. As such the more mobile sections of the community have traditionally made use of this tenure which allows swift entry and exit. High levels of tenant turnover within this sector can be attractive to potential landlords who will see as unlikely the possibility of a long-term tenant inhibiting their ability to liquefy their assets through sale of the property once the market price is at a level which makes selling attractive.

The supply of owner occupied housing

Unlike most of the rest of Europe and North America, most new building in the United Kingdom is speculative. As such the provision of new housing within this tenure is largely based on expectations of future price changes. These expectations in turn depend on the flow of funds to housing finance markets, the current level of vacant dwellings for sale, and the time taken to sell current houses. Unlike many other markets where an increase in demand will result in a fairly swift increase in supply, supply in the housing market is relatively inelastic (i.e. does not respond quickly to price changes) due to the lead-in periods necessary to construct new housing stock. Housing developers will find the conditions for construction more favourable in a situation where the building societies and banks are able or willing to lend sufficient funds to potential buyers.

The availability of such funds has an impact on the price of property, as will the availability of vacant dwellings for sale, and the time taken for current houses to sell. Clearly, at times where market conditions are such that large numbers of vacant dwellings are taking a relatively long time to sell, the development of new homes will be discouraged. Equally, in a situation where there are fewer properties on the market, and they are selling fairly quickly, there will be an impact in increasing prices which will in turn encourage the development of new properties for sale.

Allied to these factors, the costs of land, construction costs, and the cost of borrowing (interest rates) will all impinge on the decisions of developers, as will the availability of finance to builders, which in turn will be affected by the costs and prices outlined above. It is clear then that each of the different factors influencing the cost of developing and the anticipated profits to be made from investing in new development are all closely linked and in many ways interdependent.

Developers will also take account of the profitability of other work – non-residential building work – in deciding whether to develop further housing. The market conditions were such in the mid-1990s, following the hangover after the 1980s boom, that major companies such as Tarmac Construction made the decision to get out of house construction altogether.

The inelasticity of the housing market is a product of the time lags and delays caused by factors such as planning controls, seasonal factors and occasional shortages of labour and materials. Each of these factors will also have an influence on the rate at which new housing enters this sector.

As with other types of housing tenure government policy has an impact on the supply of owner occupied dwellings. One of the major policy initiatives in this area has been the right to buy provisions that were considered earlier in relation to the demand for accommodation. Right to buy sales contributed markedly to the increase in the number of dwellings in the owner-occupied sector during the 1980s and into the early 1990s. Some of those properties purchased by tenants will have also found their way into the private rented sector. The rate at which properties are being bought rose steadily from 1980, reaching a pinnacle of 139,722 dwellings bought during 1989. The level of sales has steadily reduced since that peak, with sales still above 41,000 each year during 1992, 1993 and 1994. However, the policy has clearly played a major part in expanding the supply of accommodation to owner occupation (*Housing and Construction Statistics*, 1995).

Low cost home ownership schemes will also affect the supply of new housing. Schemes such as do-it-yourself shared ownership (DIYSO) have been moderately successful in increasing the numbers of owners. The DIYSO scheme allows potential buyers who cannot afford the full cost of purchasing to buy a proportion of the house (typically 25 per cent or 50 per cent) with a housing association buying the remaining portion. The owner/tenant then pays mortgage payments in relation to any money borrowed to buy their owned portion, and rent to the association in respect of the rest of the property. Such schemes allow for the purchase of increasing portions of the dwelling as the household's income increases until 100 per cent is owned.

Supply within existing stock

The supply of existing housing depends heavily on current market conditions and the general economic climate. When incomes are rising and there are expectations of price increases, the supply of houses will also increase, as existing owners choose to sell and 'trade up'. Conversely, falling incomes (in an economic recession) and falling prices will cause a reduced supply, as households choose to delay selling.

The supply of social rented housing

New building

Unlike the other tenure types social rented housing, whilst it has always operated within the context of the market, is far more dependent on political and adminis-trative decisions, from central government, local government and statutory funding bodies such as the Housing Corporation. The new building of social rented hous-ing in the United Kingdom has been solely dependent on government policies in relation to borrowing and capital finance. Since 1979 policies to reduce levels of borrowing by local authorities have reduced their ability to provide new housing for rent, in line with a general trend in Conservative government policy toward the pri-vatisation and deregulation of housing provision. At the same time the initial encouragement to housing associations to take over the role of the main developers of new social rented housing has decreased with the increasing emphasis on private finance as grant levels have gone down. In addition, in any particular local area the political views of the local authority will also have had an impact on the types of development and the way in which that development is carried out.

Supply within existing stock

The supply of social rented housing is also affected by the use made of existing stock. The first key factor is the size of the housing stock. Clearly the more social rented housing stock there is, the more likelihood of housing within that sector becoming available to meet demand. This is not to suggest, however, that size is the only determining factor. Clearly, the level of turnover within the stock is important. For example, a social landlord with a large stock in which there was no turnover is never going to be in a position to meet the housing needs of any but its existing tenants.

An example will illustrate the impact of turnover and its relationship to stock size. Assume that there are two social housing landlords, one with a stock of 20,000 properties and the other with 5,000 dwellings. If the smaller landlord has a turnover of 10 per cent of dwellings during a year, this would equal 500 properties becoming available for reletting. If during the same period the larger landlord has a turnover of 2 per cent of its dwellings, this would equal 400 homes available for new letting. Leaving aside considerations of the popularity of areas with these respective turnovers, it is clear that in terms of total dwellings being supplied from within the existing housing stock for letting, turnover can have a bigger impact than total stock alone.

Related to the issue of turnover is the mobility of existing tenants. Traditionally, social rented housing has been more difficult to gain swift access to than private rented accommodation, due to the often bureaucratic processes used to administer the rationing process. This has tended to reduce the use of social rented housing among the most mobile groups in society. However, a certain level of mobility will obviously occur, and will influence the level of turnover in the housing stock. As the level of mobility among tenants increases, whether due to factors such as tenants moving to seek employment elsewhere or tenants choosing to leave the tenure to move into other accommodation, then there will be an increase in supply of dwellings from within the existing housing stock.

Just as the rate of construction of new dwellings affects the level of supply, so the rate at which accommodation leaves the social rented sector will have an impact. Earlier there was consideration of the impact on the supply of owner-occupied dwellings of the provisions of the 1980 Housing Act, which gave certain social rented housing tenants the right to buy their homes. There has at the same time been a substantial reduction in the numbers of social rented dwellings.

As noted above, whilst the numbers of properties owned by both local authorities and housing associations being bought by tenants under the right to buy has fluctuated year by year, there has been a steady continuing sale under this policy. At the same time the number of new properties being produced within the social housing sector has been consistently substantially lower than the number of properties leaving the sector. During 1993 there were 51,193 new social housing completions, falling to a figure of 35,500 during 1994 (*Housing and Construction Statistics*, 1995). The net result of this disparity has been a reduction of the number of properties in the social rented sector.

Levels of supply will in addition be influenced by the void management policies of social landlords. Clearly, efficient policies will reduce void times to ensure swifter availability for renting of properties vacated. The policies of the landlord will also have a differential impact on the availability of dwellings for different groups within the population. If a landlord has a policy of allocating dwellings only to tenants above a certain age, or with certain family characteristics, then clearly those who fall outside those limits will have less access to the stock of social rented housing. Similarly an increased willingness on the part of the landlord to transfer tenants between properties will increase the supply of accommodation appropriate to the needs of tenants and potential tenants.

Changes in housing supply between tenures

So far there has been consideration of a range of factors which might affect the rate at which housing becomes available within each of the types of tenure. There is, however, scope for substantial movement of properties from one tenure to another. The total number of dwellings in Great Britain has steadily increased throughout the late 1980s and into the 1990s. For example, in 1984 the total national housing stock stood at 21.653 million; by the end of 1994 the figure had increased to 23.469 million. At the same time it is clear that the stock of owner-occupied dwellings, and the stock within the housing association sector have increased throughout this period. The stock within the owner-occupied sector has risen from 12.914 million to 15.591 million, whilst the stock held by housing associations has increased from 525,000 to 874,000 during the same period. The stock of dwellings in the private rented sector has fallen slightly in number from 2.29 million to 2.278 million, although this has not been a steady decline – within the period the stock fell to a low point of 2.065 million by 1989, rising again by 1994. The only sector to have experienced substantial reductions during this period is the local authority housing stock, falling from 5.924 million to 4.726 million between 1984 and 1994 (Housing and Construction Statistics, 1995).

Many of these developments, particularly increases in housing stock within tenures, can be seen to be the result of new building specifically for a particular sector. There can, however, be substantial movement between tenures. The English House Condition Survey of 1991 showed, for example, that between 1986 and 1991, 1.3 million dwellings changed tenure (English House Condition Survey 1991, 1993, p. 5).

The next section considers some of the factors affecting the movement of dwellings between different tenures and the impact that such movements have on the supply of accommodation.

Public renting to owner occupation

The legislation introducing the right to buy can be seen as part of a government policy to increase levels of owner occupation and reduce the role of local authorities in the provision of accommodation. Following the introduction of the policy through the 1980 Housing Act, the government repeatedly increased the levels of discount in order to further encourage tenants to take up the option. Originally discount levels were such that after two years as a tenant the property could be purchased with a discount of 33 per cent of the value of the property, rising initially to a maximum of 50 per cent depending on length of residence. The Housing and Building Control Act 1984 increased the maximum discount to 60 per cent, with a maximum discount of 70 per cent of property value being introduced for tenants of flats with the Housing and Planning Act 1986.

During the same period changes to the financial controls exerted over both local authorities and housing associations had the effect of encouraging increases in rent levels and thus encouraging qualifying tenants to buy. The net result was an increase in the stock of owner-occupied dwellings as the stock of social rented housing reduced.

Council renting to housing association

Large-scale voluntary transfer (LSVT) has been an increasing response by local authorities to restrictions on their access to resources to repair and maintain an increasingly ageing housing stock. The process involves the sale of housing stock to another landlord – usually a housing association. There have been a small number of transfers to existing housing associations, but most have been to associations established especially for the purpose. Such associations are council sponsored and tend to be staffed by former employees transferred by the local authority, often operating in the same office facilities formerly used by the authority.

Council renting to the private rented sector

Developments in housing policy since the election of the Conservative government in 1979 have been firmly rooted in an overriding ideological drive toward the privatisation of state institutions – including those responsible for the delivery of welfare services – and the removal of regulation in many areas of the economy, to allow market forces to take a dominant role. A key development within the 1988 Housing Act was the first major attempt on the part of the government to privatise the administration of local authority housing with the introduction of the 'tenants' choice' provisions. Under tenants' choice, alternative landlords had the power to bid for a housing estate. The government's commitment to 'bringing housing back to the community' led to the introduction of tenants, ballots on whether they wished a proposed transfer to a new landlord to take place. Despite a voting system which some commentators denounced as undemocratic – with every abstention being counted as a vote in favour of change – the provisions had very limited success and were eventually abolished in the 1996 Housing Act.

A further policy measure supporting the drive toward privatisation of the administration of local authority housing has been the introduction of compulsory competitive tendering for housing management services. The first tranche of contracts to be put out to tender for operation from April 1995 were largely won by 'in-house' bids from existing local authority housing departments, as very few outside bidders entered the process. A small number of private companies were successful in taking over housing management services at the margins. However, housing associations largely avoided the first round, except where specifically invited by local authorities wishing to divest the housing management function.

A Government White Paper, *Our Future Homes: Opportunity, Choice, Responsibility – The Government's Housing Policies for England and Wales*, published in June 1995, proposed that local authorities be given the power to transfer their housing stock to local housing companies which will be able to draw in private funding, thus ironing out some of the current cost difficulties of LSVT. Support in some form for this initiative from both the Chartered Institute of Housing and the Labour Party suggest that housing companies in some guise will be part of the future funding mechanism for social rented housing.

In addition, there has been the privatisation of other forms of public-rented stock, such as Police, Forrestry Commision and Ministry of Defence housing, to new private landlords. Some of this stock has since moved into owner-occupation.

Private renting to owner occupation

There is a continually fluctuating relationship between the private rented and owner-occupied tenures with properties moving between the tenures depending on a range of factors, including the conditions in the markets for both tenures and the impact of government intervention. Traditionally, the net total movement has tended to be from renting to owned properties. A property might transfer from the private rented sector into owner occupation when a tenant leaves and the landlord considers the market conditions are right to sell to a home owner rather than reletting. Alternatively, the landlord might sell to a sitting tenant who then becomes an owner occupier.

Research by Holmans, based on Census data, has shown that between 1971 and 1981 the net transfer from private renting to owner occupation was 60,000 dwellings per year. This level of transfer continued through the early 1980s but slowed to the middle of the decade, and was reversed, with a net movement from owner occupation to private renting of 10,000 during 1989 (Holmans *et al.*, 1994).

After 1989 the net flow of transfers was from owner occupation back into private renting after continuous regular movement in the opposite direction. The main factors at the root of the reverse after 1988 are the deregulation of most new private lettings from January 1989, under the terms of the 1988 Housing Act, and the slowing down of the market for owner-occupied dwellings.

As discussed earlier, the numbers of privately rented dwellings fell during the mid-1980s. At this time there was a lot of activity in the owner-occupied market, and rising house prices. Clearly such conditions encouraged landlords to sell up, transferring properties to owner occupation, and encouraged sitting tenants to buy.

International comparisons

The proportion of owner occupation has increased by 21 per cent since 1969 to the current situation in which around 70 per cent of households in the United Kingdom live in owner-occupied dwellings. There is an interesting comparison to be drawn with other Western European countries such as the Netherlands, with 46 per cent, and France, with 54 per cent, to suggest that high levels of owner occupation are not inevitable in Western industrialised societies.

Turning from a consideration of the overall proportion of the population living in owner occupation to consider the rates of change in this tenure over a period of time, some interesting facts emerge.

During the two decades ending in 1990 owner occupation in Great Britain increased by 21 per cent. At the same time the tenure increased in France by 12 per cent, the Netherlands by 18 per cent, and Germany by only 1 per cent (Coles, 1991).

Coles has suggested that there would appear to be a link between levels of increased demand for owner occupation and the rate of inflation in particular national economies. As he has demonstrated, the three European Union countries with the lowest inflation rates over the past two decades, Denmark, Luxembourg and (West) Germany had the lowest levels of increase in levels of owner occupation. Over the same period, Portugal, Great Britain and Ireland, who all had relatively high inflation rates, have seen markedly high increases in levels of owner occupation. From these figures we can conclude that there is a high probability that at times of high inflation residential property can be seen as a sound investment which will retain its value in 'real terms' as other investments 'lose' value due to the effects of inflation.

An examination of the proportions of the national stock in the private rented sector across Europe again shows some interesting comparisons. In Germany 46 per cent of the housing stock is privately rented, with 25 per cent in France, 16 per cent in the Netherlands and 8 per cent in the United Kingdom (The Netherlands' Ministry of Housing, Physical Planning and the Environment, 1992).

This data shows a marked difference in the United Kingdom compared most other industrialised Western European nations. Some commentators have suggested that the low level of private renting in the United Kingdom is linked to the tradition of rent control and greater security of tenure than other countries. It is concluded that such measures have discouraged investment in private landlordism in this country. As Coles has illustrated, however, rent controls have been imposed in many other European countries. Instead, he points to the existence of subsidies for private landlords, in the form of depreciation allowances in many of the other countries, which have not been available in the United Kingdom. Such measures will act as a further incentive to private landlords to continue their investment in the tenure and not to sell off properties into the owner-occupied sector.

2.6 Assessment of housing need

Many of the factors affecting 'demand' for housing, both overall and within the different tenures, were considered earlier in the chapter. There was also consideration of the impact of price and affordability on the ability of individual households to make their preferred housing choices. As discussed during the introduction to this chapter, inherent in the market system is a requirement for households to have the ability to pay for their preferred accommodation if such housing desires are to be transformed into demand. Analysis of market conditions such as price levels, and effective demand (i.e. demand which is backed up by the ability to pay) can only give part of the picture of the overall levels of housing needed, and what types of accommodation are required. It cannot give the full picture because any such consideration will not take account of those households in need who do not have the finance required to satisfy their needs. Instead it is necessary to draw together information from a number of sources in order to arrive at a complete assessment of housing need.

Traditionally, many local authorities in the United Kingdom relied on their waiting lists as a measure of housing need. They would often base decisions on new building on the perceived shortfalls reflected through the types of accommodation, and in the locations, for which they had the greatest numbers registered on waiting lists. During the immediate post-war period, when large-scale local authority housing development was taking place – particularly in Scotland and the North of

England – the numbers of applicants for whom the authority could not provide accommodation was often the major factor influencing the type of new development taking place. At the same time many local authorities had waiting lists through which property allocations were solely based on date order. Many authorities had restrictions on who could join their lists with, for example, applicants having to have reached a certain age or to have lived in the local area for a given period of time before becoming eligible to register on the list. Such restrictions would clearly distort any assessment of 'need' using the lists as a basis.

As the role of local authorities as developers of new social rented housing has diminished they have been subject to increasing encouragement from central government to expand and develop their role as 'strategic enablers'. Whilst the strategic planning role had already existed for local authorities for some time the emphasis on this aspect of their activity was brought into sharper focus by government proposals in the 1987 White Paper, *Housing: The Government's Proposals*, which specifically stated that:

> 'the future role of local authorities will essentially be a strategic one: identifying housing needs and demand encouraging innovative methods of provision by other bodies to meet such needs, maximising the use of private finance, and encouraging new interest in the revival of the independent rented sector.'

The crux of this role, then, is for authorities to take overall responsibility for assessing the level of housing need within their area, and for the encouragement of partnership arrangements with both the private sector and housing associations to facilitate the development of accommodation to meet that need.

It was noted earlier that the Census measure of the total numbers of the population will not give a fully accurate picture of the level of demand for housing. It is, however, a useful starting point for the analysis of housing needs. The Census data that were considered earlier in relation to the total population, numbers of households and household size give a useful basis for assessment, looking at the way in which the population is structured in terms of the age profile and the way in which households are structured. Factors such as the birth rate and mortality rates can also contribute to building up a picture of likely future housing need in terms of overall stock, and also the types and sizes of dwellings which will be required.

Guidance issued by the Department of the Environment in 1980 recommends that local authorities begin by looking to forecasts of the total population and number of households to establish the total number of households in need of housing. The guidance also suggests that authorities should go beyond this to consider indicators of need for housing among those currently living in different tenures. These would include direct indicators, such as the numbers of people on waiting lists, and levels of homelessness; and indirect indicators, such as the numbers of people on low incomes, and the numbers of elderly people in the local area.

The guidance also suggests that authorities should reach some conclusions on the proportion of households who could meet their needs through owner occupation and how many would be looking to rented housing. The financial aspects of the local authority strategic planning role are considered in detail in Chapter 3.

Two further valuable sources of information to assist when identifying housing need are the English House Condition Survey, and the General Household Survey, which addresses the issue of density of occupation (levels of overcrowding and under-occupation) using the 'bedroom standard', working on the premise that the crucial indicator of whether housing space available fits the needs of the household is the availability of bedrooms. The bedroom standard used in the General Household Survey is a concept which is used to estimate occupation density by allocating a standard number of bedrooms to each household in accordance with its composition. The age, sex and marital status of each household member are considered, together with their relationship to each other. In calculating the bedroom standard:

> '... a separate bedroom is allocated to each co-habiting couple, any other person aged 21 or over, each pair of young persons aged 10–20 of the same sex; and each pair of children under 10 (regardless of sex). Unpaired young persons aged 10–20 are paired with a child under 10 of the same sex if possible or allocated a separate bedroom. Any remaining unpaired children under 10 are also allocated a separate bedroom.' (English House Condition Survey, 1991, 1993, p. 33.)

This standard is then compared with the actual number of bedrooms (including bedsitters) available for the sole use of the household, and any deficiencies or excesses calculated.

The General Household Survey, which was last undertaken in 1994, shows the variation from the bedroom standard within each of the housing tenures in Great Britain. Its findings show that only a very small proportion of the housing stock is over-crowded in the sense that it falls below the bedroom standard (those with one or more bedrooms below the bedroom standard). The survey showed that among households in the owner-occupied sector in Great Britain 18.5 per cent were living in accommodation which equalled the bedroom standard; 79.5 per cent were under-occupying, and only 2 per cent had one or more bedrooms less than the standard. Among council tenants 96 per cent were living in dwellings which were equal to, or had more than the standard, with only the remaining 6 per cent living in overcrowded conditions. Housing association tenants fared slightly better, with only 4 per cent occupying overcrowded housing, findings which might be expected with the newer, and therefore generally more recently allocated dwellings within that tenure. As such the survey findings indicated that the local authority and housing association sectors have more overcrowding than the owner-occupied sector.

Findings for the private rented sector give some interesting insights. The unfurnished rented sector is similar to owner occupation with a lot of underoccupation, 59 per cent of occupying households were found to have one or more bedrooms to spare, whilst 36 per cent were equal to the bedroom standard, and only 4 per cent were overcrowded. By contrast the furnished rented sector has the most overcrowding and the least underoccupation; with 7 per cent lacking at least one bedroom, and only 38 per cent found to be underoccupying. Such findings might be expected given the preponderance of sub-divided houses with flats and bedsitters in this sector (Office of Population and Census Surveys, 1995).

In 1991 the Census showed that there were 21.9 million households in the United Kingdom. At the same time there were 23.115 million dwellings in the country. At first glance these figures would suggest that there is a net surplus of dwellings, and therefore that there should be no homelessness, at a time when there are still large numbers of homeless households approaching local authorities for assistance and people sleeping on the streets. There are a number of reasons for this apparent disparity. First, the growth of population and of pressure on the availability of housing varies from area to area, and houses may not be where people need them. Secondly, as households and their preferences change, the types of housing contained in the stock may be different from what is needed but generally the housing stock can only be changed quite slowly. Finally, and most crucially, there is the issue of access to housing. Housing may exist but may be inaccessible to those who need it and the kinds of households increasing most quickly make this problem particularly acute.

Each of the different mechanisms detailed above can be used together to build up a picture of housing need. It is important, however, to realise that the assessment of need is only the start of the process of achieving the satisfaction of those requirements. As there is a limited stock of housing available there are rationing mechanisms, both through the market for owner occupation and private renting, and through a mixture of market factors and administrative procedures within the public rented sector.

2.7 Implications of tenure on housing quality

As has already been considered, there are a range of factors influencing the supply of dwellings to each housing tenure. A further issue for consideration is the impact of such socio-economic and demographic factors on the quality and standard of the accommodation within each tenure. A useful starting point in any consideration of the quality of accommodation is to look at a definition of what might be considered to be standards of 'reasonableness' or 'fitness' in relation to dwellings.

The English House Condition Survey considers whether dwellings have a range of basic amenities, which are defined as:

- a kitchen sink;
- bath or shower, within a bathroom;
- wash hand basin;
- indoor W.C.;
- hot and cold water supply to washing facilities.

The last survey in 1991 found that 205,000 dwellings, 1 per cent of the total housing stock, lacked basic amenities. It was found that 0.8 per cent of owner-occupied dwellings, 0.7 per cent of local authority dwellings, and 3.9 per cent of privately rented dwellings lacked one or more of the specified facilities; equivalent to 101,000, 29,000, and 64,000 dwellings respectively. The housing association sector was found to have only 5,000 properties deprived of basic facilities, marginally over 0.5 per cent (English House Condition Survey, 1991, 1993).

From this data it can be seen that the tenure with the highest number of dwellings lacking one or more basic amenities was the owner-occupied sector. It must be borne in mind, however, that as this is by far the largest type of tenure in England, in proportional terms the private rented sector would appear to be the worst placed with 3.9 per cent of its total stock lacking in basic amenities.

Local authorities in England and Wales have powers under the Local Government and Housing Act 1989 to take action if a dwelling is classed as 'unfit'. This is defined by the Act as a dwelling which fails to meet the following standards:

- structural stability;
- freedom from serious disrepair;
- freedom from damp;
- adequate provision for lighting, heating and ventilation;
- adequate piped supply of wholesome water;
- satisfactory facilities for the preparation and cooking;
  of food including a sink with hot and cold water;
- suitably located W.C.;
- suitably located fixed bath or shower and wash hand basin supplied with hot and cold water and effective drainage.

Premises are unfit for human habitation under the terms of the 1989 Act if they fail to meet one or more of these requirements, and as a result are not suitable for occupation.

The measure of condition of dwellings in Scotland is defined in Section 86(1) of the Housing Scotland Act 1987. A dwelling is defined as meeting the 'tolerable standard' if it:

- is structurally stable;
- is substantially free from rising or penetrating damp;
- is satisfactorily provided with natural and artificial lighting, ventilation and heating;
- is adequately supplied with wholesome water within the house;
- is provided with a sink with a supply of hot and cold water;
- has a water closet for the exclusive use of the occupants and satisfactorily located within the house;
- has an effective drainage system for disposal of foul and surface water;
- has facilities for the cooking of food within the house;
- has satisfactory access to all external doors and outbuildings.

Failure to meet any of these requirements results in the dwelling being classified as below tolerable standard.

A survey undertaken for Scottish Homes, and published in 1995, indicated that amongst the sample researched 4 per cent of dwellings were below tolerable standard (BTS). The 1991 Census indicated that there were 2.15 million dwellings in Scotland. The House Condition Survey findings would therefore translate to around 86,000 dwellings failing to meet the tolerable standard throughout the country. Of those dwellings failing to meet the standard the largest single reason was dampness, from which 52 per cent of BTS dwellings suffered. A further 18 per cent had inadequate lighting, ventilation and heating (Scottish Homes, 1995).

Data from the English House Condition Survey suggests that there is a correlation between the age of dwellings and their 'fitness for habitation'. The survey found that 17.9 per cent of dwellings constructed prior to 1850 were unfit, reducing to 8.4 per cent of those built between 1919 and 1944; 5.3 per cent of those built between 1945 and 1964; and only 2.2 per cent of dwellings constructed since 1964 (English House Condition Survey, 1991, HMSO, 1993).

As might have been anticipated the proportion of the housing stock which is unfit reduces as consideration turns to properties of more recent construction. There are, however, a number of factors in addition to age which impact on the standard of dwellings. The English House Condition Survey gives information on the household make up of those households in the worst 10 per cent of dwellings. Consideration of these data provides some useful insights.

The survey showed that the groups most strongly represented within the worst 10 per cent of the housing stock are single person households, with 17.5 per cent in poor condition. Also strongly featured are single parents with 11.2 per cent, and single older person households with 11.3 per cent (English House Condition Survey, 1991, 1993). This state of affairs might not be surprising as both groups will tend to have low incomes and are therefore less able to afford to repair and maintain their homes. A further function of the likelihood of low incomes among the group is the possibility that they may be restricted to the choice of poor quality housing when initially looking for a home.

Survey data would also suggest that age and income levels are key factors as to whether owner occupiers are likely to carry out repair and maintenance work on their homes. As income increases the likelihood of people spending more money on repairs to their property increases. Data from the survey suggest that households in the lowest income bands were most likely to live in the worst dwellings. This would suggest that those with the lowest income are able to afford only the worst property and are less able to afford repairs.

As owner occupiers age the likelihood of spending money on repairs would appear to decrease. A greater proportion of both the elderly and the younger age groups were found to live in the worst dwellings. As with income, this suggests that the dwellings these groups inhabit were in poorer condition to begin with and that repairs are less likely to have been carried out (English House Condition Survey, 1991, 1993).

There is also a link between age and income. The younger the occupier is, the more opportunity there is to earn money which might be spent on improvements in the house. In the same way that the above data shows the link between the income and the dwelling condition of owner occupiers, there will also be a link between the availability of finance to landlords and stock condition. If finance is available to landlords, in both private and public sectors there are more options available to them in maintaining their dwellings. In relation to local authority landlords there is a crucial impact of government financial controls in determining the amount of resources available to repair and maintain the stock. An associated factor will also be the spending decisions made by local politicians in how to ration and allocate the central government determined total sum.

A further influence on private landlords' decisions to spend on maintenance will be the rate of return on rented accommodation. In the past there has been a relatively poor rate of return for private landlords, and therefore a lack of incentive to invest in improving the condition of housing stock among this group.

As the owner-occupied sector has increased, an increasing proportion of home owners will be relatively poorer. Some commentators have noted that the Conservative government's push to increase the owner-occupied sector has taken numbers beyond limits which are sustainable by the market. In the worst cases the result might be repossession for those encouraged to take on financial responsibilities they cannot afford to meet. For others the impact will be a lack of ability to meet the costs of repairs and maintenance.

The house price boom of the 1980s, fuelled by the government's fiscal policies and an ability of mortgage lenders to advance larger and larger sums, resulted in many new home owners experiencing negative equity, with their homes being of lower value than the mortgage loans secured on them. It has been estimated that, in early 1997, around 925,000 home owners were in negative equity situations in which they are barely able to maintain mortgage payments, with no spare disposable income to meet the costs of repair and no scope for borrowing to improve or maintain the dwelling.

Further reading

Birchall, J. (ed.) (1992) *Housing Policy in the 1990s*, Routledge, London.

Clinton, A. (1989) *Housing Statistics: A Guide to Sources*, Institute of Housing/CURS, London.

Fallis, G. (1985) *Housing Economics*, Butterworth, London.

Maclennan, D. (1982) *Housing Economics: An Applied Approach*, Longman, London.

Malpass, P. and Murie, A. (1994) *Housing Policy and Practice*, 4th edn, Macmillan, Basingstoke.

Smith, M. E. H. (1989) *Guide to Housing*, 3rd edn, Housing Centre Trust, London.

Smith, M. E. H. (1995) *Second Supplement to the Third Edition of the Guide to Housing*, Housing Centre Trust, London.

Chapter 3

FINANCING SOCIAL HOUSING

3.1 Introduction

For more than a decade, changes to the arrangements for the finance of social housing have been at the forefront of fundamental government reforms of housing policy. These funding developments have affected all aspects of social housing provision and service delivery. This chapter aims to provide an overview of the main features of housing finance for social housing in the United Kingdom, and to highlight the key reasons for some of the changes which have been made.

It begins by considering the nature of housing and the reasons *why* housing finance is an important policy issue, and it then examines the influence of the economic context within which it operates. It considers the nature of public finance for housing and looks at the specific arrangements for the funding of both the development and rehabilitation of social housing by both local authorities and housing associations. These are *capital* finance issues.

The chapter also looks at finance for spending on management and repairs and maintenance, called *revenue* spending, for the two main types of social housing organisations. It examines the importance, for housing organisations, of budgets and budgetary control in managing financial resources and achieving financial objectives. It considers the arrangements for the provision of personal, financial subsidy to tenants, the housing benefit system, as well as for owner occupiers. The chapter concludes with a brief summary of the overall effects of recent changes to social housing finance for housing markets in the United Kingdom.

The nature of housing and the need for finance

The term housing finance includes *all* sources of funding for housing, whether public or private. Housing is a commodity much like any other, in that it can be produced, bought and sold. The production of housing – building homes – requires that building materials are bought and labour is paid to assemble the materials. Someone must provide the finance for this process. The dwellings may then be sold in private *markets*, and the purchasers – whether landlords or individuals – will have to pay the supplier. On the face of it, this is no different to the production of any other item. So, why is *finance* such an important issue in housing markets?

Housing is expensive

What distinguishes housing from other commodities is its high price. Housing is a very expensive item to produce. For most households, it is by far the most expensive item in their household budget. Indeed, a study for the Joseph Rowntree Foundation (a major sponsor of research into housing) found that households spend between 15 per cent and 30 per cent of their incomes on housing (Maclennan *et al.*, 1991).

The high cost of housing means that those who wish to *buy* property invariably have to find *external* sources of finance to help them, usually borrowing funds from financial institutions. In the UK, building societies and commercial (high street) banks are a major source of *private* finance for housing, and loans for house purchase comprise two thirds of all household debts (Maclennan *et al.*, 1991.) An entire industry has grown up around the need for private loans for house purchase.

However, housing is not simply a *consumer good*, wanted only for the *service* it provides in giving households shelter and security. It is a very durable commodity; with proper maintenance, it lasts for a very long time. This means that people view housing as an *asset*; they can put money into housing, and feel reasonably secure that, at some future date, they can sell the property and get their money back. So, housing is also an *investment* good, and over half of the wealth of British households is held in the form of housing (Maclennan *et al.*, 1991.) Unlike assets such as stocks and shares, however, the service which housing provides can be used by someone other than the owner, without it (necessarily) affecting its ultimate asset value. This means that property owners can either live in the dwelling themselves as owner occupiers or they can let someone else live there as tenants for a regular payment – a rent.

Renting permits those who either cannot afford to buy, or do not wish to buy, to obtain the services of a home. However, since housing is bought as an asset by landlords, they will wish to ensure that the income they earn from it, the return on their investment, is at least comparable with the *return* from other investments. If it is not, they will cease to keep their housing assets, and sell them to invest their money elsewhere.

House prices (or rents) in private markets

The term private (or 'free') markets refers to markets which are not subject to outside control, for example by the government. In the absence of any public sector regulation, private buyers and sellers can behave as they wish. In these types of markets, as explored in Chapter 2, the price of anything is determined by the interaction of *supply* (the goods or services offered by the sellers) and *demand* (the willingness and ability of buyers to purchase or pay rent).

In housing markets, the way that changes in demand and supply affect prices can be observed most easily in owner-occupied markets. When very many people are keen to buy, prices are pushed up – as was seen during the housing 'boom' of the mid-to-late 1980s. Conversely, when the demand for owner-occupied homes collapses (perhaps due to increased interest rates causing an increase in the monthly loan repayments, or rising unemployment causing falling household incomes), prices will be driven down. This happened in the United Kingdom from 1990, as Table 3.1 shows.

Table 3.1 Average United Kingdom house prices[a]

Year	Index	Year	Index
1985	50	1990	100
1986	57	1991	99
1987	67	1992	95
1988	84	1993	92
1989	101	1994	94
		1995	94

Source: adapted from Wilcox (1996) based on Council of Mortgage Lenders data derived from the DoE/BSA sample survey.
[a]Mix adjusted index 1990 = 100

The index provides a useful way of demonstrating real price changes after allowing for inflation. House prices in the base year (in this case 1990) are given a value of 100. Real prices in all other years, after allowing for inflation, are then expressed as a proportion of the base year's values. So, for example, house prices in 1993 in real terms were only 92 per cent of 1990s prices. The index has been 'mix adjusted' because the data on which it is based is a sample of properties on which building societies have given mortgages in that year, which may not be a representative mix of the stock of property types and their values.

When landlords let properties in private rented housing markets, assuming there are no *rent controls* (price ceilings set by the government), a similar process operates. As identified above, rents must offer a reasonable return on the investment made by the landlord. If private market rents fall to levels which do not provide a sufficient return to landlords, they will withdraw from renting, causing the *supply* to fall. This will ultimately cause rents to rise again, until the supply from landlords prepared to stay in the market just equals the demand *at the market rent*. However, at this rent, there may still be many people who wish to rent, but who cannot afford the price set by the market. They may have a *need* for housing, but cannot turn this need into a *demand* for housing. This is the case in many parts of the United Kingdom. There is a shortage of decent homes available at rents which many people can afford. So rents like house purchase prices are expensive; unless landlords receive a reasonable return they will not let property.

Access problems for low income groups

Since access to private housing markets, whether rented or owner-occupied, depends on the *ability to pay* the market rent or price, it is clear that low income households will be unable to afford decent housing. Before the public sector became involved in the provision of finance for housing, families with low incomes were forced to live in very overcrowded, poor quality properties, often sharing with a number of other families.

The government first became committed to the provision of finance for house building after the end of the First World War. It provided *capital subsidies* toward the cost of building council homes, which is examined in some detail in Chapter 1. Later, councils were urged to introduce *rent subsidy* schemes, in the form of rent rebates. Public finance was now to be used not simply to *provide homes* but also to *reduce weekly housing costs* for households. The current provision of public finance for housing still has these two distinct elements. This is examined further in Section 3.3.

In recent years, the main role in developing new, social housing has switched to voluntary, non-profit organisations, the housing association movement. Local authorities have increasingly been forced to take an *enabling* role, facilitating housing produced by other providers. However, whether the social housing provider is a council or housing association, the finance is still (largely) from the public sector – central or local government. The public sector's total resources are limited. Central government and local authorities must act within the constraints determined by broader economic factors, such as how well the United Kingdom economy is doing, and whether there is ample employment which generates more tax revenues from income tax, VAT, etc. The next section, therefore, considers the importance of the wider economic context to housing.

3.2 Housing in the economic context

Section 3.1 began by pointing out that housing is a commodity which must be produced like any other. However, it is a very expensive item, and the production process takes a relatively long time because of its complexity. (This process is examined in detail in Chapter 4.) As a result, housing construction is a very important *industry*, with a significant impact on the national economy. It is a large employer and, on average, the value of housing output (new build and renovation) exceeds 4 per cent of total, national output – commonly called *national income* or Gross National Product (GNP). But, as with any industry, it is not immune from developments in the national economy. The national economy tends to grow unevenly; it is subject to *cyclical* patterns, with periods of strong growth followed by periods of falling output, or *recession*.

As the economy grows, output is rising, so more income is created. Higher incomes mean higher tax receipts for central government. The demand for many goods, including housing, grows strongly too, which stimulates higher levels of output from the construction industry. However, since new housing takes a long time to produce, the main initial effect of rising demand is to push up house prices, as more buyers chase the same number of properties. As shown in Table 3.1, this could be seen clearly during the late 1980s, when despite rising housing starts, house prices rose dramatically.

When the economy ceases to grow, and then goes into recession, there is falling output. This means higher unemployment and lower incomes. Uncertainty leads households to put off buying property or moving to a larger, more expensive home and renovations are delayed. This results in a collapse in the demand for housing output. The construction industry is forced to reduce output, which adds to the growing numbers of unemployed. This, of course, further reduces national output and incomes.

At the same time, house prices face downward pressure as demand falls. In a severe recession, as during the early 1990s, house prices may even fall in real terms (see Table 3.1). This means that after allowing for inflation (the general increase in prices felt across the whole economy), housing becomes cheaper relative to other goods and services. Unemployed owner-occupying households, unable to afford their mortgages, may be repossessed – which means that the institution from which they borrowed the finance for the home takes *possession* of it, in order to sell it and re-coup the loan. The 'owners' are evicted. Similarly, unemployed renting households may fall into rent arrears, and may be evicted as a result. This increase in *homeless* households generates higher demand for social housing provision, as local authorities have a *statutory duty* to provide accommodation for certain *priority groups* (see Chapter 5), and housing associations also are expected to provide housing for these households.

It is evident that during these booms and slumps, public sector income is rising then falling. However, public sector *expenditure* tends to move in the *opposite* direction to income. Higher levels of unemployment mean falling tax receipts, but this also means higher expenditure on *welfare payments*, such as unemployment benefit and housing benefit. Government expenditure is rising whilst it is earning less from revenue. It can choose to fill the gap by more borrowing – increasing the *public sector borrowing requirement*, the PSBR – or it must reduce public expenditure. This choice depends on the policies of the government for the whole economy, known as macro-economic policies.

The impact of the government's macro-economic policies

Macro-economics is concerned with the operation of the economy as a whole. In the United Kingdom during the 1950s and 1960s, the main macro-economic concern of the government was unemployment. In recession, falling output meant rising unemployment. This also meant falling government revenues from taxes. In an effort to maintain output and employment levels, the government would attempt to make up for the fall in private expenditure by raising public sector spending. This, of course, necessitated an increase in public sector borrowing, the PSBR, because public sector receipts were falling at the same time. This *demand management* approach was first advocated by an influential Cambridge economist called John Maynard Keynes, following the Great Depression of the 1930s. He argued that the government must *manage* demand, and be prepared to borrow during recession, if such economic catastrophes were to be avoided.

However, by the mid-1970s, the government was faced with a new and persistent concern: that of chronic inflation. Inflation is a sustained increase in the general price level, such that goods in general become relatively more expensive over time. By the end of the 1970s (due partly to government policies as well as huge increases in the price of an essential raw material, Middle-East oil), inflation in the United Kingdom reached record levels approaching 25 per cent per annum. This meant that, each year, goods in general were costing a quarter more. The key macro-economic goal now became low inflation.

Reduced public expenditure and borrowing

The views of *monetarists* such as the American economist, Milton Friedman, became more influential at this time. They argued that inflation was due to increases in the supply of money in the economy, fuelled significantly by increased public sector spending and increased borrowing. Therefore, the key role for the government was to spend less and curb borrowing. Keynesian demand management approaches were viewed as anathema to anti-inflationary government policies.

Monetarists argued that the more that the government borrows, the more that it has to pay to induce people to lend. In other words, *interest rates* have to rise. This has implications not only for government costs, but for all industries' costs. Some firms may be put out of business as a result, and households with mortgages will certainly face higher repayments. Hence, recent government policies have focused on controlling public spending in order to reduce the amounts borrowed by the public sector. This has implications for all aspects of public expenditure, of course, and not just housing.

Private finance

During the past decade, the government has attempted to replace some elements of public spending with private finance. The *private finance initiative* (PFI) has encouraged private finance for the provision of a variety of goods and services previously paid for solely by public funds, such as new road-building. Private finance has also been encouraged for housing provision, with a growing emphasis on partnerships between local authority and private providers, as well as encouraging housing associations to employ private finance. This is examined in more detail in later sections.

The role of interest rates

Apart from controlling government expenditure, interest rates have been used as a key weapon in the fight against inflation. If inflation is rising, an increase in interest rates deters borrowing, which reduces the amount of money available to spend. Less money to spend means less demand, and so less upward pressure on prices. In the United Kingdom, a substantial part of consumer spending is undertaken with borrowed money, most importantly in housing markets for home purchase and for home refurbishment, but also for goods such as cars and major household items. Hence, increasing interest rates and so raising the cost of borrowing should reduce demand and limit the upward pressure on prices. Reduced consumer spending should also force firms to remain more competitive if they are to continue to sell their goods. Hence, the use of interest rates as an anti-inflationary weapon is assumed to be beneficial to all aspects of the economy.

Table 3.2 Average regional house prices in England (£)

	1989	1990	1991	1992
North	37 374	43 655	46 005	48 347
Yorks and Humberside	41 817	47 231	52 343	52 278
North West	42 126	50 005	53 178	56 377
East Midlands	49 421	52 620	55 740	54 599
West Midlands	49 815	54 694	58 659	57 827
East Anglia	64 610	61 427	61 141	56 770
Greater London	82 383	83 821	85 742	78 254
Rest of South East	81 635	80 525	79 042	74 347
South West	67 004	65 378	65 346	61 460

Source: adapted from Table 42a, Wilcox (1996)

Unfortunately, as we have seen over recent years, the emphasis on interest rates as an economic weapon has had major implications for private housing markets. High interest rates were blamed for the collapse of housing markets at the end of the 1980s, as households were deterred from entering owner occupation or moving home. House prices fell in many areas, though the worst effects were felt in the southern parts of England, where prices had previously risen the most. This is shown in Table 3.2.

Rising interest rates meant rising mortgage costs, causing repayment problems for large numbers of households. This resulted in rising numbers of house repossessions by lenders, increased homelessness, and increasing mortgage arrears – see Table 3.3. Private sector housing output also fell as a result.

Table 3.3 Repossessions, homeless acceptances and cases in mortgage arrears

	Total repossessions (UK)	*Homeless acceptances (GB)*	*Cases in mortgage arrears (UK) 12+ months*
1990	20 640	171 576	36 100
1991	47 940	178 867	91 740
1992	68 600	178 686	147 040
1993	60 500	166 394	151 810
1994	48 660	150 301	117 110

Source: adapted from Wilcox (1996), *Roof* (June and July 1996)

The impact of specific government micro-economic policies

Micro-economics focuses on the operation of specific sectors within the economy. From 1979–1997, the Conservative government was ideologically committed to private markets. This arises from a belief that private sector firms can, in general, perform better than public sector organisations, because the desire to earn *profits* will provide an incentive to be efficient. Hence, the government pursued a number of policies which were intended to improve the operation of the 'supply side' of the economy, by increasing incentives to individuals and private sector firms to encourage enterprise by rewarding individual effort.

Supply-side policies have included reduced rates of taxation to improve work-incentives and turning some aspects of the public sector over to the private sector, by a range of 'privatisation' initiatives. The key goal has been for the public sector to withdraw from much of what it previously provided, to become instead an *enabler*, essentially funding and regulating key aspects of the private sector. These goals have been pursued vigorously in the case of council housing, principally (though not exclusively) through the policy of *right to buy*, the right of council tenants to purchase their homes at a substantial discount, and so become owner occupiers.

The desire to improve incentives has also resulted in an increased emphasis on the 'better-targeted' individual housing subsidy, housing benefit, rather than general subsidies to housing construction costs. These issues are explored in more detail in subsequent sections.

3.3 Public finance for housing

The public sector may finance housing in two key ways:

Firstly it can pay for, or provide subsidy towards, the building (and rehabilitation) of houses. Thus, it can help to create housing *assets*, increasing the *stock* of housing – the total quantity available.

Principally, it can do this by:

- building council housing;
- subsidising housing associations to build housing, with housing association grant (HAG), now called *social housing grant* following the 1996 Housing Act;
- providing subsidy to private sector developers, usually in specific circumstances, such as for redevelopment in run-down inner city areas;
- offering renovation grants and some tax concessions to private landlords and owner occupiers.

Secondly, it can provide personal subsidy for individual households, both tenants and owner occupiers, towards the costs of purchasing housing *services* – mortgage repayment costs or rents.

It does this by:

- paying a financial subsidy to tenants with low incomes, in the form of housing benefit
- subsidising *all* owner occupiers, principally by reducing their liability to pay taxes, for example with mortgage interest tax relief (for those with mortgages) and exemption from capital gains tax liability;
- reducing (or eliminating) the costs of local taxes on housing, the council tax, for low income households in the form of council tax benefit.

Spending on the creation (or protection) of assets is called investment, or *capital spending*. Finance which subsidises the cost of housing services, whether mortgage costs, rent payments, or repair costs, is called *revenue spending*. Hence, public finance for housing contains both capital and revenue elements.

Planning public expenditure on housing

The government's plans for expenditure on housing are set out in their Annual Expenditure Plans, which cover spending by all government departments. These receive Parliamentary approval following the Chancellor's Budget Statement in November each year. Most of the funding for housing comes via the Department of the Environment (DoE), the Scottish Office and the Welsh Office. These spending plans permit the government to plan their borrowing needs, the PSBR, with greater certainty.

In real terms (expressed at 1993/4 prices), public expenditure on housing declined from £11.7 billion in 1980/81 to £5.4 billion by 1994/5, which is a real fall of 53.9 per cent (Wilcox, 1996). However, personal subsidies to housing costs have been rising, and housing benefit costs were expected to reach £14,200 million in Great Britain by 1997/8 (Wilcox, 1996).

'What has occurred has been a major transfer of resources from those programmes conventionally defined as public expenditure on housing (mainly subsidies to public sector housing and new capital investment) towards other expenditure (Housing Benefit and support to owner occupiers).' (Malpass and Murie, 1994, p. 109.)

This means that, in recent years, there has been a significant shift in the focus of housing finance from capital programmes to revenue spending.

The following sections examine the financial regimes within which planned public expenditure on social housing takes place, by both local authorities and housing associations. As has been seen, the distinction between capital and revenue spending is an important one, and there are specific requirements affecting both types of spending by both types of organisation. We first examine the regimes which govern spending by local authorities, then move on to the requirements for housing associations.

3.4 Finance for local authorities

Capital Finance

The background: increasing central government controls
The arrangements for capital finance for council housing reflect the recent Conservative government's determination to control public sector spending. As noted in Section 3.3, this applies not just to spending on housing, but to all aspects of local authority expenditure.

Prior to 1989, the government had tried various measures to control total housing *expenditure* by local authorities. Borrowing was permitted only for 'prescribed' capital spending, but local authorities were very creative in finding ways around these controls, for example, by using leasing schemes (a form of long-term 'renting') for capital items, which evaded the borrowing controls. In addition, the government had placed restrictions on the amounts of capital receipts – income from the sale of council housing and land – that an authority could spend. (This did not apply in Scotland, where sales were generally lower.) Only 20 per cent of sales receipts in any one year could be used for prescribed capital spending. However, unspent capital receipts could be carried forward to the next financial year, when a further 20 per cent of this could be spent, and so on. Through this 'cascade' effect, local authorities were eventually using up all of their unspent receipts. For these reasons, reforms were introduced in England and Wales in the Local Government and Housing Act of 1989. This *new financial regime* was intended to control spending more precisely.

Controls on the sources of capital finance after 1989
Local authorities have a number of possible sources for capital finance and the post-1989 financial regime placed constraints on them all. These are borrowing, capital grants, capital receipts and revenue income.

Borrowing
This is the main source of funding for capital spending by local authorities, because capital spending on housing is very costly and local authorities do not have sufficient

internal funds (largely rent income) to pay for capital works. The government controls the annual amount which can be borrowed for housing capital expenditure, via an annual allocation of 'credit approvals', following a bidding process (see below).

However, it must also be recognised that borrowing for *capital* purposes has *revenue* implications. The loans have to be repaid, and an annual amount must be set aside from revenue (current) income for this purpose. Controls on local authority revenue accounts have had the effect of severely limiting the freedom of local authorities to 'vire' (or switch) funding between these different accounts. Effectively, then, the authority must be sure that total rent income can support any loan repayments for overall housing capital expenditure.

Capital grants

A few specific capital grants are available from central government sources, either for purposes viewed as desirable by central government – such as partnership schemes and tenant involvement initiatives – or for defined areas of expenditure which the government wishes to support, such as private sector renovation grants. These are allocated competitively, as part of the capital bidding process.

Capital receipts

Capital receipts arise when any assets, such as houses and land, are sold. The main source of capital receipts has been the sale of council housing to tenants, through the right to buy policy. Over time, this policy has had a very large impact on council housing in the United Kingdom, reducing the United Kingdom council stock by an average of 24.2 per cent between 1981 and 1992.

Controls on the use of capital receipts were strengthened by the 1989 Act. English local authorities could use only 25 per cent of housing sales (but 50 per cent from land sales) to fund capital spending, with the remainder used to pay off past debts or simply to earn interest for the local authority. In Wales, 50 per cent from house sales could be spent, and 30 per cent from others. This means that some capital receipts are defined as 'useable' (for local authority expenditure) while the rest are not.

As a result, some authorities have been able to allocate their non-useable receipts to repay historic housing debts. This means, of course, that the 'unused' receipts are not necessarily available to be spent on housing at some future date, because they have already been spent to pay off debts.

There was a so-called 'capital receipts holiday' during 1993, when *all* new capital receipts could be used for capital purposes. However, council house sales were falling by this time, so the extra funds were not as significant as might at first appear. In addition, the sums were offset by planned reductions in the *future* spending plans of local authorities, so the 'holiday' merely brought forward council spending plans.

The system in Scotland, which permitted councils to use all of their receipts continued until 1996/97, and because they were always wholly 'useable' (from 1982/3), the problems generated elsewhere in the United Kingdom by the cascade effect did not arise. However, from 1997/98 it was intended that as in England 75 per cent will have to be used to repay debts.

Right to buy sales are now declining, and the previous Conservative government introduced a variety of other schemes to transfer stock from local authority control –

such as housing action trusts (HATs) and tenants choice, permitting tenants to choose their new landlord (subsequently abolished in the 1996 Housing Act), large-scale voluntary transfer (LSVT) is beginning to have a more significant impact in England. By 1994/5, LSVT had raised £1,618.6 million (Wilcox,1995), which potentially releases around £400 million (25 per cent) for new spending by the local authority. While some has been used for projects other than housing, many authorities have used substantial amounts to provide grants (in the form of LA HAG) to the new housing association, to help to fund renovations and new building. This is examined further in the final chapter.

Revenue income

Revenue income is largely income from council rents, and revenue accounts are examined next. Local authorities are permitted to make *revenue contributions to capital outlays* (RCCOs), but the revenue account for council housing, the housing revenue account (HRA) is now 'ring-fenced'. This means that income from sources other than council housing, such as the council tax, cannot be used to subsidise the HRA. So, any contribution to capital spending from the HRA must come from rents.

This initially provided an important means by which council rents were levered upwards, as they were increasingly forced to make RCCOs to cover urgent spending. The government wanted to see rent increases, so that council rents would better reflect the value of housing. However, more recently, the government was concerned that local authority rents are rising too rapidly, as councils continue to use this source of funding to pay for expensive renovations. We return to this point in the section on revenue funding.

Capital accounts

All authorities must keep a record of capital spending in a separate capital account. This records the annual amounts spent on capital works as well as the sources used to finance the expenditure, identified above.

In Scotland, the capital account is divided into Blocks A and B. Block A is for expenditure on council housing and is also known (confusingly) as the 'HRA' element of capital expenditure. This is because any borrowing for council stock (in the capital account) will appear as annual debt repayments in the housing revenue account (HRA). Block B is for expenditure on other stock, such as private sector renovation grants or mortgages for right to buy purchasers. This is also known as the 'non-HRA' element. A small amount of virement (transfer) may be permitted between the two blocks of capital expenditure.

The allocations process for capital spending

The process for allocating the government's planned capital expenditure on council housing to specific local authorities differs somewhat in each part of the United Kingdom, with slightly different rules, different names and different time scales. In Northern Ireland, 'council' housing is developed and managed by the Northern Ireland Housing Executive (NIHE), rather than by local authorities. The description which follows is based largely on the capital allocations arrangements in England. However, the general approach elsewhere is similar. Over recent years, the process has become increasingly competitive, with larger proportions set aside each year for specific, competitive allocations.

The stages in the process are as follows.

1 Submission of a housing strategy and plan

The first stage requires that each local authority (and the NIHE) produces an annual housing strategy and plan, called the *Housing Investment Programme (HIP)* in England, the *Housing Strategy and Operational Programme* in Wales, the *Housing Plan* in Scotland, and the *Annual Housing Strategy* in Northern Ireland. This sets out the local authority's assessment of housing need in its area, together with proposals for a capital programme to implement its *housing strategy*.

A good plan will have several features:

- A number of relevant local authority departments, such as social services and planning as well as housing, will have contributed to its preparation.
- It must identify housing needs across all tenures in the local authority area. This explains why many local authorities now undertake detailed surveys of housing need in their areas, so that any assertions in the plan can be justified.
- It must take into account the relevant housing association development programme – the planned capital spending – for housing associations in the area (this is examined in the next section).
- It should identify opportunities to promote specific government housing policies, such as the increased involvement of the private sector in housing provision and initiatives to involve tenants.

The plans identify specific local authority schemes for redevelopment, major repair, new heating systems, etc. Often, it will be work which is 'rolling-on' from the previous year. Nowadays, local authorities can afford to undertake very little new building – this has become almost the exclusive preserve of housing associations.

2 Evaluation of the plans

The plans are assessed by the DoE, the DoE in Northern Ireland, Scottish Office or Welsh Office as appropriate, so that the allocation of total expenditure (determined by the central government) between local authorities and to the NIHE can be determined. The 'quality' of the housing plan will help to determine each council's allocation, subject to the overall spending limits in the government's expenditure plans. This means not only the quality of the preparation of the HIP submission, but also the extent to which the authority's plans are likely to further central government objectives for housing – such as increasing the role of private finance. The quality of the authority's management, as reflected in performance data, will also be taken into account. This is examined further in Chapter 5.

3 Annual capital guideline

After the plans have been assessed, each authority is allocated an annual capital guideline (ACG) for housing. This is based partly on a 'needs' assessment, arising from the general needs index (GNI) – an attempt to assess local authority needs in the context of national criteria of need, taking account of factors such as the proportions of ethnic minority households in the area. There is also a discretionary element, based on the quality of the authority's housing plans and the perceived success of their previous capital projects.

The ACG is the total permitted spending, in cash terms. It is not, however, scheme specific. It is up to the local authority to determine which of the proposals in its capital programme it will fund. Only the overall level of capital spending is determined by the government. This is quite different to capital funding for housing associations which, while there is an overall limit dictated by the approved development programme or ADP, is largely a project-based system. In general, housing associations have to obtain specific approval for each scheme they undertake, as will be seen in the next section.

In recognition of the fact that some authorities used leasing agreements to get around previous attempts to control capital spending, the ACG includes any commitments which the authority might have for leasing charges. Large leasing costs mean that less is available for other spending.

Part of the ACG is an allocation of specified capital grants (SCGs), which are specifically for private sector renovation grants. Even though renovation grants are now means-tested, these allocations are seldom sufficient to meet demand, with the result that many authorities are forced to operate 'waiting lists' for grants to improve private housing.

The ACG is further reduced by the anticipated amount of 'useable' capital receipts which a local authority will have available to spend, receipts taken into account or RTIAs. This means that if receipts from sales are lower than expected, the authority might well find itself short of capital funds.

It is then clear how much of the ACG local authorities will require in the form of 'credit approvals' for permitted borrowing. Broadly, the formula is:

$$\text{Credit approvals} = \text{ACG} - \text{SCGs} - \text{RTIA}$$

However, there is no obligation to spend housing capital receipts on housing projects. Indeed, it has been calculated that, nationally, around £200 million 'could have found their way into boosting council investment on leisure centres, town halls and other council services' (Wilcox, 1995, p. 20).

4 Credit approvals

These take two forms:

(i) *Basic credit approvals* (BCAs) are allocated to permit local authorities to raise the remainder of their capital guideline by borrowing. The overall BCA relates to all of an authority's capital spending, not only on housing, and (as with capital receipts) there is no obligation to spend the housing element on housing, so that these can be used for other types of capital spending. However, the government is likely to take account of any reduction in permitted spending by a local authority when it next assesses spending allocations for housing, so few authorities are likely to underspend their housing allocation.

Although in theory other types of (non-housing) BCAs can be used for housing projects, in practice limits on the amount of loan repayments which are eligible for subsidy in the revenue account – from which loan repayments for housing are made – constrain this possibility.

(ii) Supplementary credit approvals (SCAs) are allocated in addition to particular local authorities for specific programmes. However, SCAs are not additional spending permissions, but are 'top-sliced' from the total (national) provision for credit approvals. They have the effect of reducing the total amount available for BCAs, and are an attempt to target some of the borrowing more precisely to favoured programmes. These will be programmes which meet to government's broad housing objectives, including features such as tenant involvement and private sector partnerships, with some private finance provision.

In Scotland, preferred programmes include support for work in partnership areas and rural development initiatives. In England, they have been used largely for urban area initiatives such as *estate action*, though these are now subsumed into a single regeneration budget (SRB), allocated by multi-department 'government offices' in the English regions. Thus, SCAs for estate action now come from the SRB, and have to compete with many types of projects other than housing, such as economic regeneration and community development projects. Evidence so far suggests that housing is obtaining fewer funds than in the past, when there were specific allocations for housing programme funding.

If BCAs or SCAs are not used in the year in which they are allocated, they are 'lost'. Furthermore, future credit allocations are likely to be reduced if an authority is seen to be 'underspending' its allocations.

Sources of borrowing

The local authority treasurer is responsible for all borrowing by a local authority. It is the task of the treasurer's department to ensure that the authority obtains its funding at a fair price (rate of interest) and at timely intervals, that is, it should not unnecessarily be taking out loans which are not immediately needed. The treasurer must also ensure that all rules affecting the operation of accounts are complied with.

The borrowed money is placed in the local authority's loans fund. Local authorities have a major advantage over housing associations, in that they represent a much more secure 'home' for investments, so generally are able to obtain much more favourable rates of interest. Local authorities have a much larger *asset base* (the total amount of capital assets owned), so are viewed as very low risk by lenders.

Local authorities have two main sources for borrowing, as set out below.

I Capital markets

Local authorities can issue their own financial instruments, such as bonds, which are sold on the *capital markets*. These are national markets through which organisations can raise capital finance. Hence, local authority bonds must compete with borrowing by central government and large private sector firms.

These financial instruments guarantee an annual amount of interest, based on current, general interest rates (otherwise, they will not attract buyers). The interest is paid each year, but the capital borrowed is only repaid after a pre-determined period of time, usually after a long period of up to sixty years. This ensures that there is considerable security and stability for the authority, in terms of the annual costs of loans. In the meantime, the original purchaser can sell the bond to someone else (who then receives the interest payments), so the bonds are *tradeable* on the capital markets. This also enhances their attractiveness to lenders.

2 The Public Works Loan Board

Finance for this fund is borrowed by the central government, so it should be a cheaper source than the local authorities' own external borrowing – a government is even more of a safe bet! Each authority receives a quota allocation from the Board, based on its capital programme and existing debts. The Board will also provide short-term emergency funding – i.e. it acts as *lender of the last resort* for local authorities, should an authority find itself temporarily short of funds.

The impact of the post-1989 regime on local authority capital finance

The ability of local authorities to fund capital spending on housing has been severely curtailed by recent government policies. Local authorities have now virtually ceased to build new homes. House completions by all local authorities in Great Britain were only 1,623 in 1994, compared to 76,997 in 1980 (Wilcox, 1995). Even in Northern Ireland, where (due to the very small role of housing associations) allocations to the NIHE have been maintained at relatively higher levels, completions have declined by over two thirds, from 2,507 in 1980 to 810 in 1993.

The decline in capital funding has put severe pressure on renovation programmes, and many local authorities have increasingly resorted to increasing rents to fund expensive rehabilitation from revenue sources. As ever greater percentages of local authority tenants are now in receipt of housing benefit, there is an awareness that most tenants will not themselves have to pay for these rent increases. Unfortunately, for those not in receipt of housing benefit who have to pay these higher rents this is providing a greater incentive to move out of council tenure, via right to buy or the cash incentive scheme (by which tenants may obtain a cash grant to buy in the private sector). If this occurs, it will provide a further twist to the 'residualisation' spiral, the process by which council tenure is increasingly the home of the most disadvantaged and poorest households in the United Kingdom.

The increased use of competition to allocate capital funds has had the effect of forcing many local authorities to pursue projects which are favoured by the government, involving tenant participation of some kind together with housing association and private sector involvement. Other authorities have chosen to pursue large-scale voluntary transfer, transferring all of their stock to (in general) a newly created housing association, with fewer restrictions on spending. Such schemes to promote tenure transfer are examined in the final chapter.

Local authorities are now permitted to create *local housing companies*, which could remove them from central government borrowing controls. This issue is also examined in the final chapter.

Revenue finance

What is local authority housing revenue?

Revenue finance is funding for the provision of housing *services*, rather than for the provision of the housing assets.

Revenue *expenditure* includes spending on management (staff, offices and running expenses), the maintenance of council housing and annual payments of interest on debts.

Revenue *income* is obtained from local taxes (the council tax), rents, housing subsidies from the government, interest received from mortgages (granted for right to buy purchases) and interest on any unused capital receipts.

Local authorities are required to maintain two quite separate accounts for revenue finance:

- *The housing revenue account* pays for all services to the local authority's council housing tenants. The main source of income is rents from council houses and government subsidy.
- *The general fund account* is the main revenue account for the whole council, which also funds general housing services which are provided for private sector residents of a local authority (such as advice centres and help for the homeless). The main source of income is the council tax, uniform business rates (the tax levied on firms in the local authority area) and central government grants.

The housing revenue account (HRA)

The main elements in the HRA are shown below.

Expenditure

- Loan charges. The cost of repaying the money borrowed to pay for capital spending. These changes are often the largest item of spending and can vary slightly with interest rate levels, as new debt is taken on.
- Repair and maintenance costs. This covers day-to-day repairs and planned maintenance programmes (such as re-painting), but *substantial* improvements would be capital expenditure.
- Management costs. The costs of paying employees, office expenses, staff training, and so on.
- Revenue contributions to capital outlays (RCCOs). The local authority may transfer revenue income to fund capital projects; this has become commonplace since capital accounts have been subject to such severe restrictions (as examined above).

Income

- Rents and charges to council tenants.
- Housing revenue account subsidy (housing support grant in Scotland). An annual payment from the government to the local authority. It is supposed to cover the difference between 'notional income' and 'notional expenditure'.

Because of the rules by which the government now calculates subsidy, rent income has become relatively more important and voids and arrears will have a major impact – see below.

- Interest received. Paid to the council for mortgages and other loans. (Interest received from invested capital receipts from the sale of housing assets must be paid to the general fund.)

Housing revenue account subsidy

This subsidy from central government was originally intended to help to provide councils with a 'level playing field' in the provision of services to council tenants. It was recognised that, for various reasons, some councils would necessarily incur higher costs (e.g. due to higher costs for building and land, resulting in higher loan costs) or may receive less income than others. Therefore, it was fair that central government took a role in redistributing some income to councils.

Like the system for capital finance, the revenue arrangements underwent substantial revision in 1989. To explain why, we need to examine briefly the operation of revenue funding before 1989.

The pre-1989 revenue subsidy system

The housing revenue subsidy following the 1980 Housing Act was in two main parts:

- housing subsidy, to restrain rent levels;
- rent rebate subsidy, to reimburse the council for actual rent income lost through rent rebates to tenants – the forerunner of housing benefit.

Essentially, the housing subsidy element was a deficit subsidy to compensate councils for any shortfall in income compared to expenditure. The government calculated subsidy on the basis of the estimated income and expenditure for council housing, assuming also a contribution from the general rate fund – as the general fund was then called. Since a key aim of the subsidy system was to increase council rents, the government assumed both rising rent levels and increasing subsidy from the general rate fund in making the subsidy calculations, i.e. it used 'notional' figures to calculate the anticipated deficit, rather than real ones. This meant that subsidy could be progressively withdrawn. Any council which chose not to increase rents in line with the assumptions could increase general fund contributions and/or reduce costs.

In the event, council rents rose rapidly, and eventually many councils became ineligible for subsidy – there was no longer a notional deficit. This meant that the government had lost its ability to influence council rent levels in all but 95 councils by 1987/8. In some cases, rate fund contributions had grown well beyond the assumptions made for subsidy purposes. In others, they were well below the notional figure. Some councils, still in receipt of subsidy, were transferring funds out of the HRA into the general rate fund. It became clear that the subsidy was not necessarily being used for the purposes intended.

It was also recognised that the substantial transfers to or from the general fund were making it impossible to assess how efficient and effective the council housing service was. It permitted the real performance of housing managers to be obscured. It was decided to make councils more accountable for their housing services, by ensuring that it became clearer how much they were spending, where it came from, and on what.

The post-1989 revenue subsidy system

The Local Government and Housing Act of 1989 introduced significant changes to the revenue subsidy system in England and Wales; as with capital spending, the central aim of the new revenue subsidy was greater control over council spending by the government. Thus:

- rents should increase, to reflect more closely the real value of council housing;
- councils would be forced to become more efficient in their delivery of the service, so management and maintenance allowances would be constrained;
- expenditure would become more transparent; it would become clearer just what councils were spending their rent (and other revenue income) on;
- all councils would be brought back into entitlement to subsidy; this would restore the government's ability to apply an upward lever on council rents.

Features of the revenue subsidy system

There is now only one subsidy, the HRA subsidy. This includes:

- A rent rebate element, to repay housing benefit costs for council tenants (since local authorities pay this on behalf of central government).
- A general housing element to cover any income deficit, *which can be negative if a surplus is anticipated*. This has had significant implications for local authorities, as examined below.

The HRA is 'ring fenced' to prevent contributions from the general fund (which includes council tax receipts and other sources of local authority revenue income).

Local authorities receive *specific* annual allowances for management and maintenance costs, rather than general ones, applicable to all, as before.

Each authority has an annual *guideline* rent, which may increase each year. For example, in 1992/3, guideline rent increases were between £1.20 and £4.50; in 1994/5, between £1.50 and £2.90 (Aughton and Malpass, 1994).

The calculation of subsidy

The calculation is complex, and the amount of housing revenue account subsidy can vary significantly between local authorities, often bearing little relationship to each local authority's actual spending. The calculation requires the determination of the figures in a notional housing revenue account for each local authority, not the actual HRA. The level of subsidy is set to cover the difference between these 'notional' amounts of income and expenditure.

Notional income

Rent The average amount of rent the authority should be charging is assumed to reflect the market value of the council's housing stock, as measured by the valuation of houses and flats recently sold under the Right to Buy. The calculation is undertaken as follows:

- the value of each council's stock is estimated;
- based on this, the *total* value of council housing in the United Kingdom is estimated;
- from this, the total required council rent income is assessed;
- the value of each council's stock as a percentage of total council stock values is assessed;
- the council's rents are assumed to contribute this percentage of total rent income;
- the council's total rent is divided by the number of dwellings, to give a notional average rent.

If a local authority charges less than the notional average rent to its tenants, the subsidy will be less than is needed to balance the account. There will be insufficient income into the housing revenue account, and costs will have to be reduced to balance the account, or rents increased.

Arrears The government assumes that all the rent is gathered; there is no allowance for arrears. This is intended to place some pressure on councils to ensure that rents are collected efficiently. Average rents will, of course, have to be higher to cover any sums lost through arrears.

Voids The government allows the local authority to have 2 per cent of its property empty (void) over the year. If the authority has a higher voids level, then rents of existing tenants will have to cover the rents that would have been paid on those extra void properties. This is intended to provide an incentive for councils to become more efficient, in turning around empty properties quickly.

Notional Expenditure

Management costs The government also calculates an allowance for management costs, taking into account the characteristics of the authority's stock. If a local authority decides to spend more than its notional allowance on management, then rents will have to be higher than the notional average rent to balance the housing revenue account.

Repair and maintenance costs The government calculates the notional amount that the local authority should spend on maintenance. Again, if the council decides that it needs to spend extra on maintenance (for example, to turn void properties around faster), then rents have to cover the extra costs.

Capital spending (RCCOs) The government does not allow for any extra spending on capital projects outside the credit approval system. If the local authority decides to make a revenue contribution to capital spending, then rents have to cover that extra money. As examined above under capital finance, this has become an increasingly important source of funding for capital spending by local authorities.

Loan interest repayments The allowance for loan repayments will reflect the government's capital spending guidelines for the authority. The limits to this mean that, if the authority uses more of its BCAs for housing than the government intends, the additional costs of the loan repayments will not be allowed for in the calculation of subsidy; rents will have to increase to fund these additional repayments. This provides a significant restraint on capital spending beyond the guidelines.

The effects of the new HRA subsidy

The subsidy for housing benefit payments – the rent rebate element – is generally positive, since most councils (except those which have transferred all of their stock through a large scale voluntary transfer) have some tenants (now, a majority) in receipt of benefit. But the assumptions about rising notional rents (rising incomes), and strict limits on management and maintenance allowances (expenditure), have resulted in the general housing subsidy element becoming negative in a number of cases, i.e., the HRA is assumed to have a *surplus* rather than a deficit. Since HRA surpluses are not permitted, and funds cannot be transferred to other accounts, the notional negative general subsidy is deducted from the rent rebate subsidy, so that the total HRA subsidy may not cover the full costs of housing benefit payments. *This means that some of the rent payments of tenants who are not receiving housing benefit have to subsidise those who are.*

This has, of course, necessitated large rent increases in some local authority areas. Rents have also had to increase to fund essential maintenance not covered by the allowances and to pay for additional subsidies to the capital account, also hit by government controls. In both England and Wales by 1990, average rents already exceeded guideline figures and the gap has continued to grow. These rent increases have resulted in increased numbers of tenants eligible for housing benefit (see Section 3.7) providing a further push to the spiral of rent increases.

By 1993/4, notional HRA surpluses exceeded notional deficits by £66 million; nationally, then, HRAs were assumed to be in overall surplus. According to Aughton and Malpass, the notional English HRA surplus 'is projected to rise to a massive £688 million by 1996/7, by which time council tenants paying rent will be bearing 28 per cent of the cost of housing benefit for other council tenants' (Aughton and Malpass, 1994, p. 46).

Housing support grant in Scotland

The Local Government and Housing Act did not apply in Scotland, so the system there is essentially the 1980 system, but with some adjustments. The HRA subsidy is called housing support grant. The Secretary of State for Scotland has had the power to limit rate fund contributions to the HRA since 1985/6. This has had the effect of causing Scottish rents to rise, but they still remain well *below* English and Welsh rents, and generally below the guideline figures. For example, in 1994, average weekly rents in England were £35.90, £34.11 in Wales, but only £27.79 in Scotland (Wilcox, 1996).

This may be due, partly, to the fact that Scottish local authorities have until 1997/98 been free to spend all of their capital receipts (see Section 3.5), so there was not the necessity to make substantial revenue contributions to capital spending. However, council housing is a much larger proportion of total housing provision in Scotland than in England or Wales, and it is possible that the political commitment to higher rent levels there is weaker.

The general fund account

The general fund is the main revenue account for all of a council's services in England. The housing element of provision from the general fund will depend, to some extent, on the local authority's perceptions of the requirements of its residents. The main housing elements of expenditure likely to be found in the general fund account are shown below. This also identifies the main sources of income to the general fund. Some are general local authority income, and others come from housing specific sources. .

Expenditure
* Renovation grants paid to private owners for essential repairs to their dwellings.
* Slum clearance of private sector dwellings; this has fallen to extremely low levels.
* Housing advice services. This might include the cost of providing housing aid centres, and grants to private bodies to provide advice.
* Housing benefit payments. These are rent rebates paid to private sector or housing association tenants.
* Housing benefit administration costs. Local authorities administer the entire housing benefit system for the government.

Income:
* Revenue support grant. The main source of revenue income for councils. This is examined in more detail below
* Council tax. The local tax paid by local residents in the area; the government sets an annual limit to any increases ('capping'), so the local authority has little freedom to set charges.
* Uniform business rates. The local tax paid by businesses. The government felt that some councils were overcharging business taxpayers, so the rate is now set centrally by the government who then determines how large a share is paid to each council.
* Rents and charges. For temporary accommodation for the homeless.
* Interest on mortgages to private owners (rarer now), loans to housing associations and interest from the invested portion of non-useable capital receipts (from the sale of council housing and land).
* Housing benefit subsidy. Repayments from the government of rent allowances paid to private and housing association tenants.
* Housing benefit administration subsidy. This subsidy does not cover the full costs of administration for most councils. This is examined in Section 3.7.

The calculation of Revenue Support Grant
The revenue support grant (RSG) is based on standard spending assessments (SSA). This is the amount which the government believes will permit each council to deliver equal service provision, having regard to the needs in the area. However, as with most attempts to relate spending to needs, there is much controversy about the adequacy of the indices of needs, with apparently 'needy' areas receiving lower assessments than apparently wealthy areas. Some councils also feel that they are 'classed' inappropriately, such as non-urban rather than urban.

The SSA is then reduced by:

* the 'local contribution'; the amount which the government determines can be raised from the council tax.

a payment from the UBR (uniform business rate) pool, which is the 'local' tax charged to businesses; this is also determined by the central government.

This determines the amount of RSG.

The effects for local authorities

It can be seen that local authorities have lost the ability to control most of their general fund income, including the sources which formerly were entirely controlled by them, the council tax and uniform business rates. Only the level of charges, such as rents from temporary accommodation, remains under their direct control. Furthermore, many would argue that the assessments for revenue support grant have not recognised sufficiently the ever widening scope of local authority responsibilities, for example, community care responsibilities, or Children Act requirements. There have been some recent examples of councils declaring that they are unable to fulfil their obligations to (generally very vulnerable) recipients of community care, because the 'money has run out'.

Within the general fund, housing services have to compete with all other types of council provision. Increased expenditure on one element generally demands reduced expenditure elsewhere. This is the main reason why some councils have made significant cut-backs to their provision of housing services to the private sector, closing advice centres or hostels for the homeless, for example.

3.5 Finance for housing associations

Capital finance

Like local authorities, the arrangements by which housing associations obtain capital finance for housing have seen significant changes in the 1990s. In order to understand the reasons for these changes, as well as to appreciate their implications for housing associations, it is necessary first to explore the previous arrangements.

The background: the pre-1988 regime

The Housing Corporation (HC) is now the main funding body for housing associations in England. However, when this body was first set up in 1964, it aided specific activities, such as co-ownership housing, throughout the United Kingdom.

The Housing Act of 1974 introduced *housing association grant* (HAG). This provided a large capital subsidy from the public sector to housing associations registered with (and hence, regulated by) the HC for capital projects. Housing associations were now expected to make a real contribution to social housing provision. Housing association rents, like most private sector rents, were to be controlled *fair rents*, determined by rent officers. As a result, the funding process operated as follows:

1. The housing association applied to the HC for approval to build a scheme; if accepted, the association borrowed finance from the HC to pay for development costs as the scheme progressed.

2. On completion, the rent officer determined the *fair rent* for the scheme. Fair rents were assessed on the assumption that no shortages existed, so were well below market rents.

3. The annual income from the rents was then offset against management and maintenance costs, together with a 4 per cent allowance for voids and bad debts.

4. The remainder of the rent income was assumed to be available to make annual loan repayments to the HC. The amount of loan which this payment would support was calculated; all scheme costs above this were met by HAG.

Problems with the pre-1988 regime

- It was very expensive for the government; latterly, as much as 90 per cent of the scheme cost was funded by the public sector in the form of HAG.
- There was little incentive for associations to control development costs; basically, If costs rose, so too did HAG. Hence, the risks lay entirely with the government.
- Rents were re-assessed periodically by local rent officers, who determined the 'fair rents'; with inflation, these were rising, but the sums repaid to the HC remained at the same level as originally determined. For example, in 1978, the average housing association fair rent in England and Wales was £10.08; ten years later, in 1988, this had grown to £24.75. This meant that associations were generating ever larger rent surpluses. This led to a requirement (in the 1980 Housing Act) that housing associations pay surplus rent incomes into a *grant redemption fund*, either for return to the government, or to fund activities such as major repairs which would otherwise attract grant funding.
- Rents bore no relationship to scheme costs, though they were nevertheless generally higher than council rents (for example, in 1988, the average council rent was £18.74, six pounds a week less than the average housing association fair rent). To a government committed to greater market provision, so that prices would better reflect true costs, this was unacceptable.

It was decided that a new approach was necessary. The government wished to expand the role of housing associations, but without substantial increases in HAG costs. It also wanted to provide incentives to housing associations to achieve better value for money. As a result, the 1988 Housing Act and Housing (Scotland) Act introduced a 'new regime' for housing association finance, designed to address the main problems of the previous system.

Features of the post-1988 regime

The grant rate

The proportion of the costs of a scheme to be paid by HAG are determined at the start, set by the applicable *grant rate*. Grant rates are revised annually and usually downwards. Initially, a target of 75 per cent (of scheme costs) was set for England, 85 per cent for Scotland, but trust rates in 1997/98 in England for general needs housing were set at 44.4 per cent in the North of England and 64.6 per cent in London.

Private finance – 'mixed funding'

Most associations are expected to supplement HAG by borrowing funds from private sector lenders, so-called 'mixed funding'. However, the government recognised that some very small associations were unlikely to be able to offer the security required by private financial institutions, so they remain with a new version of *public funding* – they can borrow the extra funds needed from the HAG funder or local authority.

Major repairs fund

Associations are now required to fund major repairs costs for schemes largely themselves. Under the pre-1988 regime, grants were available from the Housing Corporation. Now, all new schemes have to contribute to a *major repairs fund*, so that the association can build up sufficient funds to pay for all future work.

Higher rents

New lets (and re-lets of old regime properties) are *assured* tenancies, instead of the old housing association secure tenancies. These can be let at *higher rents*, which better reflect the scheme costs, because they are not fair rents under the control of the rent officer. Furthermore, whereas fair rents can be re-assessed only every two years, new regime rents can be revised annually.

Rents have to cover:

- the repayments of the private loan;
- management and maintenance costs;
- an allowance for voids and arrears;
- a sum to be set-aside for future major repairs; the suggested figure varies by funder, for example, 0.8 per cent of current construction costs (and fees) for new build and 1 per cent for rehabilitation schemes in England, compared to 0.7 per cent in Scotland for all schemes.

By far the largest element in this rent calculation is the loan repayment. The lower the grant rate, the larger the private loan. This increases the repayments, so rent levels are higher. In contrast to local authorities, few associations operated rent pooling systems, which shares the costs of more recent, higher-cost developments between all tenants. With rapidly rising new rent levels, many more associations are now operating rent pooling.

Cost controls

The funding bodies introduced *cost indicators* for different types of development, to control scheme costs more effectively. These vary between different local authority areas, depending on local cost conditions (including land costs). Ordinarily, the costs of any proposed development must be within the relevant cost limits.

Risk of cost-overruns

Once the level of HAG is determined, in general, cost-overruns have to be at least part funded by the housing associations. Over-runs of up to 30 per cent may be allowed (i.e. costs of up to 130 per cent of the original estimated scheme costs), but *half of* the extra has to be paid by the association. This is intended to provide a strong incentive for associations to keep a tight control over scheme costs.

New funding bodies

To implement the new regime, two new statutory funding bodies were created: Tai Cymru (Housing for Wales) and Scottish Homes (from the old Housing Corporation in Scotland and the Scottish Special Housing Association). As a result, Scottish Homes (SH) differed from the other funders, in having its own stock to manage, as well as overseeing housing association activity in Scotland. SH was expected to transfer its stock to other landlords in time. In Northern Ireland, the Northern Ireland Housing Executive (the provider of 'council' housing in Northern Ireland) has powers to approve housing association developments, but these are funded directly by the DoE in Northern Ireland. The Housing Corporation was retained as the funding body for England.

The capital funding bidding process

The new regime completely reversed the previous process by which grants were allocated to specific schemes, in that, in the past, the amount of grant was determined *at the end* of the development period, once the fair rent had been determined and all costs were known. HAG was a *residual* sum. The new system sets HAG at the *start*. It is *pre-determined*. It is then up to the housing association to ensure that costs were constrained within these limits. Rents are determined at the *end*, at the level needed to cover all annual (revenue) costs.

The precise details of the allocations process differs between each of the funding bodies, and is also subject to regular revisions. Hence, all that we can provide here is a *general* indication of the stages in the process. The process examined below is based on the Housing Corporation's requirements, but the other funders have adopted similar approaches. Note that HAG is now called social housing grant (SHG) by the Housing Corporation and Tai Cymru, but for simplicity, the term HAG is used to apply to all funders.

1. The government determines the total expenditure available for housing associations; the relevant statutory funders then issue an *approved development programme* (ADP) (or similar), setting out the amounts available for each type of project.
2. Each housing association bids for a share of the ADP, indicating the types of schemes it intends to develop and for what sums; this bid is judged both on past performance and on how well it conforms to the relevant local authorities' housing strategies (examined in Section 3.4). Some funders have also recently introduced rent limits – examined further below.
3. Once it receives its overall annual allocation, the housing association applies for detailed approval for each project; it submits details of estimated scheme costs, which, in general, must be within (or preferably below) the relevant *cost indicators* determined by the funding body. The calculation of total scheme costs must also allow for any interest charges which will have to be paid on money borrowed to finance the development period.

4. If this receives *scheme approval*, the funder undertakes to provide an amount of HAG, based on current grant rates for the type of development and the amount originally bid for. (In England associations are encouraged to bid for lower amounts of HAG.)
5. The association arranges private finance for the remainder of the scheme's costs; as noted earlier, at least half of any cost over-runs have, in general, to be borne by the association (e.g. from cash reserves).
6. HAG is released in pre-determined proportions at various stages in the scheme's progress. Costs beyond this have to be temporarily covered by the association, by borrowing and/or from reserves.
7. On completion, the private finance is released to the housing association, and monthly repayments of the loan and interest commence.

Rent limits

Rent limits have been introduced by some funders due largely to the increasing proportions of housing association tenants on housing benefit (see Section 3.7). It became apparent that there were reducing incentives for associations to curb rents, if very few of their tenants would actually have to find the costs of the higher rents. It also meant that the actual cost to the government was very much higher than simply the HAG costs, as there was a rising revenue cost in the form of a rising housing benefit bill.

The first funding body to attempt to tackle this was Tai Cymru. In 1994, it introduced limitations on the size of housing associations to which it would give HAG. It wished to fund only those associations with annual development programmes in excess of £3 million. These were approved development bodies (ADBs). Associations with smaller programmes would have to join with an ADB to gain funding. However, for 1995/6, they also introduced a new requirement in relation to rents. Funding would be offered only if rent levels were reasonable – called rent-bidding. This made it very difficult for even ADBs to be sure that they could achieve programmes requiring £3 million in funding. As a result, approved developer status has been abandoned, but rent-bidding continues.

Similarly, the Housing Corporation introduced a form of rent limits from 1996/7, in the form of *benchmark rents*. These are related to the cost of development for the type of scheme, the relevant Total Cost Indicators (TCIs). Associations have to take these figures into account when setting rents for new schemes, and their bids are examined in the light of proposed rent levels. If rent levels for a project exceed benchmark rents, the additional rent is assumed to attract housing benefit, and the annual value of this is calculated and added to the social housing grant (SHG) bid as a capital sum. So, for example, if the SHG bid is for £2 million, but rents are above the benchmark, the capitalised value of anticipated additional housing benefit costs is added to the £2 million SHG, to give the total, real capital cost to the government. Another association, bidding for more SHG but with lower rents, might therefore seem to be offering better value.

From 1997/8, there are additional controls on association rent levels for all new housing association schemes in England. The association must charge the rent indicated in the bid to the HC, and thereafter, rent increases must not exceed the rate of inflation + 1 per cent. Thus if inflation were 2 per cent, the maximum rent increase that year would be 3 per cent.

The calculation of HAG

1 Cost indicators

Cost indicators are devised by each of the funding bodies to reflect estimated development costs in particular areas. They may be revised periodically, down as well as up if appropriate (for example, some English cost figures declined between 1993/4 and 1994/5).

Each funder has their own particular system, though in general, the cost indicators will vary by:

- the nature of the development (new build or rehab);
- the location (council district);
- the type of tenant (family or special needs);
- the size of dwellings.

Scottish Homes, for example, has *total indicative costs* (TICs), with separate amounts for new build and rehabilitation schemes. These are further varied for *density* (dwellings per hectare) and *dwelling size* (number of persons), as well as special provisions for elderly and other schemes.

In England, there are *total cost indicators* (TCIs):

- the base figure varies by council district and dwelling size;
- key multipliers vary the base figure, to take account of the nature of the development (new build, rehab, package deal, etc.);
- supplementary multipliers allow for special needs' requirements, such as lifts and communal areas.

The association must generally demonstrate that the scheme's costs are within (or below) the indicative costs.

2 Grant rate

The grant rate is the proportion of scheme costs which will be provided by HAG. So, the maximum payable is:

$$\text{Cost indicator} \times \text{Grant rate.}$$

If estimated scheme costs are lower than the indicative costs, then the maximum HAG is

$$\text{Estimated costs} \times \text{Grant rate.}$$

As a simple example, suppose that scheme costs are assessed as £400,000, and this is within the cost indicator for the type of scheme and number of dwellings. If the current grant rate is 50 per cent, then the amount of HAG payable is:

$$£400,000 \times 50\% = £200,000.$$

Grant rates vary considerably between funders. They have fallen fastest in England. For example, in 1995/6, in most London boroughs, the grant rate for a three bed-room property was 64 per cent, compared to 48.5 per cent for the same sized property in most northern districts. Housing associations in these areas in the north must now find *more than half* of the costs for properties of this type from private sources and, as indicated previously, they may bid for lower grant rates. Scottish Homes' grant rates have remained higher, but at the end of 1994, they announced that there would be a 'managed downward trend in the overall HAG rate' (Scottish Homes, 1994). For 1996/7, Scottish Homes' average grant rate was 68 per cent, compared to 56 per cent for the Housing Corporation.

Every cut in grant rates potentially puts up rents for new association properties. For example, in response to the proposed 4 per cent reduction in grant rates in Wales for 1995/6, the Director of the Welsh Federation of Housing Associations claimed that this would increase rents for new homes by 'at least £4 a week' (quoted in HA Weekly, 16 December, 1994). However, in the light of expanded attempts to control rents (examined above), the main alternative for associations is to try to reduce scheme costs. There are concerns that this is leading to reduced design and construc-tion standards in some cases. In response to these concerns, in July 1995, the National Federation of Housing Associations (now, the National Housing Federation) proposed new minimum design standards, but such constraints are not favoured by the DoE. However the Housing Corporation has issued scheme development standards (SDS) which all new housing association schemes in England must meet.

Private finance

As we have seen, with the decline in HAG rates, virtually all associations must now obtain some private finance for new development. Indeed, a number of housing associations have developed some schemes without any HAG at all, raising all of the finance privately (sometimes in conjunction with a private development com-pany), and charging market rents.

The need to access private funds has forced a more 'business-like' approach on many housing associations. Private lenders view associations as they would any company seeking finance from them. They want to know that their funds are secure, and that the borrower will be able to repay as agreed. In short, they seek always to minimise any risk that they could lose money. This means that they want detailed financial information about the 'company', including rent levels and details of its other housing assets. Associations with a large asset base (generally, a large stock, with high proportions dating from pre-1988) are, therefore, more likely to be viewed favourably by private financial institutions, because this will help to reduce any risk of default (failure to repay). The need for a secure asset base has helped to stimulate a series of mergers between associations in recent years.

Business plans

The requirements of private lenders generally include a business plan prepared by the association. Business plans set out the present state of the organisation, indicate plans for the future, and, most importantly, show how those plans can be achieved. Most housing associations now produce business plans. Indeed, in Scotland, Scottish Homes require that all associations have an annual business plan as part of the bidding process for capital funds. This must identify the housing association's objectives, the housing needs to be met and proposed tenure and dwelling mixes. Planned schemes must be consistent with the agreed business plan. This was intended also to be of value to private lenders, but in practice, research for Scottish Homes in 1994 suggested that the associations' business plans often fail to include sufficient financial information to satisfy private financial institutions (Scottish Homes 1994a).

Effects for housing associations

Rising rents
As we have seen, the main result of mixed funding has been rising rents for housing association tenants. Table 3.4 shows that, as a percentage of average male manual earnings, the new assured rents have been steadily increasing, though by much less in Scotland due to much lower dependence on private finance.

Table 3.4 Rents as a percentage of average manual male earnings (housing association assured rents)

	1989	1990	1991	1992	1993	1994	1995
England	11.2	12.1	13.3	14.5	16.3	16.2	16.5
Wales	12.4	13.7	14.5	15.6	16.4	15.9	14.8
Scotland	9.0	9.1	9.4	9.4	10.1	10.6	10.6
N.Ireland	10.5	10.7	10.7	11.0	11.7	12.3	12.6

Source: adapted from Wilcox (1997)

However, even these figures disguise the full impact of mixed funding, because:

- These are *average* rents; new rents are generally higher than the previous average, around £10 a week in 1993 (Wilcox, 1996).
- This is based on *average male* earnings; many housing association tenants earn well below average earnings, and many are female – whose earnings are well below male figures.

There are real concerns now about whether housing association rents are *affordable*. The National Housing Federation (formerly the National Federation of Housing Associations, the NFHA) suggests that rents are 'affordable' at up to 25 per cent of *net* income (i.e. take-home pay). Average earnings are based on *gross* (before tax and other deductions) figures. According to Aughton and Malpass (1994):

'By the middle of 1993, over 70 per cent of new assured tenants were paying rents above the affordable level, as defined in the new NFHA policy.'

As a result, by 1995 around 80 per cent of new housing association tenants were on housing benefit (Joseph Rowntree Foundation, 1995b).

The important issue of affordability is taken up again in Chapter 7.

Increased risks

The issue of risk has become very significant for housing associations. Risks have greatly increased in two main ways:

Capital risks As identified earlier, associations must bear at least some of the risk of costs rising during the development phase. The desire to reduce these risks has contributed to the increased use of approaches to development which reduce the overall time period, and offer greater certainty about costs. Arrangements such as *package deals* or *design and build* contracts combine much of the design and construction elements, so that the association can agree a fixed price for everything in advance. These are examined further in Chapter 4. As noted above, there are also some fears in relation to design and construction standards, as there may be a temptation to 'cut corners' in an attempt to curtail costs. In England, where grant rates have fallen fastest, there has been a reduction in rehabilitation work, simply because this is inherently more at risk of cost increases, as new and unforeseen problems emerge. New build is less risky.

As time goes on, it is also becoming more difficult for some associations to gain private funding. Much of their existing stock has already been used as security against earlier loans. Additionally, in England in particular, where grant rates have fallen fastest, the loans required are now a much larger share of total scheme costs.

Revenue risks There is a growing body of anecdotal evidence from housing associations that rapidly rising rents have increased the difficulties of letting in some areas. Increasingly, it is only households entitled to full housing benefit (where benefit payments cover all of the rent) which can afford new housing association properties. In areas with depressed property markets in particular, new housing association rent levels may be well above what is considered 'usual' in the area. Indeed, there are growing fears in some areas that rent officers may fix rent ceilings for housing benefit (which is examined in Section 3.7) below current association rents for new lets. This would mean that housing benefit would not cover all of the rent, and tenants may fall into arrears and eventually have to quit. This leaves housing associations with an uncertain future in relation to rent income – and lenders share this concern.

Significance of size

As examined above, private financial institutions, in general, adopt a very cautious approach to lending funds. They prefer to have a large amount of *security*, to guarantee that they will get their money back whatever happens. Small associations, with few assets, can offer little extra security; furthermore, they might be considered more at risk of failure – going bankrupt – which has resulted in a certain amount of merger activity between housing associations, keen to expand their asset bases.

In England, with a large number of small-to-medium sized associations, a new financial institution was set up under the 1988 Act, specifically to help these housing associations to access private funding. The Housing Finance Corporation (THFC) assembles the funding requirements of a number of associations into one 'package', and then finds a private lender willing to lend on this larger portfolio of schemes. Other associations also join together to make collective applications for private funding.

Development programmes

Table 3.5 indicates planned spending by housing associations in Great Britain over recent years. The proportionate growth in the use of private finance is very clear, particularly in England and Wales. Since Scottish Homes grant rates have remained higher, levels of private finance remained lower for longer.

Table 3.5 Planned gross investment by housing associations (£ million)

	Total England	Wales	Scotland	Privately financed England	Wales	Scotland
1987/88	1020	72	132	0	8	0
1988/89	1109	80	164	100	8	0
1989/90	1492	112	213	150	22	10
1990/91	1602	149	243	175	33	37
1991/92	2151	186	271	240	53	42
1992/93	3605	247	313	950	73	55
1993/94	3231	211	327	1000	70	54
1994/95	2899	197	350	1050	65	81
1995/96	2544	166	363	1000	65	94
1996/97	2295	151	320	1050	60	83

Source: adapted from Wilcox (1997)

The peak in England in 1992/3 reflects the *housing market package* (HMP), introduced by the Housing Corporation at the end of 1992. Housing associations received £577 million in HAG (plus the private finance raised) to purchase housing on the open market. This was primarily an attempt to boost the depressed market for owner-occupied housing, and the funds were deducted from future planned housing association spending. These HMP homes have generated some management difficulties for housing associations, since they are very often single dwellings in scattered locations, with different construction methods and differing maintenance requirements to the rest of the association's stock.

Planned expenditure for 1996/7 showed significant reductions over 1992/3, in the order of 36 per cent in England and 39 per cent in Wales. The balance between rented housing and shared ownership initiatives was also further skewed toward ownership initiatives – some 21 per cent of funds in England for example in 1995/96. Some of these schemes release properties for new tenants, but do not all result in new homes being built. By 1997/98 housing association planned expenditure was further significantly reduced with large reductions in HAG amounting to a £1 billion cut across the United Kingdom as a whole (*Inside Housing*, 29 November, 1996). In the light of these cuts the significance of private finance seems set to increase.

Revenue finance

Income and expenditure account

The revenue account for housing associations is the property revenue account, now called the income and expenditure account in England, so that it is more like the revenue account of a private sector landlord.

The main sources of *income* and categories of *expenditure* are shown below. The revenue accounts of housing associations are not subject to the strict controls placed on local authority housing revenue accounts. On the contrary, they are encouraged to make surpluses, to ensure that they generate sufficient funds to pay for future major repairs. In contrast, local authorities are not permitted to put money aside for *future* capital expenditure, though they may, of course, contribute to current capital spending, with RCCOs.

Expenditure:

- Loan repayments. This is an increasingly significant element for many housing associations, due to the requirement (under the new regime) to obtain an element of private finance for capital spending. Generally, loan repayments include elements of both capital and revenue. Housing associations can not borrow over such long periods as local authorities and will generally have to pay higher rates of interest to reflect higher risks.
- Management costs. These are actual costs rather than allowances; furthermore, costs are generally higher than for most local authorities, reflecting the much smaller size of most association stock, with fewer possibilities of 'economies of scale' in management.
- Maintenance costs. Allowances are also defined. However, maintenance is not a significant problem for most housing associations, because, being relatively recent social housing providers, they generally have much newer stock than most local authorities.
- Major repairs' provision. The statutory funding bodies make recommendations about the amounts to be set aside from *post-1988* schemes; schemes completed before this (with no private funding) make contributions to the rent surplus fund (examined below). Increasingly associations will set up designated reserves for major repairs rather than establish a major repairs provision. This has the effect of boosting surpluses and reserves.

Income

- Rents. Some rents from pre-1988 schemes will be *fair rents*, determined by the rent officer, but rents on all assured (post-1988) tenancies are determined by the association. Rent setting issues are examined briefly below, as well as in Chapter 5. Voids and arrears will reduce rent income.
- Revenue deficit grant. This is available for pre-1988 schemes, where the fair rents do not cover all expenditure. However, it is reduced by any reserves available to the association. The need for this has diminished, because most old schemes now have assured re-lets (at higher rents), and in any case, fair rents have been increasing significantly.
- Interest. Payable on cash investments.

Rent setting

Housing associations are free to determine rents for all post-1988 properties, but these are expected to remain 'affordable', though this has never been defined by the government. Housing association rents are now well above local authority rents in most areas, caused primarily by mixed funding – the need to repay private loans.

As identified in the last section, the statutory funders are at last beginning to take an interest in rent levels, with the introduction of 'rent bidding' and limits to rent increases. However, associations would argue that the problem lies not so much with rent setting as with declining (capital) grant rates, which require that rents support ever larger private loans.

Rent surplus fund

In the last section we identified that, as rents increased on pre-1988 schemes, housing associations started to make a surplus of income over expenditure. They were required to pay this into a *grant redemption fund*, to permit the government to make use of these surplus funds. The 1988 Housing Act replaced this with the rent surplus fund (RSF).

The RSF applies only to pre-1988 schemes, in which some tenants are likely to remain on fair rents (in secure housing association tenancies), whilst others (in re-lets) will have assured tenancies on rents determined by the housing association.

The *relevant income* is the anticipated gross rent income from these schemes. This is reduced by the schemes' *relevant expenditure*, which includes:

- an allowance for voids and arrears;
- allowances for management and maintenance costs;
- loan charges (the public sector loan element);
- any service charges.

The remaining income is net income. This is shared:

- 80 per cent to the major repairs fund;
- 20 per cent to reserves.

Initially, in England, the Housing Corporation retrieved some of the income from the RSF. However, this provided little incentive for housing associations to increase rents on older schemes. There was not the lever of (private) loan repayments to force rents up. Thus, the 20 per cent allowance for reserves was intended to offer this incentive.

The effects for housing associations

One of the main effects of the post-1988 regime for revenue funding is that rent-setting policy has now become a major issue for housing associations. In the past, rents were determined by the rent officer, so associations did not need to concern themselves with rent setting. Now, for post-1988 schemes and re-lets of old schemes, the association must set its own rents. This requires the determination of a rent-setting policy.

Rents on new schemes funded by private finance must generally be able to cover all scheme expenditures, but, as we have already seen, these have been increasing substantially, as grant rates have declined (see Section 3.6). However, housing associations may choose to reduce the rents payable on new schemes by cutting scheme costs, or making contributions from their reserves – in effect, contributions from the rents of other tenants. Some form of rent-pooling is now allowed, in recognition of the fact that existing tenants in older properties may be paying significantly less than new tenants. A major issue is how to set rents fairly under a pooled system and what factors to vary rents for and by how much. These issues are examined in Chapter 5.

A report for the Joseph Rowntree Foundation, *Rents and Risks: Investing in Housing Associations*, 1995 (by researchers from Cambridge University) found that most associations have built up healthy revenue reserves, by pushing up rents on older stock as it is re-let. (Contrast this with the situation for local authorities, which cannot retain surpluses in their HRA.)

However, the research found that rents had been rising, on average, at about 3 per cent faster than private sector rents, and are rapidly reaching market (private sector) rent levels. In some areas, such as the North East of England, they have already done so. As a result, around 80 per cent of association tenants are now on housing benefit. This is, of course, the primary reason for the introduction of rent limits by the statutory funding bodies. With the likelihood of increased restrictions on benefit payments – examined in Section 3.7 – some associations may find it increasingly difficult to let their high rent properties. In addition, some associations have variable rate private loans, which means that loan repayments from the revenue account would rise considerably if interest rates increase in future.

So far, the use of subsidy from the rents from earlier, cheaper schemes has permitted many associations to continue to develop and keep rents (relatively) down. However, as the report suggests:

'One must ask whether it is economically or politically desirable that the poor in lower cost areas should be having to pay for the poor in low income/high cost areas'. (Joseph Rowntree Foundation, 1995.)

3.6 Planning and controlling expenditure

Housing organisations, just like any private firm or individual, have to plan how they will spend their financial resources. Someone (or group, such as the management committee) must take decisions about priorities for expenditure, and must plan to ensure that income will be sufficient to cover this.

Sections 4 and 5 identified the ways that social housing providers bid for and are allocated capital finance; however, having received these funds (or the prospect of them), they will have to plan how they will be spent, on what, and when. Similarly, for revenue finance, they must determine income levels (principally by setting rents) based on the amount they wish to spend. This means that they have to prepare budgets, for both capital and revenue spending, which set out planned income and expenditure.

Budgets

The treasurer or finance director will have to compile capital and revenue budgets for the whole organisation, which identify broad categories of expenditure and income, approved by the relevant Committee.

The time period covered by the budget may depend on its purpose. Generally, revenue budgets are *annual*, covering the organisation's *financial year* (April 1998 – March 1999, for example). Capital budgets may cover a longer period, say two to five years, to reflect the time scale of capital projects.

These main budgets may be specified in a number of ways:

- By department. For a local authority, the council's budget will be allocated to particular departments, such as housing, social services, environmental services, etc.
- By location. A large organisation may need budgets for each *location*, such as a budget for each area office. Many local authorities have *decentralised* their housing budgets, so that smaller units (the area office, or the estate) are responsible for the allocation of their own budgets, within the overall limits defined by the centre.
- By category. This focuses on the *nature* of the income or expenditure, known as *line-items*. For example, in a revenue budget, line items might include employees (salaries, wages, pensions, etc.), office expenses (stationery, telephones, etc.), staff travel/transport costs, repairs and maintenance.

The process of budget preparation

There are a number of possible approaches to preparing a budget. These include incremental budgeting, planning programming budgeting systems and zero-based budgeting.

Incremental budgeting

For revenue budgets, this is a fairly common approach. It takes the *current* budget as the starting point, and concentrates on the *elements which need to change* in the budget. For example:

- costs may be rising due to inflation, or falling because prices (e.g. for maintenance) have become more competitive;
- employees may be entitled to increments, increasing the salary costs;
- there may be a need for new/additional services (e.g. for community care provision, or tenant involvement initiatives);
- income may be falling, for example due to reduced revenue grants.

Each line-item in the budget is adjusted for these changes. Of course, if income is static or falling, and costs are rising, then further adjustments will have to be made. Some elements may need to be reduced. For example, it may be decided to close a hostel, or to make some staff *redundant* (in which case, redundancy costs will have to be taken into account).

This approach concentrates attention on the *reasons for change*, but its essential assumption is that service provision will continue as before.

Planning programming budgeting systems (PPBS)

This approach is particularly relevant for capital budgeting, because it focuses on the *objectives* of the organisation, and identifies *alternative ways* of meeting these objectives. For example, the objective of providing 200 new dwellings may be met through a number of different possible programmes. The costs of each of the programme elements are identified, and compared to their possible benefits – the expected output. This enables the organisation to allocate capital resources between different programmes effectively. However, in practice, it is a difficult approach to implement, firstly because the objectives of organisations are usually complex and difficult to define precisely and secondly, because the outputs from *services* (such as housing) may be difficult to measure.

Zero-based budgeting

This approach starts with the assumption that *nothing is essential*. Each element of cost is identified and compared to the benefits which it provides. This is useful where *alternative levels of provision* are possible for each function, since it makes explicit the benefits and costs of each alternative. Alternatives are identified as *decision packages*, and are assessed against stated criteria, for example, the need for the activity (is it a statutory requirement?), its political acceptability, its contribution to the organisation's objectives. The decision packages are then *ranked in priority order*, and resources allocated to agreed budget levels (i.e. the anticipated capital or revenue funds).

The advantage of this approach is that it focuses attention on *value for money*, and develops a questioning attitude in the organisation – is this activity *really* necessary? However, it is also very time consuming, and may require a large amount of *subjective* assessments, permitting decision makers to favour 'pet' interests.

Budgetary control

Having *set* the budgets – i.e. set out anticipated income and expenditure, and ensured that they balance (are equal) – the management must ensure that each budget is *monitored* regularly. Responsibility will vary, depending on the 'level' at which the budget is set. For example, the treasurer is responsible for the *whole* of a local authority's budget, and must maintain regular checks to ensure that overall spending is constrained within budget limits. A number of local authorities operate *decentralised budgets*, which permit particular managers (on an estate or in an area office) to control their own budgets. These will have to be monitored regularly, not just by the managers responsible, but also by *their* managers.

If it seems that a budget is in danger of becoming overspent, then urgent action must be taken to adjust planned expenditure so that it remains on target. If this is not possible (for example, if storm damage has resulted in much higher than expected expenditure on repairs), then the 'higher' level of management control needs to be alerted, so that other budgets can be adjusted.

Perverse incentives?

While budgets must be monitored with the intention of ensuring there is no overspend, the goal is not necessarily to spend less than the amount allocated. Particularly in the case of capital projects (with credit allocations from the government), anything unspent is 'lost'. Similarly, an area manager who spends less than the revenue budget allocation may find the office budget cut in the next year, particularly if the incremental approach to budgeting is adopted.

Far from ensuring that money is spent sensibly, this will provide a *perverse incentive* to spend any excess money urgently, and possibly wastefully, before the end of the budget period. Any system of budgeting which penalises saving in this way will virtually guarantee waste.

Cash flow

It may not be sufficient simply to monitor overall spending to ensure that it remains within budget particularly in the case of a housing association. Budgets may need to be monitored to ensure that *at any one time* it does not spend more than the resources available, i.e. the *cash flow* of the organisation must be monitored.

If there are expected to be insufficient receipts to cover payments in a particular time period, the organisation will need to decide whether it can:

- delay some payments, until the cash flow situation improves;
- obtain temporary finance to cover the shortfall (which is much easier for a local authority);
- permanently reduce some planned spending.

For capital projects, it is particularly important that a housing association monitors its cash flow, because the amounts involved are potentially very large. Usually, they will undertake a *cash flow analysis*, which sets out anticipated payments and receipts *in each time period* (e.g. each month). The building contractor may need to receive regular payments for work completed (called *interim payments*, and examined in Chapter 4), but income may not be received until much later, since HAG is paid at much less regular stages, called *tranches*.

Having completed the cash flow analysis, the association may find it has to *delay* some activity – such as the start date for a particular project – in order to ensure that sufficient funds remain in the capital account each month. Alternatively it may need to arrange additional, temporary borrowing. Any association which fails to do this risks bankruptcy, if it tries to spend more than the resources it currently has available.

This contrasts with the situation for a local authority housing department, which does not have to concern itself in the same way with 'day-to-day' sources of funding for expenditure. The treasurer is responsible for monitoring the cash flow for the whole authority, and has access to short-term borrowing to accommodate any short-term deficiencies. The main concern is that, over the financial year, the budget for the whole authority is balanced.

3.7 Individual subsidy for housing services

Subsidy for tenants: housing benefit

What is housing benefit?

Housing benefit (HB) is the main personal housing subsidy payable to tenants, whether in the social or private sectors. It is a *means tested* subsidy, so applicants must have relatively low incomes to qualify. The government has been committed to 'better targeting' of housing subsidy in order to reduce spending. This has meant a reduction in general capital subsidies to housing – so called 'bricks and mortar' subsidies – because these cannot be directed to specific tenants. Instead, the government has chosen to increase social housing rents (as identified in Sections 3.4 and 3.5), so that the price for those who can afford to pay more closely reflects the real value of the housing provision. For those tenants unable to pay the increased rents, housing benefit would be available to 'take the strain'. In the private sector also, the abolition of rent controls, in the form of 'fair rents' for private sector tenancies from 1989, has resulted in rising numbers of tenants on housing benefit.

The present housing benefit scheme was introduced in 1988, following a rationalisation of the means test requirements for different types of benefit. The test is now the same as for income support (for unemployed households) and family credit (for low-income working households). Generally, anyone entitled to housing benefit will also receive council tax benefit (CTB), a reduction in the amount of tax payable to the local authority for local services, but this is also available to low-income owner occupiers.

How is housing benefit assessed?

There are four key elements in housing benefit assessments:

1. The household's expenditure needs

The government determines what each household reasonably needs to spend each week on essentials (excluding housing costs), and these figures are revised annually. There are two elements to this:

(i) *Personal allowances*, which relate to the household size and age. For example, those under 25 (unless married) are given smaller allowances, couples get more than single households and there are additional amounts for each dependent child, depending on age.

(ii) To the personal allowances are added *premiums*, to reflect the additional expenses of some household types and members. For example, in 1996, these applied to single parents, single pensioners and disabled persons.

2 Eligible housing costs

This is the usually the rent payable (including necessary service charges) unless the sums exceed reference rent levels (see below). If there are non-dependent adults living in the claimant's home (such as able grown-up children or grandparents), they are assumed to make some contribution to the rent (even if they don't), which varies with their income. So *non-dependent deductions* will reduce eligible costs. Single applicants under the age of 25 are expected to share accommodation, so the full rent is not allowable. Their eligible cost is based on the average cost only of a room in shared accommodation.

3 Income

Since housing benefit is means-tested, this means that the income of the household must be assessed to determine whether it is sufficient to cover expenditure needs and housing costs.

Income includes:

(i) Earnings, pensions, benefits and any other regular or irregular earnings. In an attempt to offer some incentive to claimants to take employment, there is an *income disregard*, i.e. a small amount of any earnings is not taken into account.

(ii) An assumed amount of interest received on capital or savings above £3,000 (even if no interest is actually received). If capital exceeds £16,000, the household is ineligible for housing benefit.

4 The taper

If households have income in excess of the expenditure deemed necessary, they are expected to contribute 65 per cent of this toward their housing costs. In other words, for each £1 of income above the maximum permitted amount, the household loses 65 pence of it for housing costs. This is known as the *taper* – the rate at which benefit is withdrawn for each £1 increase in income. The severity of the taper contributes significantly to the *poverty* and *unemployment traps*, see below.

Steps in the calculation

1 Assess income
- Calculate income, from wages, benefits, pensions, etc. and add assumed income from capital,
- Deduct any *income disregard* – the actual amount depends on the household type (single, couple, etc.).

2 Assess expenditure needs
- Calculate the value of relevant *personal allowances*.
- Add any relevant *premiums:* this gives the *applicable amount* of income thought to be needed by the household for essential expenditure.

3 Calculate excess income
- Deduct the *applicable amount* from the *income*.

4 Assess eligible costs
- These are mainly rent payments and some service charges. If the accommodation is thought to be unreasonably large or expensive, the rent officer can *determine* what the rent should be, so a lower amount will be payable.
- Deduct any *non-dependent deductions* to give the eligible costs.

5 Deduct 65 per cent of excess income from eligible costs
- This is the entitlement to housing benefit.

Any household with an assessed income (less non-dependent deductions) which is equal to or lower than the applicable amount will be entitled to full housing benefit, i.e. 100 per cent of the rent will be paid. Other households, with excess income, may be entitled to *partial* housing benefit, i.e. some contribution to rent costs.

Who is ineligible?

There is a wide range of exclusions. Some of the more important are:

- those with capital in excess of £16,000 (as identified above);
- full-time students;
- people in residential care;
- those who do not have a 'commercial arrangement', e.g. are living with a close relative;

- persons from abroad; which does not include people such as EU nationals and some asylum seekers who have applied for asylum on entry to the United Kingdom.

Who allocates housing benefit?

As identified in Section 3.4, housing benefit is administered by local authorities on behalf of the government. Housing benefit 'payments' to council tenants simply reduce (or eliminate) their weekly rent, and this appears in the HRA. Private and housing associations tenants receive actual payments from the local authority, and this is recorded in the general fund. The cost of administering housing benefits also falls on the general fund, though local authorities receive payment for this service from the government.

Housing benefit is very expensive to administer, because the calculation (as shown above) is complex and it is time consuming for staff to check all of the relevant items. Each small change in income or other circumstances will require a new assessment to be made. This sometimes results in considerable delays in assessing housing benefit entitlement, which leaves many claimants without sufficient resources to pay their rent. These delays can leave private tenants at risk of eviction, and it may cause housing association arrears figures to rise.

Complaints reached such a level that, in 1993, the DSS issued new guidelines to local authorities. These said that:

- Housing benefit claims should be determined (i.e. assessed and a decision made) *within 14 days.*
- The award should be made *within 14 days,* or 'as soon as reasonably practicable thereafter'.
- If claims could not be settled within 14 days, local authorities should make *interim payments*; a failure to do so 'is likely to incur the wrath of the ombudsman' (the official 'watchdog' who investigates complaints about local authorities).

In their defence, local authorities would point out that payments made by the government for the administration of housing benefits claims are inadequate. In addition, there are frequent eligibility changes. In the context of continuous pressures on authorities' revenue resources (examined in Section 3.4), they cannot put extra resources into this activity, not without some other aspect of council services suffering.

The claims process

There are two routes into housing benefit, for the tenant in receipt of income support, the other for tenants not in receipt of income support.

Tenants in receipt of income support automatically receive a housing benefit claim form from the Benefits Agency, which assesses income support claims. This results in a two-stage process, because, having been investigated by the Benefits Agency, they are then reinvestigated (about some aspects) by the council. Furthermore, there may be delays in the Benefits Agency forwarding housing benefit claims to the local authority, which further delays housing benefit payments. Local authority performance indicators (see Chapter 5) include 'percentage of HB claims processed within 14 days', but this *excludes* any delay by the Benefits Agency.

Tenants not in receipt of income support must apply directly to the local authority. The authority is responsible for producing its own housing benefit claim forms, and while some are very good, others may be complex and very difficult for tenants to complete. There is also a problem of lack of awareness for tenants as many will simply be unaware that they may be eligible for housing benefit.

Reference rents

If a local authority believes that the rent is unreasonably high, or the property is too large for the household (i.e. it is *underoccupied*) it can ask the rent officer to determine a reasonable rent. For new claimants from January 1996, however, there is a system of *local reference rents*. These apply both to new claimants and existing claimants who move, though claimants in supported and sheltered schemes are exempt. The reference rent means that:

- Housing benefit is calculated by reference to the *general* level, the mid-point, of private sector rents in an area.
- Housing benefit payments are a maximum of the reference rent, plus half the difference between actual and reference rents (i.e. tenants can choose to fund half of any excess rent).
- Local authorities will have some discretion to pay above the maximum.

The scheme is intended to provide tenants with an incentive to negotiate lower rents with landlords, as well as to ensure that they do not occupy a property which is too large or luxurious for their needs. However, there are concerns that this system creates real hardship for some claimants, forcing them into poorer quality accommodation or else into greater poverty, by having to fund any excess themselves from incomes which are already extremely low. In some areas, the shortage of accommodation is so acute that it is unrealistic to expect that claimants can find cheaper properties to rent. If a tenant feels that the reference rent is unfair, they may ask for a second opinion from another rent officer, but some feel that this provides insufficient protection for vulnerable households.

There are also fears that, if local authorities refer some housing association rents, these may be above the reference rent level. If so, tenants on full housing benefit would no longer get all of their rent paid, leading to rising levels of arrears. Since 'average HA rents are already at or above private rented sector rents in some areas' (Chartered Institute of Housing, Consultation Response, April 1995), these proposals could make it extremely difficult for some housing associations to let new, high-rent properties; potential tenants on full housing benefit could find their housing benefit payments falling *below* full rent levels. Private lenders will be fearful of lending in these circumstances. This could, therefore, have a significant impact on the development programmes of some housing associations.

Problems of the present housing benefit system

The housing benefit system creates a number of different problems for the administrators of the system, for claimants and for the government. These are as follows.

Perverse incentives for administrators

It has been claimed that some problems with the administration of housing benefit arise simply because of the perverse incentives which are built into the present arrangements. Some examples, identified in *Roof* (Nov/Dec 1993) include:

- Local authorities should not reclaim any overpayments due to their own error, but there is no penalty for doing so; on the contrary, the falsely reclaimed sums may be kept.
- There is no time limit on re-claiming (unavoidable) overpayments, which can arise when, for example, a claimant's income changes. Thus there is no incentive for local authorities to deal promptly with these. This can result in very large bills for claimants.
- Backdated claims attract only 50 per cent subsidy from the government, which provides a huge *dis*incentive to address them.

Low levels of take-up

This is a problem common to all means tested benefits, because many people entitled to them do not apply. This can be for a number of reasons, including ignorance, a fear of bureaucracy, an inability to complete the claim forms or a resentment of what is perceived as 'charity'.

According to *Roof* (Nov/Dec 1993), around 17 per cent of eligible tenants do not claim, which amounted to £900 million in unclaimed housing benefit in 1993. This suggests that many households are struggling to pay rents which they really cannot afford.

Disincentive to work

This arises because of the operation of the *poverty and unemployment* traps. When income rises, whether by taking a job (and leaving unemployment) or taking a better paid job, the combined effects of withdrawal of benefit and extra taxes can leave the household little better off. The housing benefit *taper* was identified above as 65 per cent. It is likely that other benefits (such as council tax benefit) will also be withdrawn.

The combined effects of the withdrawal of benefit and extra taxes for working households who earn more, called *the poverty trap*, is illustrated in Table 3.6. This shows

Table 3.6 The housing benefit poverty trap. Cumulative deductions from £1 extra gross earnings 1994

	Family	Single/couple
Increased tax		
Income tax @ 20%	20p	20p
National insurance @ 10%	10p	10p
Net earnings	70p	70p
Reduced benefit		
Family Credit @ 70% taper	−49p	0p
Housing benefit @ 65% taper	−14p	−45.5p
Council tax benefit @ 20%	−4p	−14p
Increase in net disposable income	**3p**	**10.5p**

that a family is left with only 3p from each £1 of additional income, as a result of increased liability for taxes and withdrawal of benefit, to which housing benefit makes a substantial contribution. Even a single person or couple is only 10.5p better off.

The *unemployment trap* has a similar effect to the poverty trap. For those who are out of work, the loss of benefit coupled with the requirement to pay taxes can mean that they are actually *worse off* as a result of getting a job. Housing benefit and council tax benefit are likely to reduce considerably; unemployment benefit and income support will be lost, but a family may be able to claim a (much smaller) family credit. They will then have to pay income tax (at least 20 per cent) and national insurance contributions (10 per cent). The overall effect may well leave them worse off, and that is before the additional costs of employment, such as clothing, travel, lunches etc., are considered.

The effects of rising rents on work incentives

The disincentive to work provided by housing benefits has been considerably worsened by rising levels of rent in social tenures. Table 3.7 shows that the main effect of rising rents is to considerably *extend the breadth* of the poverty trap. This arises because, for those on full housing benefits, all of any increase in rent is paid by housing benefits. Rising rents simply increase the amount of household costs paid by the benefit system. This means that the wage that has to be earned to compensate for loss of benefit rises with every rent increase. In the worst case, Table 3.7 shows that a single

Table 3.7 Gross earnings at which benefit dependency ceases at different rent levels (1994/95), pounds per week

Rent	Couple over 18	Gross earnings Single parent (one child under 11)	Single parent (two children under 11)	Couple (two children, one under 11, one 11–15)
30	153	112	93	123
40	177	185	165	202
50	200	215	227	248
60	224	239	250	271
70	248	262	274	295
80	271	286	298	319
90	295	310	321	342

Source: adapted from Wilcox (1996)

parent with two children paying £90 rent would need to earn £321 per week to remove themselves from benefit dependency and escape the effects of the poverty trap. Few single parents (predominantly female) could ever aspire to such earnings!

Recent research for the Joseph Rowntree Foundation found that around half of all households on benefit calculated whether they would be better off before accepting employment, with owner occupiers more likely to accept work regardless of financial implications than tenants. This suggests that the work disincentives generated by the benefit system are indeed significant for many households, and it was particularly marked in the case of single households (Ford and Kempson, 1996).

Disincentive to economise

Since housing benefit pays the full cost of rent increases, it has been suggested that this provides a *disincentive to economise* on housing, i.e. it encourages households to take accommodation which is too expensive and/or too large for their needs. The removal of rent controls may have permitted some private sector landlords to charge exploitative rents and the availability of housing benefit has enabled tenants readily to accept these inflated rents. It is also possible for claimants to move to better properties, offering standards of accommodation well above their needs. This is the primary reason for the introduction of reference rents, examined above.

Rising rents further reduce incentives to economise. Once the household is eligible for housing benefit any increase in rent after this is paid by housing benefit. Thus, at low rent levels, there *is* an incentive to economise (move to a cheaper property to save money) due to ineligibility for housing benefit; but as rents rise the household becomes eligible for housing benefit, which will meet any rent increases.

However, research by Peter Kemp at the Centre for Housing Policy at the University of York (Kemp, 1995) found little evidence that this was actually happening. The main reasons why tenants took properties where the housing benefit payment was later restricted was because:

- they did not know in advance what rent was acceptable;
- there was a shortage of other accommodation.

Tenants may now ask for a pre-determination (by the rent officer) of the allowable rent before they commit themselves to a tenancy.

The high costs of housing benefit

By 1997/8, housing benefit costs are projected to reach £13,300 million (Wilcox, 1996, Table 103). The main effect of rising rents has been to greatly extend benefit dependency. By 1993/4 in England, an average of 66 per cent of local authority tenants, and 60 per cent of housing association tenants, were in receipt of housing benefit. For *new* association tenants, in new mixed funded schemes, this rose to 83 per cent (DoE, 1994).

The government required rents to rise as part of its strategy to make social housing rents reflect the real value of housing more accurately, and private rents to rise to increase incentives to private landlords. As a means to promote this, it reduced *general* capital and revenue subsidies. However, this change in focus has had the effect of causing the social security bill to escalate to what are viewed as alarming proportions – hence the recent moves to cap rent levels in both local authority and housing association properties.

Subsidy for owner occupiers

This text is primarily about social housing, so this chapter is largely devoted to issues affecting the finance of social housing. However, it is important that this is viewed in the context of resources made available to other tenures, so that a comparison can be made. Owner occupation was viewed, for many years, as the 'preferred tenure' by the Conservative government, which explains why owner occupiers have tended to receive a wider range of subsidies than social housing tenants. Furthermore, most of these are general subsidies, available to any household; they are not means tested, and, as a result, may offer higher levels of subsidy to the wealthiest households in the United Kingdom.

The range of subsidies available to owner occupiers includes:

Mortgage interest tax relief (MITR)

This is available to all owners with a mortgage and gives exemption from paying income tax on any income used to pay the interest payments on a mortgage. Due to rapidly expanding home ownership, the costs of this rose dramatically throughout the 1980s, to peak at £7.7 million in 1990/1 (Wilcox, 1996).

As a result of the spiralling cost of MITR, the government has adopted two approaches to drive it down:

1. Holding down the maximum eligible mortgage to £30,000, despite house price rises, which mean that many households have much larger mortgages than this.
2. Reducing the rate of tax subsidy; in 1996/7, this was only 15 per cent for all claimants, so the income used to pay interest is no longer fully exempt from tax. Until 1990/91, higher-rate tax payers could gain tax relief at their highest rate, so for them this is a considerable reduction.

As a result of these changes, as well as considerably reduced interest rates in the early 1990s, MITR had been reduced to an estimated £2.8 billion in 1995/96, and the annual average subsidy had fallen from £820 to £270 (Wilcox, 1996).

It should be noted that the system was constructed so that potentially more subsidy went to the higher income groups, for two reasons. Firstly, the larger the mortgage (up to the £30,000 limit), the larger the subsidy, despite the fact that a bigger mortgage implies a higher income. Secondly, those without a mortgage do not benefit. While the absence of a mortgage might suggest a higher income, many elderly people have repaid their mortgages but nevertheless have very low incomes, and they gain nothing from this subsidy. It is also regressive in a regional sense, because those with mortgages in London and the South East of England gain a relatively higher share, reflecting higher house prices.

Capital gains tax exemption

When most assets are sold, any gain in value (after allowing for inflation) – the capital gain – is subject to tax. In the case of the only or main dwelling of an owner occupier, this tax is waived. This represents a significant subsidy, and is doubtless part of the reason why housing as an asset is more attractive in the United Kingdom than many other assets, such as stocks and shares. However, since this is a tax *exemption* rather than a payment, estimates of the cost of this subsidy are difficult to make or obtain, and its value will fluctuate considerably depending on the state of private housing markets and hence the numbers of homes sold.

Again, it should be noted that the greater the value of the property sold, the larger is the value of this tax exemption. This suggests that it is the richest who gain most, with the poorest owner occupiers gaining relatively little in comparison.

Exemption from Schedule A income taxation

Since owner occupiers choose to take the benefits of the value of their properties' services 'in kind' – instead of renting the homes out to earn rent income – they used to be charged income tax on the 'imputed' (estimated) value of those services. From 1963, however, this tax was abolished for owner occupiers. Again, it is very difficult to assess the value of this tax exemption, because it would involve estimating the 'rental value' of all owner-occupied homes in the United Kingdom, and then making some assessment of the likely tax liability of each individual occupier (since some may have insufficient income to be eligible to pay tax in any case, and others would be liable at the highest tax rate of 40 per cent). However, we can be certain that this represents a substantial saving for owner occupiers, especially for those in expensive properties – again, predominantly in London and the South East – indicating that the richest gain most.

Income support for mortgage interest payments

Unlike most of the other subsidies available to owner occupiers, this is a means-tested benefit, provided only to those on income support – the unemployed, sick, or disabled. Claimants must have assets (excluding the house) valued at less that £8,000. From 1987, the scheme paid half of all mortgage interest payments for sixteen weeks, and the full amount thereafter. As the numbers of unemployed owner occupiers rose during the recession at the end of the 1980s, however, the government sought ways to reduce the cost of this benefit, which had reached about £1.1 billion by 1994.

- A mortgage ceiling of £150,000 was introduced in 1992, reduced to £100,000 in 1994.
- From October 1995, new borrowers are ineligible for any interest payments for nine months. For pre-existing borrowers, there is no entitlement for four months, and only 50 per cent for the next four.

It was the Conservative government's belief that private insurance should be taken out to cover mortgage interest for the first nine months, but many commentators have suggested that this fails to recognise that the most vulnerable mortgagors will find insurance difficult or too expensive to obtain.

As a result, these new rules suggest that owner occupiers will be much more vulnerable to repossession if they become unemployed in future. While the intention was to improve work incentives, research for the Joseph Rowntree Foundation in 1989 and 1993 indicated that unemployed home owners, capable of working, were, generally, actively seeking work. Furthermore, a majority of claimants are those who are unable to work: 17 per cent elderly, 12 per cent disabled and 21 per cent single parents in 1994. Maclennan and More (chapter on housing in the Public Services Yearbook, 1995/6) argue that, in the light of this, there is a limited economic case for the reform.

Improvement grants

These means-tested grants are available for essential repairs to properties, to help to bring them up to acceptable standards. They include assistance with the provision of essential sanitary facilities, adequate heating and hygienic kitchen facilities, and are available to low-income landlords as well as owner occupiers. However, as identified earlier, only a limited amount of *specified capital grants* are made available by the government to local authorities for these purposes, so in practice, many authorities have to operate a waiting list. The relatively worsening condition of property in the private rented and owner-occupied sectors suggests that this present system is failing to address the problem of poor house condition in the private sector sufficiently well.

Comparison with subsidies for tenants

It is useful to compare the subsidies available to owner occupiers with those available to tenants, and to examine how these have been changing. However, it should be noted that assistance with owner-occupiers' costs excludes all of the tax *exemptions* identified above, as well as improvement grants, since these are available also to landlords. This means that Table 3.8 generally understates the subsidies available to owner occupiers.

Table 3.8 Assistance with housing costs (£ million at 1995 prices)

	Home owners	Council tenants	Private tenants (including HAs)
General subsidies			
1989/90	6810	809	55
1996/97	2660	−551	−
Means tested			
1989/90	353	2940	1006
1996/97	900	5429	3909
Totals			
1989/90	7163	3749	1061
1996/97	3560	4878	3909

Source: adapted from Wilcox (1997)

This table indicates that:

- Subsidies to private tenants have risen fastest, due to the abolition of rent controls; this includes housing association tenants.
- Subsidies to council tenants have remained fairly static in real terms, though the balance has shifted considerably from general (HRA) subsidies to means tested (housing benefit) subsidies. This reflects both the decline in capital subsidies and council rent increases, resulting in more tenants claiming housing benefit.
- While the general (MITR) subsidy to owner occupiers has been falling, the means tested income support for mortgage interest has been rising – reflecting the increased proportions of unemployed owner occupiers.

These changes are a reflection of the broad policy shift to the 'better targeting' of subsidies, away from general subsidies, to means tested subsidies. It has had the result of reducing the subsidies to owner occupiers, though, as identified above, this is grossly understated without some recognition of the value of tax exemptions.

3.8 Conclusion: the changing allocation of housing finance

This chapter has shown that there have been significant changes in the allocation of housing finance over recent years, which have had an impact on many parts of the housing system. These changes result largely from two specific economic goals of the last Conservative government, explored in earlier sections. We summarise below some of the key financial effects of these developments.

Objective 1: a reduced role for the public sector

Effects:

- A significant reduction in capital spending on new homes by local authorities.
- Initially, increased finance for new social housing provision by housing associations, with an expansion of capital funding (via housing association grant, or HAG).
- The transfer of social housing stock to owner occupation (via policies such as Right to Buy), or to new, private sector landlords, with policies such as large scale voluntary transfer (LSVT) and housing action trusts (HATs). This is discussed in more detail in the final chapter.
- An increasing role for private finance for social provision, with *mixed funding* required for housing associations, and an increasing emphasis on *partnerships* with the private sector for local authorities.
- An attempt to encourage private renting, with rent controls largely removed and some fiscal (tax) incentives for private landlords (such as the business expansion scheme and investment trusts).
- More recently, a reducing total sum available for housing association capital spending on social rented housing, as funds are switched to ownership initiatives.

Partly as a result of this latter development there has been increasing support for housing associations by local authorities. For example, local authority HAG was forecast to provide 11,000 housing association dwellings in 1995/6 in England (Public Expenditure Survey Report, 1995/6).

Objective 2: better targeting of subsidy

Effects:

- A switch to 'market rent' policies for social housing, with changed revenue subsidy policies, intended to force both local authorities and housing associations to increase rents.
- An increased emphasis on *personal* housing subsidy via means-tested benefits (principally housing benefit), for those tenants unable to afford market rents.
- Reduced universal, capital subsidies for both local authorities and housing associations (which are subsidies available to all tenants).
- An extension of some forms of subsidy to selected owner occupiers (such as Right to Buy). While the value of one of the older subsidies (*mortgage interest tax*

relief) has been declining, this has been supplemented by a wide variety of special schemes to encourage social housing tenants to become owner occupiers.

These policies have had the effect of causing expenditure on housing benefit to increase dramatically, because for those on benefit, the whole of any increase in rent is paid by housing benefit increases. Until 1990/91, they also resulted in dramatic increases in the cost of subsidy to owner occupiers, with the cost of mortgage interest tax relief (MITR) soaring. This caused the government to introduce measures to limit the rate of income tax on which MITR was payable from 1994, as well as to limit the maximum eligible mortgage. Nevertheless, this subsidy alone is estimated to have cost £2.76 billion in 1995/6 (Wilcox, 1996).

We are now in a situation in which most forms of financial subsidy are under strain, with declining public resources available to all tenures. The extent to which private finance can fill the gap is now in some doubt. It does seem that new initiatives are urgently needed, which goes some way to explaining why LSVT and local housing companies have emerged as a favoured way forward for many local authorities concerned about the continued, adequate provision of social housing. At the centre of these moves is a debate about the definition of the PSBR, which means that borrowing by local authorities for expenditure on their housing stock is deemed to be public expenditure. These issues are examined further in the final chapter.

Further reading

Chaplin, R. *et al.* (1995) *Rents and Risks; Investing in Housing Associations*, Joseph Rowntree Foundation, York.

Ford, J. and Wilcox, S. (1992) *Reducing Mortgage Arrears and Repossessions*, Joseph Rowntree Foundation, York.

Garland, D. and Parker, J. (undated) *Managing Housing Budgets in a Competitive Environment*, Chartered Institute of Housing ADC, Coventry.

Garnett, D. Reid, B. and Riley, H. (1991) *Housing Finance*, Longman/Chartered Institute of Housing, Coventry.

Gibb, K. and Munro, M. (1991) *Housing Finance in the UK: An Introduction*, Macmillan, Basingstoke.

Hills, J. (1991) *Unravelling Housing Finance*, Clarendon Press, Oxford.

Housing Finance, Quarterly Journal of the Council of Mortgage Lenders.

Maclennan, D. (1994) *A Competitive UK Economy: the Challenges for Housing Policy*, Joseph Rowntree Foundation, York.

Malpass, P. (1990) *Reshaping Housing Policy*, Routledge, London.

Meen, G. and Wilcox, S. (1995) *The Cost of Higher Rents*, National Federation of Housing Associations, London.

Pearce, B. and Wilcox, S. (1991) *Home Ownership, Taxation and the Economy*, Joseph Rowntree Foundation, York.

Chapter 4

DEVELOPING SOCIAL HOUSING

4.1 Introduction: the context of social housing development

Social housing development may involve the provision of new dwellings, or the rehabilitation of existing buildings. The ability of housing organisations to engage in development work is highly dependent on the policies of the central government. It is central government which, largely, control 'the purse strings' for capital spending, spending on housing assets.

As identified in earlier chapters, the emphasis of recent government policy has been on local authorities as *enablers* of social housing development, rather than as providers. They have been encouraged to sell land cheaply to housing associations, and to transfer part or all of their stock to associations for rehabilitation. *Partnership* initiatives, which involve private sector developers, are encouraged, with some government finance specifically targeted to this approach to development. As a result, local authorities have virtually ceased to build new housing. By 1995, local authority housing *starts* had declined to tiny amounts: 605 in England, 376 in Scotland, and 53 in Wales. Even in Northern Ireland, where 'council' housing is developed by the Northern Ireland Housing Executive and the housing association movement has remained very small, starts had fallen to 1071 by 1994 (from a high of 4,357 in 1983) (Wilcox, 1996). Local authorities now struggle, under severe financial restrictions (see Chapter 3), to refurbish their ageing stock.

Housing associations were encouraged to take over the main role of developing new social housing, initially via a huge expansion in housing association grant (HAG) from the government. More recently, with the advent of *mixed funding* and the use of private finance, HAG levels have been declining significantly. Nevertheless, housing associations remain the main providers of *new* social housing in the United Kingdom starting 41,679 new homes in 1994, compared to 2,204 by local authorities

This chapter aims to describe the main features of the *process* of developing or rehabilitating social housing schemes. It begins by identifying the key people who will need to be involved in housing development, and then examines the main stages in the process. The intention is to provide an overview of this whole process, to promote an awareness of the essential features, rather than confer expertise in specific aspects of construction. For reasons of space, it has not been possible to include information about different construction technologies, which are many and varied. The repair and maintenance of social housing, which directly involves many more housing managers, is examined in Chapter 5.

4.2 What is the housing development process?

The housing development process includes all activities which are necessary to achieve the construction of a new housing scheme or the refurbishment of existing dwellings. The stage with which everyone is familiar, when construction work actually begins on site, is in reality the final stage of a long and complex process. Many separate issues first have to be resolved by the housing organisation, and most of these decisions will require the advice and assistance of a number of other parties, with different skills and areas of expertise. This section begins by identifying and briefly describing the main people with important roles in the process. Their specific responsibilities at each stage will become clear later, as the process itself is examined.

The main parties to the process

The client
The client requires the development, initiates the process and pays for the design and construction.

This may be a person or organisation. The client must ensure that everyone involved in the scheme's design and construction is very clear about the requirements for the scheme, by setting them out in a number of clearly defined ways, which are examined as the process unfolds. Housing organisations are usually represented in this role by one or two people, sometimes employed in a separate development section, known as the *client's representatives*. Housing managers may be involved in some or all of the activities required of this role.

Parties employed or engaged by the client
The client employs a number of professionals to direct and manage the development process. Some large social housing organisations may have a number of their own 'in-house' consultants, able to provide all or most of the specialised roles. Many others will undertake insufficient development work for it to be worthwhile to employ specialist skills internally, so they will need to employ external specialists.

The consultant
The consultant generally designs the development and oversees its construction.

This person (or persons) is most often an *architect*, who has detailed knowledge of both house and estate design, so can advise on the best solutions to development problems and issues. When the development is a rehabilitation project, a *building surveyor* will usually be involved with the architect, or may replace the architect in the consulting role. This is because building surveyors have detailed knowledge of *existing* buildings, both of their design and of the sorts of problems which arise from this. Building surveyors are also employed by social housing organisations to inspect property which needs repair, so will often work with housing managers engaged in maintenance work. This is examined in Chapter 5 on managing social housing.

The quantity surveyor

The quantity surveyor (QS) is the client's cost consultant.

The quantity surveyor costs the designs prepared by the main consultant, ensures that *value for money* is being obtained, and later, values construction work as it progresses to permit payments to be made to the contractor. Although the QS will have to work closely with the architect, she or he must be appointed separately by the client, because the QS checks that the architect's design is within the organisation's cost limits and/or offers good value for money. For rehabilitation projects, the building surveyor will usually also undertake the QS role.

Other consultants

Other consultants may be necessary for some projects.

For example, where there are difficult site conditions, such as old mine workings, a *civil or structural engineer* may be engaged to undertake detailed examination of the site and advise on the design of the buildings' foundations. This professional can also advise on buildings which have special structural requirements, such as high rise flats. *Electrical and/or mechanical engineers* may be needed when there are lifts; *landscape architects* specialise in the external areas of an estate; and *highways engineers* can resolve complex road layout or access difficulties. Generally, the main consultant will advise when any of these are necessary.

The contractor

The contractor is the organisation which undertakes the construction work.

Sometimes, in the case of a local authority, the contractor appointed will be the in-house 'direct works' section, but in most circumstances, an outside contractor – a building company – will be engaged. It is important that the client and consultant maintain good communications with the contractor, in order to ensure that the work is of the right quality and is completed on time.

The contractor's main representative on site is the *site agent*, who supervises and coordinates the work of all of the different skills, such as bricklayers, joiners, plumbers, electricians, etc.

Sub-contractors

Sub-contractors may be employed to undertake some work in place of the main contractor.

These may be *nominated* by the client, or they may be engaged by the contractors themselves, because they have greater expertise in some aspects. They operate under the direction of the lead contractor.

The clerk of works

The clerk of works closely supervises the construction work on behalf of the client.

Once the construction work is underway, it is overseen by the consultant. However, this person cannot provide close day-to-day supervision. For this reason, most social housing projects will engage a clerk of works, who is employed on the site by the client organisation, and works closely with the architect to ensure that what is built is exactly what is required by the architect's design. This role is particularly important for a rehabilitation project, because, very often, new and unforeseen problems emerge once the work begins. A poor standard of work may result, unless closely monitored.

The planning supervisor

The planning supervisor coordinates all requirements relating to health and safety matters for a scheme.

This is a recent role, required by the Construction Design and Management (CDM) Regulations from 31 March 1995. It results both from the concerns of the Health and Safety Executive (HSE) – the body which oversees workplace safety in the United Kingdom – and the European Union (EU) about high accident and fatality rates on construction sites. These regulations impose duties on clients, consultants and contractors to ensure that there are adequate health and safety controls at all stages of the development process, in order to reduce the likelihood of accidents.

This function need not rest with one person, but may be undertaken by the design team or contractor where appropriate. What is important is that someone or somebody always takes the responsibilities of the planning supervisor, and this must to be stated in any contracts (which are examined at a later stage). Under the current regulations the client has the key responsibility for ensuring that a planning supervisor is appointed and that the person or organisation chosen is competent to carry out the function.

The responsibilities of the planning supervisor include:

- informing the HSE of planned projects which are likely to last more than 30 days or involve more than 500 person working days on site (so, minor maintenance projects are excluded);
- reviewing and coordinating arrangements to avoid risks to health and safety;
- preparing a *Health and Safety Plan*, identifying potential hazards, safety issues and procedures;
- creating a Health and Safety file, containing all details about the site and the subsequent construction.

Solicitors

Solicitors are employed to advise on legal aspects and draw up contracts.

In general, a solicitor will be needed to advise on all legal constraints on a site, complete the purchase of a site or buildings, and to draw up any contracts, which specify the conditions under which the client is employing the different parties. This helps to ensure that the client has *legal redress* – can go to court for compensation – in the event of a party failing to perform adequately.

Other key public sector parties

In addition to the parties employed directly by the housing organisation, there are a number of other people whose roles are important to development. These are public sector employees with specific statutory responsibilities, i.e. they have some obligations by law for aspects of the development process. The role of the Health and Safety Executive has already been identified, in overseeing matters affecting the safety of the public and employees whilst construction work is continuing.

Development controls are intended to ensure that the quality of the physical environment is maintained and protected from inappropriate developments. Development control is the responsibility of the planning authorities, which, in general, are local authorities (though in some parts of England and Wales Urban Development Corporations and National Parks authorities have these powers). This is overseen by the central government, via the Secretary of State for the Environment. An important function of the planning system is to ensure that there is an adequate supply of land for housing. As part of this role, the planning authorities are required to draw up *development plans*, which indicate how such requirements are to be met.

In most areas, where there is only one tier of local government; there is a single (unitary) development plan. Where two tiers remain, the plans are in two parts: the first drawn up by the county council and the second, by the district council. Overall, however, all development plans must cover similar issues:

- A 'structure' plan, which defines requirements in broad terms, taking account of factors such as demographic trends, government policy and housing demand in the area. It specifies the target number of new dwellings to be permitted, which are distributed amongst the districts.
- 'Local' plans, which identify specific locations in the area considered suitable for residential development, as well as local policies for development control.

Planning officers

Planning officers are responsible for drawing up development plans and recommending whether applications relating to the types and location of buildings and the use of land should be approved.

The *planning committee* of the local authority grants approval for development, but is advised by its professional officers. A development scheme is likely to attract planning consent if it conforms to the development plans. This is intended to ensure that:

- The interests of other occupiers in the locality are protected. So, planning consent is needed for the construction of new buildings, most changes of the use of a building (e.g. from a residential use to an estate office) and for some extensions. Neighbours have the opportunity to object to any plans before they are considered by the council.
- The visual appearance and environmental quality of an area is protected.

This may result in special conditions being attached to the consent, such as a requirement to use particular types of building materials in keeping with other properties in the locality. Some sites may have specific planning requirements; for example, old trees may be protected by *tree preservation orders*, and the plans will have to include measures to protect these trees during construction work. Some buildings are *listed*, as being of special architectural interest. There are strict limitations on the extent to which such buildings can be altered by construction activity. In rural areas, where it may be difficult for local people to access housing, local authorities may require, as a condition of planning consent, that only those who live or work in the area may rent or buy. In England and Wales these are known as Section 106 agreements.

In addition to controlling the location and types of construction work, local authorities have a duty to oversee the standards of construction. These are governed by the *Building Regulations*.

Building inspectors

Building inspectors are responsible for checking that standards of construction conform with the Building Regulations.

Building Regulations' approval must be obtained for most building work and is normally obtained before any work commences. In addition, the building inspector (or other authorised person, such as a representative of the National House Builders Council) checks the progress of construction at various stages, to ensure compliance with the regulations before the next stage can commence.

Other public officers

A number of other public officers may need to be involved in some projects.

For example, properties which are intended for multiple occupation, such as flats, need to be approved by the fire service. This is to ensure that there are adequate, safe exits in the event of fire and that suitable measures are taken to deter the spread of fire, such as fire-resistant doors to hallways. The police may advise on site layout, roads, footpaths and boundary treatments as well as on security measures, such as door and window locks, alarms, and the use of video surveillance equipment.

4.3 What are the main stages in the development process?

There are a number of different stages in the process of developing a housing scheme. These can be classified in a variety of ways, but for housing managers, it is useful to conceive of three main, (largely) sequential phases.

Stage I: Initiating the development

The first stage includes all of the activities which need to be undertaken before there can be a firm decision to go ahead with the project. This involves identifying and assessing potential sites (for new build), establishing the feasibility of possible schemes, and identifying exactly what is required of the development. The consulting architect (or building surveyor) always becomes involved during this phase.

Stage II: Designing the development

This includes all of the activities which contribute to the final detailed plans for the project, generally produced by the consultant and guided by a briefing from the client. This stage will determine whether the organisation achieves the sort of new development or refurbishment that it requires, because the outcome is the final design which will be constructed.

Stage III: Constructing the development

This final stage is concerned with getting the project built. The client must first appoint a contractor to undertake the work, and there are several possible approaches to this. The process of constructing the properties is overseen by the consultant, with close supervision provided by the clerk of works.

There are some approaches which provide 'short-cuts' through the development process, by assigning some or all of the design stage to the contractor. However, the key tasks in achieving a housing development remain basically the same; it is a question more of who is responsible for undertaking these tasks at each stage. The next two sections assume a traditional approach in defining key roles; some 'short-cut' approaches are examined following the design stage.

4.4 Stage I: initiating development

What type of development is wanted?

The social housing organisation should have clear ideas about the sorts of housing needs for which it wants to develop housing. These needs are identified in the local authority's annual plans for housing – such as the Housing Investment Programme in England, or the Housing Plan in Scotland – which include data from housing associations in the area (examined in Chapter 3).

In the past, local authorities built predominantly for general (family) needs, so they produced largely two- and three-bedroom houses. It is largely these types of dwellings which have transferred out of the social sector into owner occupation via the right to buy policy. Due mainly to land constraints, most urban authorities also built flats, and during the late fifties and sixties, many were encouraged to build high-rise homes for families (with very mixed success). Since local authorities concentrated largely on housing families, many housing associations were started with the aim of meeting more specialised needs, such as homes for the elderly, or for young single people. This resulted in a much higher proportion of flats being constructed in the housing association sector.

Now, severe financial constraints mean that few local authorities are able to engage in new build, and housing associations have largely taken over the role of producing new homes for general needs, as well as continuing to provide homes for other needs groups. The proportions of houses in the housing association sector is likely to be increasing as a result. In addition, the *large-scale voluntary transfer* (LSVT) of some local authority properties to housing associations is adding significant numbers of houses to housing association stock.

Properties which are to be refurbished will often have existing tenants, who will wish to return to their refurbished homes. If, however, the properties are empty, then a decision will have to be taken about the need which it is intended they will meet, because this will affect the design requirements.

Selecting a site

For a new build scheme, having identified the type of development wanted, the process moves to identifying an appropriate site; clearly, for rehabilitation projects, the site already exists!

Finding a site

There are many different possible sources of information about sites. The main ones include:

- Individual landowners; these may be a particularly important source in rural areas, where the local authority may be prepared to grant *exceptional* planning permission for a social housing scheme.
- Estate agents, who sell development sites on behalf of owners in most areas.
- Development or construction companies, who may have land which is surplus to their requirements. This is most common when the market for speculative, owner-occupied dwellings is slow, so the contractors may be unwilling to risk building on their own account. In return for making the land available, however, they will often require that the contract to construct the properties is placed with them.
- Local authorities; they will have identified possible development sites in their area as part of their local development plan, which is examined below. It is increasingly common for local authorities to make land available to housing associations at low (or zero) prices in return for *nomination rights* over a certain percentage of lettings, often 50–100 per cent. This is the right to nominate new tenants for the scheme from their own waiting list. Some local authorities may have assembled information about development sites as a *land bank*.
- Other housing organisations (who may have been offered a site unsuited to their own requirements, but who think it may be suitable for other housing uses).

Initial site appraisal

The client, usually the development manager or holder of a similar post, needs to make an initial assessment of the suitability of the site. Key factors should be considered systematically, so that nothing of importance is overlooked. This approach also permits alternative sites to be compared more easily.

Key factors might include those set out below.

Is the site suitable?

This involves an assessment of the site from both the perspective of potential for affordable development and the needs of the customers who will be housed. These can be grouped into three main categories.

Physical features

For example, from the perspective of customer needs, a steeply sloping site is unlikely to be acceptable for a scheme of bungalows for the elderly, but may be suitable for family accommodation. The size of the site may also be important for particular uses.

A site investigation and survey will normally be necessary to identify problems such as old mine workings, or previous land-fill, both of which will add to site preparation and construction costs. The investigation involves a detailed physical examination, including possibly taking bore-hole drillings (to remove samples from well below the surface) and testing soil samples. This is undertaken by a consultant such as a structural engineer, who will produce a site investigation and survey report on findings.

Figure 4.1 shows a good site for housing development.

Accessible from existing highways?

It is essential that a site can be easily accessed from the existing road network. If new roads need to be constructed to service a site this can often be prohibitively expensive.

Location

Young people are unlikely to want to live on the outskirts of a city, but families may be quite happy with a suburban location. For the elderly, it is vital that local services, such as shops and public transport, are at hand.

Fig. 4.1 A good site for housing development, fairly level, with services readily available

Are services available?

These include electricity supplies, telephones, gas, water, and sewers. It can be expensive to provide new sources of supply, but services are more likely to be readily available in urban locations. This partly explains why development costs on rural sites tend to be higher.

Are there any special conditions?

The landowners may wish to specify the type of development which can be constructed, or there may be existing controls affecting land use, such as *covenants* which restrict rights, or existing public rights of way.

Does the likely price offer 'value for money'?

This will depend partly on current market conditions – whether or not sites are in high demand – as well as the particular features, locality, etc. of the site.

Can the properties be let at the rents which will be necessary?

This is a key issue for housing associations rather than local authorities, since they do not, in general, have such a large historic stock over which to share the costs of new development by rent pooling (see Chapter 5).

Has outline planning consent been granted?

This can be checked with the planning officers of the local planning authority. Some minor works may not require planning consent. Planning applications are usually granted, in two stages: outline and detailed. At this stage, the organisation need only be concerned that outline consent is (or will be) available, though, in practice, many housing associations will opt to obtain both stages at the start, which minimises delays.

Outline applications require:

- a brief description of the proposed development; and
- a site plan, to identify the land.

This permits the planning authority to check that the proposed development conforms to the development plans. Outline planning consents are generally granted, subject to further approval of specific items. These are called *reserved matters*. Reserved matters deal with:

- siting
- design
- external appearance
- means of access
- landscaping

If the client wishes, information about these reserved matters *can* be included at the outline stage, but this would not be usual.

Full (detailed) planning permission requires detailed information about the design, layout, and other requirements. of the development. This will usually be obtained when the detailed design has been prepared.

Local authorities have to undertake slightly different procedures for planning permission. If the development will be undertaken by the authority itself, it must obtain 'deemed consent', which requires:

- a *first resolution* passed by the housing committee;
- a *second resolution* passed by the planning committee.

The second resolution can be made only after publicity of the application, and notice being served on the owners of the land (if not the local authority). If the local authority owns the land but the development will be undertaken by someone else (such as a housing association), the second resolution may include conditions on the development, which are viewed as *reserved matters* and remain to be approved.

What requires planning consent?

The need to obtain the approval of the local planning authority applies to the following changes.

Building, extending or altering a property Some types of development, defined by Development Orders issued by the Secretary of State, do not need specific consents. For example, the Town and Country Planning General Development Order, 1988, lists 28 categories of development which are exempt. In general, these are minor alterations, so are likely to apply only to refurbishment schemes, such as:

- extensions which add *no more* than 50 cubic metres or 10 per cent of the existing building size, whichever is the greater;
- small buildings, which are 'incidental to the enjoyment of the house' such as a greenhouse or garden shed (but not a garage);
- a porch, with a floor area no larger than two square metres.

Most other changes require planning consent. *Listed buildings*, which have some special importance or architectural interest, may be removed from general permitted development. National parks, conservation areas and areas of outstanding natural beauty are also subject to specific restrictions.

Changing the use of the property In addition to the general exemptions provided by development orders, the Planning Acts define 'use classes', such as Class C3 dwelling houses, or Class C2 residential institutions. A change of use will require planning consent in most cases. So if, for example, a housing association wishes to convert a large children's home into several flats, or the housing department wishes to convert an estate dwelling into a 'neighbourhood office', it will have to obtain consent.

What if consent is denied?

If consent is refused, the applicant has the right to appeal to the Secretary of State. The appeal may be granted or refused. In recent years, the government has taken a more relaxed approach to planning issues, and appeals have had a greater chance of success.

If all elements in this initial site appraisal are acceptable, the next stage is to appoint a consultant to undertake a full *feasibility study*.

Selecting and appointing a consultant

The consultant must be reliable and responsive to the client's needs. For this reason, the client organisation should undertake some checks on any new consultant, to determine whether:

- they have previous experience of similar types of project;
- past projects were completed on time, within cost budgets and to the client's satisfaction;
- their past designs are liked by the client.

Some clients will have in-house consultants (e.g. the architect's department of a local authority), but they should nevertheless meet the standards required of external consultants.

A formal *letter of appointment* – in effect a binding contract – is not normally offered until the consultant has shown that the project is feasible and is worthwhile. At this stage, therefore, the consultant generally receives only a *letter of intent* (to appoint once feasibility is demonstrated) from the client organisation and will be working 'at risk', i.e. without a fee.

Once the organisation decides to proceed with the scheme, the consultant will receive a letter of appointment (usually agreed with the organisation's solicitor) which:

- defines the roles of client, consultant and any other relevant professionals;
- identifies the conditions of the appointment;
- specifies the fees and expenses payable;
- requires indemnity insurance, to cover the client in the event of any design failures.

This is an important document, because it effectively defines the service which the client expects of the consultant.

Feasibility study

The consultant will begin by sketching out possible estate layouts for different property types, suitable for the desired type of scheme, and identify possible construction methods. From these initial ideas, one will be selected for further consideration. This will be the scheme which appears to meet the client's requirements best, and is likely to be within the client's budget.

On the basis of this initial draft design, the feasibility of the scheme will then be assessed.

What is feasible?
In general, a project is considered feasible if:

- estimated costs suggest that it is likely that it can be constructed within budget constraints.
- in the case of housing associations, rent levels which are necessary to cover scheme costs are viewed as affordable;
- assessed levels of risk are acceptable.

Costs

The consultant will draw up more detailed drawings from the initial sketch, to show broad design details. These enable the quantity surveyor to estimate construction costs. To these must be added all additional costs, such as:

- the cost of site acquisition (purchase);
- fees for professionals, such as consultants and solicitors (to undertake the legal work);
- fees for statutory requirements – building regulations' approval and planning consents;
- interest charges on any money which will have to be borrowed during the construction phase, in order to make regular *stage payments* to the contractor as work progresses.

The social housing organisation should also consider likely future maintenance costs, and may wish to build an allowance for these into the costings; for housing associations, this is particularly important, since rents will have to cover these future costs. In general, they will also need to ensure that total costs are within the cost limits imposed by their statutory funding body, for eligibility for housing association grant (HAG).

Rents

In general, local authority rents are not directly related to scheme costs, since most operate a system of *rent-pooling*, which spreads all costs amongst all schemes. Housing association rents are usually, however, directly related to scheme costs. (Approaches to rent-setting are examined in Chapter 5.) If housing associations expect to receive HAG for the scheme, they will have to provide a feasibility report for the funding body, which shows the rent levels which will be generated by the scheme costs. They must feel confident that the properties can be let successfully at these rent levels.

Housing association rents must cover:

- loan repayments on borrowed finance, which will depend crucially on total development costs, as well as current HAG *grant rates*;
- contributions to a fund for future major repairs;
- expected future maintenance costs, which depend partly on the design of the scheme;
- management costs;
- provisions for voids and bad debts.

Risk

There are always risks that something will go badly wrong due to unforeseen factors, causing the project to be delayed or costs to rise. This is especially a risk with projects to rehabilitate existing buildings, because structural problems may only become apparent when work begins. It is largely this element of higher risk that has resulted in the decline of rehabilitation by housing associations, most of whom now, under mixed funding, must bear at least half of the risk of cost increases. This is examined in Chapter 3.

There is also the possibility that the properties cannot be let (or sold, for shared ownership projects) once completed, so these risks must be taken into account. The demand for homes to buy is affected greatly by general economic conditions, such as interest rates and rates of unemployment, none of which are under the control of social housing organisations. Under the new financial regime, housing association tenants must cover the organisation's costs via rents, so increased voids or unsold properties mean higher rents for the other tenants.

Different organisations will be able to tolerate different levels of risk. Local authorities and very large housing associations will generally have more scope to absorb higher costs than small housing associations, for whom the level of reserves to deal with possible cost increases will be crucial. The number of schemes in progress will also affect acceptable risk levels, because if the worst happened and *all* went wrong, this could create real problems.

A number of approaches to risk assessment are possible; two of the more common methods are as follows.

Sensitivity analysis This approach attempts to identify particularly high risk elements in the costs, such as void losses or the risk that interest rates will increase during the construction period, resulting in higher loan repayments. The calculations are re-worked, making different assumptions about these risk factors. So, for example, loan repayments may be calculated assuming interest rates of 8 per cent, 10 per cent and 12 per cent. Voids may be assumed to be 3 per cent, 5 per cent or 10 per cent.

It is then possible to see the extent to which the viability of the project is affected by these changes. If it became clear that, with very few changes to the assumptions, the project would cease to be feasible, then this would suggest that it was a high risk undertaking.

Rating of risk factors This is a simpler approach, which attempts to assess the *relative* riskiness of each element in the calculation, compared to other schemes. The National Housing Federation suggests an approach such as this.

Risk elements are rated on a scale of, say, 1 to 5, 1 being the least risk. This might include risks such as:

- cost increases
- problems with the contractor
- late completion dates
- letting difficulties

The overall riskiness of the project can be seen from the total score. Generally, a project with a lower risk score would be preferred over one with a high risk score.

Feasibility report

All of this information is set out in a feasibility report for the consideration of the development manager, management committee or whoever is responsible for taking decisions about development. The assumptions made for the calculations – such as interest rates, completion date, and so on – must be clearly identified. A decision is then made about whether to go ahead with the project.

Once the decision to proceed has been taken, the next step is to acquire the site, though not before outline planning consent at least has been obtained, as examined in the last section. (In reality, unless this was thought likely to be granted, the scheme would not have progressed to feasibility study stage.)

Site Acquisition

How is the price agreed?

The cost of the site may be a substantial part of total costs, so it important to obtain value for money. Before the sale price is agreed with the vendor, social housing providers *must* obtain a valuation from an 'independent' valuer, such as (in the case of local authorities) the *district valuer*, a civil servant employed by the Valuation Agency. Housing associations are not generally permitted by the statutory funders to pay a price higher than the valuer's price. In any event, it is a sensible precaution against potential corruption.

It is usual to obtain an initial *informal* valuation, to use as a guide for negotiation purposes. If the vendor's price remains above the valuation price, it *may* be possible to discuss this with the valuer, before the formal valuation is undertaken.

When seeking a valuation it is essential that the client passes all available information to the valuer concerning the site, services, legal constraints and site investigation.

What is involved in purchasing?

Before any money is paid, the client's solicitors must ensure that the vendor does actually own the land – in legal terms, has the *title* to the land. If the title is not registered (at a registry set up by the government), this will involve checking back through all previous purchases in the *title deeds* to ensure that the *title* (or right) was properly transferred. In England and Wales, this is transferred by a conveyance, in Scotland by a feu charter or *disposition*. It is important to ensure that the title has no restrictions which could prevent the development of the site.

If the title has been registered, at the Land Registry in England and Wales, or the Register of Sasines or Land Register of Scotland, then checking ownership is quite simple.

For housing associations purchasing leasehold sites in England and Wales, the statutory funders will generally require minimum lease expiry terms as a condition of receiving HAG funds. This is because the leaseholder regains ownership of the land once the lease expires. Minimum expiry times are generally shorter for rehabilitation schemes than for new build, reflecting the different life-expectancies of the two types of development.

The solicitors will then draw up a contract, and this is *completed* when payment is made and ownership is transferred in the *deeds* which confer a *title* to the land. After this, the housing organisation is free to begin construction work on the site.

4.5 Stage II: designing the development

The next step is to determine the details of the design requirements, so that the briefing (from which the consultants will design the scheme) can be prepared. This will be influenced by current ideas about what constitutes good design.

What is good design?

This is a controversial topic, because few designers can agree, objectively, about what makes a good design. However, it can be argued that if the design 'works' for its inhabitants, so that they feel that it gives them the main things that they want from a home, then it is, subjectively, a good design. This applies both to dwelling design and to external design, the physical context of the dwellings.

What do households want from a home?
Good designs seem to fulfil two key requirements:

They are functional
Homes need to provide adequate shelter, comfort and security for their inhabitants. Both dwelling and estate design can affect these functional matters.

They express symbolic and aesthetic values
Homes are also seen a physical expression of their inhabitants, so they can 'confer' social values such as status, a sense of worth and success, 'respectability'. Most people prefer to live in a 'nice' home which is aesthetically pleasing to them, and gain a sense of well-being from this. It is not only house *types* and *styles* which are important, but *locality*.

Social housing providers in the past may have overlooked some of the symbolic and aesthetic requirements of dwellings, focusing exclusively on the functional aspects of the design; for example, the tower-blocks of flats built in the 1950s and early 1960s may have been functionally good (though many were not, with problems of damp penetration and poor security, for example), but symbolically, they offered little to residents. The importance of the 'image' projected by the home is perhaps most clearly demonstrated by the actions of tenants freed from landlord constraints when they purchase under the right to buy policy; almost inevitably, the external, 'public' appearance of the property is changed, with a new front door, for example, or a porch.

Recent influences on ideas about design

Most social housing providers will recognise that some types of design seem to be associated with certain sorts of behaviour, such as the degree of neighbourliness, or problems of vandalism and other anti-social behaviour. But does the design *cause* bad behaviour? It is worth examining, briefly, some research findings which have been influential on ideas about the significance of design, because these ideas affect social housing design today.

Estate layout and social groupings
One of the most influential pieces of work to suggest that estate design influenced social groups and the sense of community contrasted life in a traditional inner-city area with that in a new suburban estate, following slum clearance. *Family and Kinship in East London* (Willmott and Young, 1957) suggested that the new estates

resulted in social isolation, in contrast to the supportive social networks which existed in the old areas. This study was influential in moving housing policy away from slum clearance to the rehabilitation of old housing areas. Where slum clearance could not be avoided, attempts were made to keep social groups of neighbours together on the new estates.

A study in the USA in 1959 found that the *layout* of homes affected the number of contacts made between residents, which in turn influenced social group formation. A later study in Essex by Peter Willmott (1963) also found that layout mattered, with short culs-de-sac best promoting community links. However, later work in the North Midlands suggested that social factors were most significant, such as class and family life-cycle stage. Where these were similar, then better social links would be formed. However, the physical environment does provide the framework within which these social links take place. Most designs today attempt to cluster dwellings together rather than stringing them out along a road, for example.

Defensible space

This concept originated with Oscar Newman's work in the USA in the 1960s, which concentrated largely on functional aspects of design. He suggested that public spaces which were not under the control of any particular residents were more vulnerable to crime. Thus, the design should ensure that someone can assume responsibility for these spaces so that they become 'defensible'.

Newman's work was partially reinforced by a study by Alice Coleman in the United Kingdom (1990), which identified problems of the surveillance of some public spaces. This resulted in greater anonymity and provided easy escape routes for criminals. However, Coleman went further, suggesting that large-scale, high-density flats *created* conditions which resulted in criminal behaviour and low levels of respect for others.

These ideas have been highly influential in recent social housing design. Few organisations would now build high-rise flats for families, and new-build design as well as refurbishment generally attempts to minimise *indefensible space*, with more private gardens, for example, and the eradication of interconnecting walkways, shared stairwells and other such features from blocks of flats where possible.

Figure 4.2 gives an example of homes clustered together, while Fig. 4.3 shows an example of one of the problems of indefensible space.

What about management?

While the ideas mentioned above have been influential, few housing managers believe that design changes are sufficient to resolve or prevent problems. Recent approaches emphasise the need for management and community as well as design initiatives for unpopular estates.

The work of the Priority Estates Project, emphasising decentralised management and tenant involvement, has been very influential, and recent policy initiatives, such

Fig. 4.2 Recent designs seek to cluster homes together, with good visibility over any public spaces

Fig. 4.3 Indefensible space creates problems – in this case of litter

as City Challenge and Estates Action in England, have emphasised the necessity of an approach which goes well beyond simple physical (design) changes for unpopular, run-down estates. Rehabilitation, whilst important, is unlikely to be enough. Recent research by Anne Power and Rebecca Tunstall (1995) confirms that local management initiatives and tenant involvement are crucial to improving unpopular estates. Issues such as these are examined further in Chapter 6.

Preparing the briefing

What is the purpose of the briefing?

The briefing is the document which lets the consultants know exactly what the client wants, so the more detailed the briefing, the better. Only if the designers are very clear about the client's requirements will they be able to produce a design which fully meets them.

Who prepares the briefing?

The briefing will be developed by the person(s) in the organisation responsible for the development, but the views of other involved parties should be considered. Over time, knowledge derived from experience of specific schemes can be incorporated into the general requirements.

In a social housing organisation, ideally those who will have future responsibility for the development should also be consulted. Managers know which design features cause management problems, and maintenance staff can advise about aspects with high maintenance costs. Indeed, some organisations attempt to adopt a *lifetime* approach to scheme costs, so that repair implications are automatically incorporated into the scheme appraisal.

Tenants' views are also valuable. For rehabilitation work, generally the people who will actually occupy the scheme can be consulted. For new build, the views of tenants on other new developments should be routinely surveyed (after a period of occupation), so that they can comment on good and bad design aspects and influence future developments.

Can the initial brief change?

In practice, the first version of the brief will usually develop over a short period of time, as new information comes to light. This will be added to the initial brief, until, eventually, the *full brief* emerges. By the time the design is complete, the *final brief* should have been amended to include all of the information given to the consultants. This is necessary so that, when the scheme is completed, the organisation can evaluate the consultants by checking whether the requirements of the final brief have been met. If they have, but the scheme is still felt to be unsatisfactory, then the fault lies with the client. The brief was not adequate. In this event, future briefs should be modified, to take account of the weaknesses identified in this brief.

What does a briefing contain?

There are usually two key aspects:

1. The *general* requirements of the organisation, applicable to all schemes, and developed over time.
2. The *specific* requirements of the particular site or property, for the particular need.

The briefing must cover *all* aspects of design about which the organisation has clear requirements and preferences. If the consultants have designed many schemes for the organisation, they may be familiar with their *general* requirements, but will still need detailed briefing about the specific requirements of this particular scheme. This fact is often overlooked when *in-house* architects are employed to design the scheme.

There are a number of possible approaches to developing specific design briefs, and they may be set out in slightly different ways. In general, they will need to cover the following.

Details about the site
This includes details such as:

- physical aspects such as location, boundaries, size, slope, aspect, soil characteristics, existing vegetation, existing buildings and whether these are to be retained, existing services and positions, etc.
- environmental aspects such as adjacent buildings and uses, local amenities such as shops, parks, bus routes, etc.
- legal aspects such as public *rights of way* over the land and ownership of boundaries such as fences.

Rehabilitation schemes will, obviously, impose many more constraints on the possible design, so the brief should identify these constraints fully, as well as indicating the changes desired.

Cost limits for the development
Most social housing organisations face severe cost constraints, which have helped them to become more conscious of *value for money* and less likely to engage in unnecessary expenditure. However, there are growing concerns about declining quality as a result, and organisations must try to ensure that the brief does not permit cost limits to reduce design standards.

Procedural aspects
This includes statutory bodies which need to be consulted, the consents required, procedures for approval by the client, and so on. In general, this will include information about the planning authority, the highway authority and public utilities (which include gas, electricity and water). If outline planning consent has been obtained, any reserved matters affecting requirements should be identified.

Time limits
The *programme* sets out *target dates* for achieving each stage in the construction process, though the consultant may negotiate about these.

Requirements of the accommodation design

This is likely to form the bulk of the briefing and is highly detailed. It must cover the following.

General requirements

Mainly for new build, general requirements are:

- Type of buildings (detached, terraced, flats, etc.).
- Dwelling numbers, mix and sizes. This will reflect the need(s) to be met as well as desired densities (number of units per hectare).
- Maximum number of storeys; higher densities may be required when land costs are very high, such as in some inner city areas, and generally require more storeys.

For all schemes, general requirements are:

- Car parking, the numbers of car parking spaces, etc.
- Other facilities, such as play areas (for general needs housing), meeting rooms (for sheltered schemes), laundry rooms (for hostels).
- Land use distribution, indicating the proportionate share for dwellings, car parking, roads and other facilities.

Dwelling design requirements

For new build, the organisation may prefer to use a previous *standard* design for each type of dwelling, because this will reduce design costs. Welsh housing associations have a *pattern book* of standard house designs, produced by their statutory funding body, Tai Cymru. However, whether the designs are to be *standard* or one-off, the same details need to be reproduced in the brief. These include:

- General design requirements, such as minimum space requirements for net floor area, storage areas, plot sizes.
- Room relationships, such as access to rooms from hallways, from room to room (e.g. kitchen may not open off living room), and external access requirements (to external doors, road, etc.)
- Requirements for living areas, such as the siting of heaters and fires, radiators, TV sockets, thermostats.
- Kitchen requirements, such as minimum provision and height of units, unit types, power sockets, sink position (e.g. in natural light), ventilation requirements, space for eating, laundry needs, work surfaces.
- Bedroom requirements such as fitted wardrobes, the position of radiators and windows, ventilation, and lighting.
- Bathroom and WC requirements for ventilation (e.g. extractor fan), sound insulation, a second WC (for large dwellings).
- Storage areas, for the storage of refuse, fuel, meters, linen, prams, bicycles, garden equipment, etc.
- Doors and window requirements such as UPVC windows to reduce maintenance costs, windows with external panes which can be cleaned from inside, security fittings.

- Provision of services, including the type of heating system, requirements for water supply, electricity and gas connections (e.g. in kitchen).

Until 1981, there were statutory minimum standards for English and Welsh local authority dwelling design, known as the *Parker Morris standards*, named after the committee which recommended their introduction. These design standards were related both to house type and number of occupants, and are outlined below. The standards were very detailed, and cost limits now preclude such generous standards, but they indicate the sorts of design detail of which consultants need to be made aware.

In addition, dwellings must be designed to permit normal activities to be undertaken in the home, so designs should be checked to ensure sufficient space is allowed for circulation of people, furniture removal, eating around a table, and other such requirements.

Social housing providers, as discussed above, are increasingly aware of the symbolic importance of design, so dwelling designs should be attractive to an average person.

A Summary of Parker Morris standards

Access requirements:

- access from bedrooms to bathroom without having to pass through another room (unless just for one or two occupants);
- separate back access, or passage through the house to the back without going through the living room;
- maximum climb of two storeys to front access.

Space standards:

- minimum areas of net space and storage space;
- kitchen space for cooker, refrigerator and washing machine;
- eating space in the kitchen, for two or more people;
- hall or lobby space for coats.

Fixtures and fittings:

- separate WC (from bathroom) for four or more person homes;
- for larger, five or more person homes, a second WC;
- handbasin with WC not adjoining the bathroom;
- linen cupboard;
- minimum provision of electric sockets, e.g. four in working area of kitchen, three in living area, two in bedrooms.

Space heating:

- when outside temperatures are $-1°C$, heating should permit kitchen and halls to be maintained at $13°C$ and living and dining areas at $18°C$.

Furniture:

- plans to show furniture (to scale);
- kitchen to accommodate a small table;

- dining table and chairs in meals space;
- in living room, two or three easy chairs, settee, TV, small tables, bookcase and other possessions;
- in bedrooms, beds to accommodate one or two as appropriate, bedside table, chest of drawers and wardrobe of suitable sizes, dressing table in double bedrooms.

Environmental design requirements

This concerns site layout, and how the dwellings will 'fit into' their surroundings. For a rehabilitation scheme, there may be little scope for altering environmental aspects such as:

- the distribution of dwellings (such as how they are to be grouped);
- vehicle and pedestrian circulation, such as footpaths, specific vehicle access needs, and adequate access for emergency vehicles (such as fire engines);
- aesthetic and social criteria, such as dwelling orientation (what they face) and any requirements for privacy and safety;
- landscape features, like existing trees, hedges, and any *preservation orders* which prevent the felling of trees;
- security.

Examples of important estate design issues are indicated below.

Estate layout: some key design issues

- Public and private distinctions. A clear distinction between the 'public' (front) and 'private' (back) areas of the dwellings is desirable, so that visitors arrive at the 'right' side and households have some private areas.
- Private outdoor space. This should consider *aspect* (preferably, an east-west orientation for the dwelling) and provide space for clothes drying and fuel, bin and garden equipment storage.
- Play areas. For family dwellings, footpaths should provide safe passage between dwellings, with areas set aside for specific play activities, preferably away from elderly residents.
- Roads and parking. Access roads should permit vehicles to be reasonably close to dwellings, so that they are visible to residents. They should also permit access to emergency vehicles. 1.5 parking spaces are commonly provided per dwelling, less for developments for the elderly. Generally, roads are now designed to curve (to slow traffic), or with speed bumps if speed could be a problem.
- Landscaping. This needs to be carefully planned to create a pleasant environment, which is easy (and cheap) to maintain, without large areas of space for which no one is responsible. It should make best use of any significant features, such as trees.

Figure 4.4 illustrates one way to reduce traffic speed, while Fig. 4.5 shows a sheltered scheme for the elderly with creative landscaping.

Construction standards

This section details any special requirements for the construction *methods and materials* to be used, which requires expertise in construction technology and is beyond

Fig. 4.4 Speed bumps (sleeping policemen) are becoming more common to reduce traffic speed

Fig. 4.5 A sheltered scheme for the elderly, which makes creative use of a very large, old (protected) tree in a circular driveway

the scope of this text. Obviously, however, requirements should reflect any knowledge acquired by the organisation from previous schemes, so that methods or materials which have caused problems are avoided. Additionally, there may be a desire to standardise some elements (such as door and window types), which will permit the holding of spare parts to be minimised, and may allow for reduced maintenance contracts to be negotiated.

As identified at Stage I, construction standards are controlled by the Building Regulations, which ensure that only safe methods and materials are used. The consultant will have to ensure that approval under the *Building Regulations (1985) Act* is obtained from the local authority.

The design drawings

Drawings are a physical representation of the scheme which is designed by the consultants. They enable the client to see what is proposed, as well as, ultimately, enabling the contractor to build according to the design.

Outline drawings

The consultant must design in line with the brief, but is free to interpret these requirements as she or he chooses. This means that, for any given briefing, a large number of possible approaches are possible. The consultant will have already produced some outline plans for the feasibility study, but ideas now need to be 'firmed-up'.

Outline plans will be sketched out, and these need to be considered by the client to ensure that they conform with the brief. If any aspect is unsatisfactory, the consultant will need to revise as appropriate.

Detailed drawings

Once the client is happy with the outline scheme, the consultant proceeds to draw up detailed drawings. These are more numerous and detailed than the outline plans, and will have to be drawn carefully *to scale*. This means that a specified distance on the plan corresponds to a larger area on the ground. For example, a scale of 1:1000 means that 1 mm on the plan represents 1 metre on the site. The smaller the scale, the more closely the two distances match. All drawings will clearly indicate the scale.

A number of different drawings have to be made, in order to give a full picture of the scheme. These drawings are submitted for detailed planning consent, and are needed by the contractor so that it is clear what is to be constructed. (In the following sections all of the drawings relate to two particular schemes: Commercial Buildings, a rehabilitation project for tenement flats in Scotland and Turnbull Street, a new build housing scheme of flats and bungalows in Hartlepool.)

The main types of drawing are illustrated as follows.

Location plan

This places the site within its locality, showing adjoining roads, buildings, etc. It indicates the position of north with an arrow, and is usually drawn to a scale of 1:2500 or 1:1250. Figure 4.6 shows a location plan for Commercial Buildings.

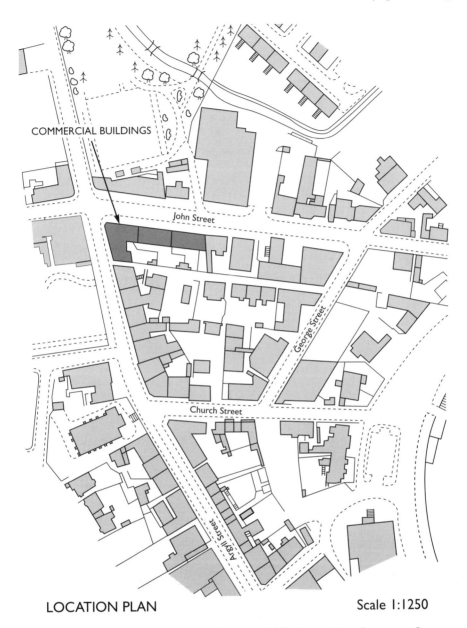

COMMERCIAL BUILDINGS

John Street

George Street

Church Street

Argyll Street

LOCATION PLAN   Scale 1:1250

Fig. 4.6 Location plan for Commercial Buildings; a rehabilitation project of tenement, flats (scale 1:1250)

Site layout plan

This shows the position of the dwellings in the site, with roads, trees, etc. indicated. The scale is usually 1:500 or 1:200. Figure 4.7 shows a site layout plan for Turnbull Street.

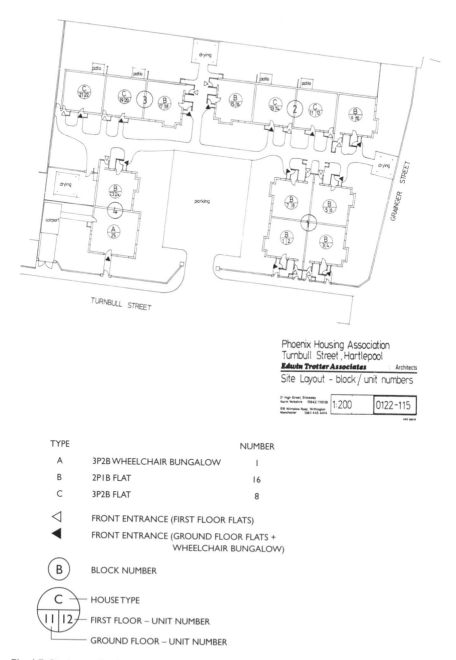

Phoenix Housing Association
Turnbull Street, Hartlepool
Edwin Trotter Associates : Architects

Site Layout - block / unit numbers

21 High Street, Stokesley North Yorkshire (0642) 710129		
818 Wilmslow Road, Withington Manchester (061) 445 4414	1:200	0122-115

TYPE		NUMBER
A	3P2B WHEELCHAIR BUNGALOW	1
B	2P1B FLAT	16
C	3P2B FLAT	8

◁ FRONT ENTRANCE (FIRST FLOOR FLATS)

◀ FRONT ENTRANCE (GROUND FLOOR FLATS + WHEELCHAIR BUNGALOW)

Ⓑ BLOCK NUMBER

C — HOUSE TYPE

11 12 — FIRST FLOOR – UNIT NUMBER

— GROUND FLOOR – UNIT NUMBER

Fig. 4.7 Site layout plan for Turnbull Street; a new build project of flats and bungalows (scale 1:1200)

Floor plans

These are produced for *each* floor of each dwelling type, at a scale of 1:100 or 1:50. Possible furniture layouts should ideally be included, so that it can be seen whether the layouts are feasible. Figure 4.8 shows a floor plan for Commercial Buildings, while Figure. 4.9 gives a floor plan for Turnbull Street.

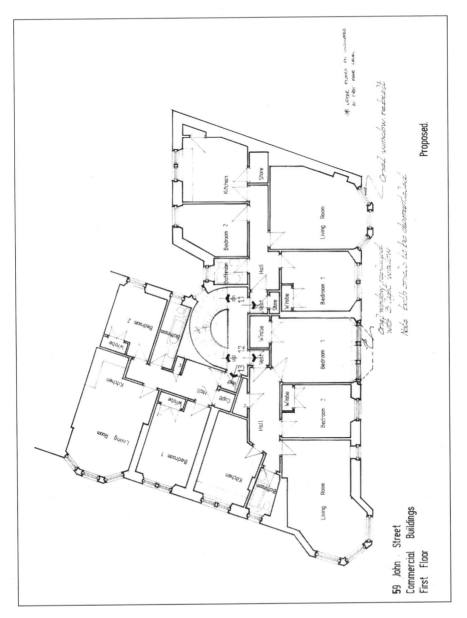

Fig. 4.8 First floor plan of Commercial Buildings

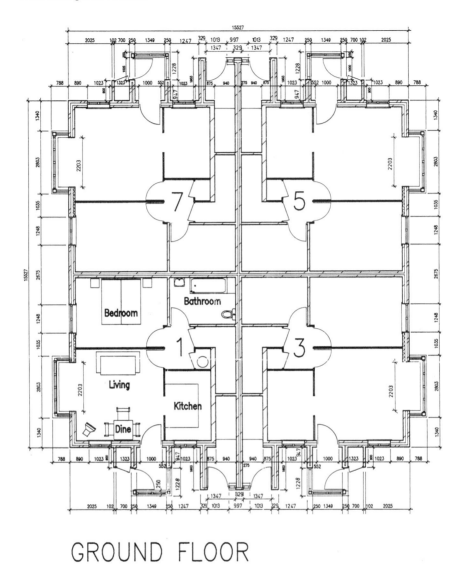

GROUND FLOOR

Fig. 4.9 Ground floor plan of Turnbull Street flats

Elevations

These view the properties from various positions, such as the front, side and rear. They give an impression of what the dwellings will look like from the outside, and will generally indicate wall and roof colours. Figures 4.10 and 4.11 show elevations for Turnbull Street while Figure 4.12 shows an elevation for Commercial buildings.

North & South Elevations

N.B. All cills to be type 1

▢   Air brick position
(see detail 0122(21)3)

e j —·— Expansion joint
(see detail 0122(21)7)

Brick type key

▤ type 1
≈≈ type 2
▦ type 3

Phoenix Housing Association
Turnbull Street, Hartlepool
Edwin Trotter Associates :   Architects

Block 1 Elevations

21 High Street, Stokesley
North Yorkshire   (0642) 710129

518 Wilmslow Road, Withington
Manchester   (061) 445 4414

| 1:75 PLT_EB1 21/12/92 AJM | 0122–121 |

Fig. 4.10 Turnbull Street elevation – North and South

East & West Elevations

N.B. All cills to be type 1

▢   Air brick position
(see detail 0122(21)3)

e j —·— Expansion joint
(see detail 0122(21)7)

Brick type key

▤ type 1
≈≈ type 2
▦ type 3

Phoenix Housing Association
Turnbull Street, Hartlepool
Edwin Trotter Associates :   Architects

Block 1 Elevations

21 High Street, Stokesley
North Yorkshire   (0642) 710129

518 Wilmslow Road, Withington
Manchester   (061) 445 4414

| 1:75 PLT_EB1 21/12/92 AJM | 0122–121 |

Fig. 4.11 Turnbull Street elevation – East and West

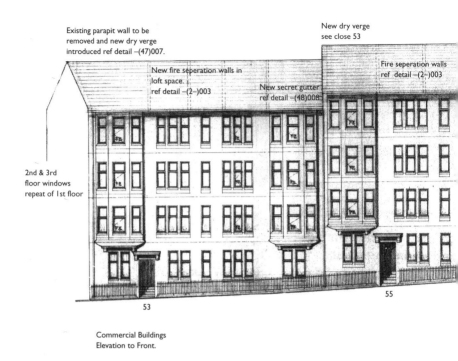

Existing parapit wall to be
removed and new dry verge
introduced ref detail –(47)007.

New dry verge
see close 53

New fire seperation walls in
loft space.
ref detail –(2–)003

Fire seperation walls
ref detail –(2–)003

New secret gutter
ref detail –(48)008

2nd & 3rd
floor windows
repeat of 1st floor

53

55

Commercial Buildings
Elevation to Front.

Fig. 4.12 Elevation of Commercial Buildings (John Street frontage)

Construction drawings

These are much more detailed drawings, which show information about methods of construction for different parts of the dwellings and the provision of services. They have to be submitted for approval under the Building Regulations, and form part of the instructions to the contractor about how the scheme is to be built. Figure 4.13a–e (see pp. 132–3) gives examples of construction drawings for Commercial Buildings.

The construction specifications

The specifications identify, in detail, the construction methods and the quality of materials to be used. These are, necessarily, highly detailed and technical. They are produced so that the contractor knows exactly what standards are expected for all work. Generally, they will incorporate all relevant national and European standards of performance, as determined by bodies such as the *British Standards Institute*. This awards products which comply with relevant performance standards – such as electrical fittings – a BS number, which refers to their standard for the product.

The sample specification for brick and block walling shown in Figure. 4.14 (see p.134) gives some idea of the sort of detail which is found in specifications.

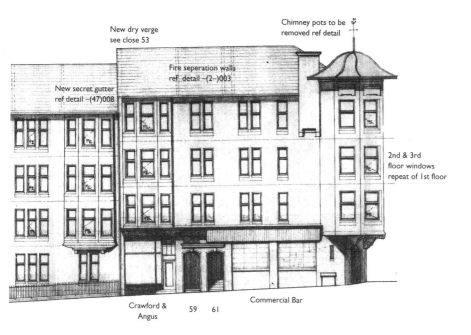

New dry verge
see close 53

Chimney pots to be
removed ref detail

Fire seperation walls
ref detail –(2–)003

New secret gutter
ref detail –(47)008

2nd & 3rd
floor windows
repeat of 1st floor

Crawford &
Angus

59   61

Commercial Bar

The role of the contractor

Traditionally, the client appoints the consultant, who undertakes the design in accordance with the briefing, as outlined above, and subsequently supervises the contractor. However, it is now more common for housing associations to be prepared to take 'short-cuts' through the development process, with contracts which give the contractor a greater role in relation to design. Some of the main, alternative approaches to the design stage include are set out below.

Package deals

These offer the quickest way to achieve a development, because a complete scheme is purchased 'off-the-shelf' from a building company. It is paid for in one lump sum, on completion, usually to the builder's own design. This largely eliminates the role of the consultant, and can offer good value for money.

Design and build

Under this approach, the contractor provides the design as well as the construction work, so this also reduces the traditional consultant's role. The client can have an input into the design, by setting out precise details of the organisation's design requirements in a briefing called the *employer's requirements*. In this case, the client is represented on site by an *employer's agent* – usually a quantity surveyor – to oversee standards of work, rather than the architect. Again, the price is usually fixed in advance.

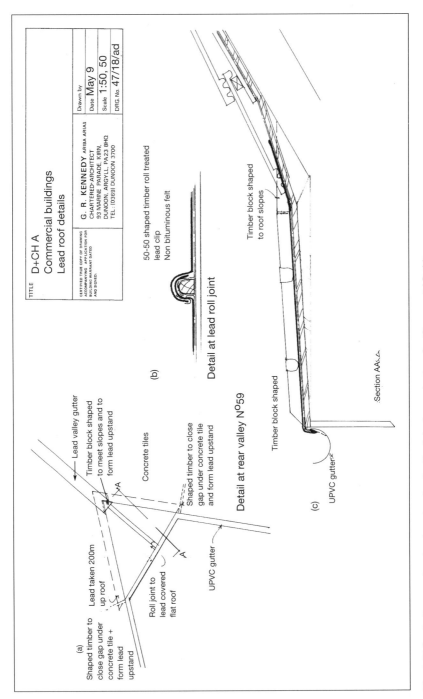

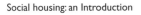

Fig. 4.13 (a–e) Construction drawings showing details of the feature lead roof at Commercial Buildings

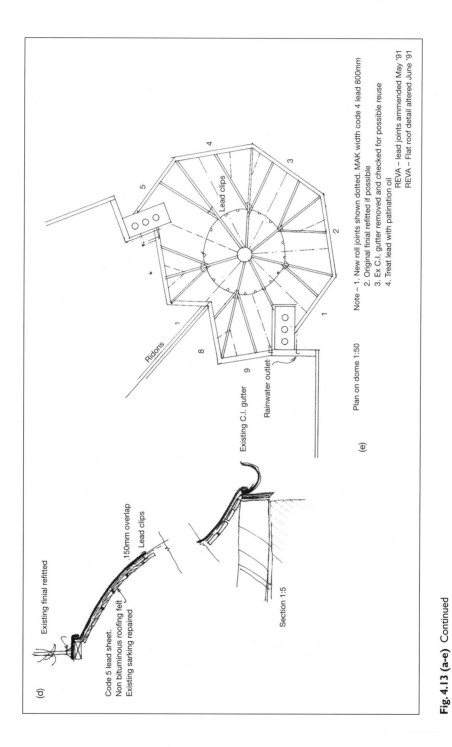

(d)

Existing finial refitted

Code 5 lead sheet.
Non bituminous roofing felt
Existing sarking repaired

150mm overlap

Lead clips

Section 1:5

Existing C.I. gutter

Rainwater outlet

Ridons

Lead clips

Plan on dome 1:50

(e)

Note – 1. New roll joints shown dotted. MAK width code 4 lead 800mm
2. Original finial refitted if possible
3. Ex C.I. gutter removed and checked for possible reuse
4. Treat lead with patination oil

REVA – lead joints ammended May '91
REVA – Flat roof detail altered June '91

Fig. 4.13 (a-e) Continued

133

F10   BRICK/BLOCK WALLING

To be read with Preliminaries/General conditions.

TYPE(S) OF WALLING

110 CLAY FACING BRICKWORK TO BRICK BANDING, AND FIRST FLOOR OF TWO-STOREY DWELLINGS – BRICK TYPE 2.
- Bricks: To BS 3921.
- Manufacturer and reference: Allow the sum of £300.00 per thousand.
- Mortar: As section Z21.
  Mix: Group 3 generally, Group 1 to cill bricks.
- Bond: Half lap stretcher.
- Joints: Flat brushed back.
- Features: As detailed elevations.

120 CLAY FACING BRICKWORK TO BRICK PLINTH – BRICK TYPE 3:
Bricks: To BS 3921.
Manufacturer and reference: Steetley Brick and Concrete Products Ltd –
Staffordshire slate-blue – Br 018.
Mortar: As section Z21.
Mix: Group 3 generally, Group 1 below dpc.
Bond: Half lap stretcher.
Joints: Flat brushed back.

130 CLAY FACING BRICKWORK GENERALLY – BRICK TYPE 1
Bricks: To BS 3921.
Manufacturer and reference: Steetley Brick and Concrete Products Ltd
Multi Red smooth – BR 003.
Special shapes: See 0122(31)7.
Mortar: As section Z21.
Mix: Group 3 generally, Group 1 to screen walls and cill bricks.
Bond: Half lap stretcher generally, English Garden wall to screen walls.
Joints: Flat brushed back.
Features: As detailed elevations.

140 CLAY FACING BRICK WORK: DPC COURSES TO SCREEN WALLS/SCREEN WALL COPINGS.
Bricks: To BS 3921.
Manufacturer and reference: Ibstock Building Products Ltd: Telford Blue BL1.
Mortar: As section Z21.
Mix: Group 1 sulphate resisting with Ronac waterproofing addictive to d.p.c courses;
Group 1 with Ronac waterproofing additive to screen wall copings.
Bond: Half lap stretcher, English Garden Wall.
Joints: Flat brushed back.
Features: As detail 0122 – 137.
Special shapes: Double Cant bricks (ref AN6) for use with coping system specification F30: 780.

310 CONCRETE COMMON BLOCKWORK TO INTERNAL PARTITIONS
- Blocks: To BS 6073: part 1. Solid no voids.
  Minimum average comprehensive strength: 3.5 N/sq mm
  Work size $440 \times 215 \times 100$.

Fig. 4.14 Specification for brick and blockwalling for Turnbull Street

–   Mortar: As section Z21.
    Mix: Group 3.
–   Bond: Half lap stretcher.

340 CONCRETE COMMON BLOCKWORK TO PARTY WALLS
    Blocks to BS 6073: Part 1. Solid no voids.
    Minimum average compressive strength: 3.5 N/sq mm, weight not less than 1900 kg/m³
    Work size: 440 × 215 × 100.
    Mortar: As section Z21.
    Mix: Group 3.
    Bond: Half lap stretcher.

350 CONCRETE COMMON BLOCKWORTH TO INNER LEAF OF EXTERNAL WALLS:
    Blocks: Lightweight aggregates to BS 6073: Part 1. Solid no voids.
    Manufacture and reference: Boral Edenhall; Reference 'LYTAG' Thermal blocks.
    Minimum average compressive strength: 3.5 N/sq mm. 7.0 N/sq mm.
    Thermal conductivity: Not more than 0.39 w/mK at 3% moisture content.
    Work size(s): 440 × 215 × 100
    Mortar: As section Z21.
    Mix: Group 3.
    Bond: Half lap stretcher.

390 ENGINEERING BRICKWORK TO MANHOLES AND BRICKWORK BELOW GROUND LEVEL.
    –   Bricks: To BS 3921, Engineering Class B – bricks to be solid with no frogs or holes.
    –   Mortar: As section Z21.
        Mix: Group 1 sulphate resisting.
    –   Bond: English bond and half lap stretcher.
    –   Joints: Flush.

Fig. 4.14 Continued

Develop and construct (or detail and build)

This approach is closer to the traditional approach. The consultant will produce *outline* designs, which will define very clearly what the client requires. The contractor then takes over and is responsible for turning these outline designs into *detailed* designs, which are then built. Again, the client is represented by an employer's agent, because the design cannot change once work commences. There is usually a fixed-price contract.

What are the advantages of these approaches?

They reduce:

• the length of the development process, which means that the client obtains a completed scheme much more quickly, and so begins to earn income sooner;
• costs, or as a minimum, offer more certainty about costs;.
• the risk that the organisation will have to find additional resources to fund extra costs, which has become particularly important with mixed funding, under which housing association grant (HAG) is set very early in the process, so additional costs must be met by the organisation.

What are the disadvantages?

They offer less client control over the design (to varying degrees), which can:

- reduce the possibility of standardising designs, fixtures and fittings, which can increase future maintenance costs;
- result in a scheme which is less suitable for particular needs than developments which are specially designed;
- eliminate the possibility of changing the design as work progresses;
- reduce possibilities to monitor and control standards of construction; this can be particularly important in rehabilitation work, where problems can easily be hidden.

4.6 Stage III: constructing the development

How is the contractor selected?

There are two main approaches to selecting a contractor:

- negotiate with a firm which is known to be reliable – a *negotiated contract*;
- request quotations from a number of firms – the process of *competitive tendering*.

Local authorities are obliged to place all work valued in excess of £50,000 out to competitive tender, so that a number of firms have the opportunity to bid for the work. The statutory funding bodies normally expect this also of housing associations. Negotiated tenders are normally permitted only when the work follows on directly from an earlier contract, or when the developer owns the site and wishes to negotiate some sort of package-deal approach, examined in the last section.

Competitive tendering

In order to reduce the possible number of tenders (or *bids*) to manageable proportions, the consultant will generally advise on drawing up a *select list* of contractors. However, it is important that there is sufficient competition to encourage keen pricing by contractors, so generally the list will consist of about six firms. Local authorities must advertise (in the European Union as well as the United Kingdom) for firms to apply for inclusion on their select list of tenderers, whereas housing associations will generally draw up a specific list for each project. However, both must undertake a series of checks, to ensure that potential tenderers are capable of undertaking the work.

Checking potential contractors

Many organisations will ask potential contractors to complete a standard 'organisation and capacity' questionnaire, which covers key aspects such as:

- financial records, with information about turnover (the value of work under-taken in a year) and financial stability (assets and debts); a banker's reference is also usually required;
- details of past experience of constructing similar projects;
- references from past clients, commenting on matters such as the quality of their work, their ability to complete on time, and their willingness to cooperate.

The client's quantity surveyor (QS) will usually also check whether the contractor's previous tender prices have been competitive.

Inviting tenders

When the selected firms are invited to tender, they are sent the *tender documents*, which are generally prepared by the quantity surveyor. They usually comprise:

- information about the site (location, characteristics);
- the detailed design drawings;
- detailed specifications;
- information about the sort of contract into which the firm will have to enter;
- a form on which the tender price is entered;
- a *bill of quantities*, which itemises all construction activities (the *quantities*), for indi-vidual pricing by the tenderer.

Having received the tender documents, the contractor will be in a position to calcu-late the likely costs of the work, and can decide whether to put in a tender. The *closing date* and *time* for receipt of tenders must be clearly specified, and the tender must be supplied in an unmarked envelope, so that the tendering firm cannot be identified until the tenders are opened.

Selecting a tender

The sealed envelopes are opened, at the appointed time, by the consultant, client, quantity surveyor and other relevant parties such as committee members. This ensures 'fair play'. The client's quantity surveyor will then check the accuracy of the prices, and having assessed whether the bids are reasonable, will make a formal recommendation about which (if any) tender to accept. This need not be the lowest price if there are suspicions that the contractor might be unable to complete the project for unrealistically low sums. If all bids are too high, the quantity surveyor will need to consider how lower bids might be obtained, for example, by making alterations to the design.

Once a tender has been accepted, but before the legal contract is signed, the consultants will undertake pre-contract planning with the contracting firm.

What is pre-contract planning?

Pre-contract planning ensures that no time is wasted; if various details are sorted out in advance, the contractor can get on with the actual construction work as soon as the contract is drawn up and signed. Pre-contract planning meetings will be arranged to sort out matters such as:

The contract commencement date

This may depend on the completion of site acquisition, or arrangements to decant (temporarily rehouse) existing tenants.

The contract completion date

Usually, the organisation will want the work to be completed as soon as possible, since faster completion means quicker letting and more rent income. If it involves the rehabilitation of existing tenanted stock, then the decanted tenants will be able to return more quickly.

The programme of work

The programme of work enables the consultant to monitor progress, and initiate appropriate steps if work falls behind.

The role of the planning supervisor

The location of this function must be clearly agreed, so that the requirements of the CDM regulations can be fulfilled.

Arrangements for informing other parties

The building inspector must be informed about start dates, so that regular inspections can be made as work progresses. In the case of existing premises, the council tax authority should be informed, as no tax will be payable. Electricity and gas companies should also be contacted to take meter readings. This will ensure that the client is not liable for unauthorised use during construction work.

Anyone likely to be affected by the construction work must be advised about works which directly affect them. This is important not simply because it is good *public relations*; the works could interfere with a neighbour's business, with perhaps serious legal implications as a result.

Site security

Building sites are regularly subject to vandalism and theft. Responsibility for secure storage for materials must be agreed, particularly in high-risk areas. Both the client and the contractor should have adequate insurance.

Communication

It is essential that clear lines of communication are established and that everyone is clear about each other's roles.

Agreeing the contract

A *written contract* ensures that all parties are clear as to what has been agreed. It reduces the possibilities of misunderstandings and, importantly, offers the possibility of *legal action* if either party to the contract fails to deliver as agreed. The contract is drawn up by the quantity surveyor, and will generally be a standard contract type, approved by the construction industry, such as the JCT (Joint Contracts Tribunal).

The contract simply sets out what has been agreed, and will cover the following:

- The *basis for payment;* the value of the contract, which will generally be for a *fixed price*.
- The *contract period*; how long the work will take.
- The *construction design* details; what, exactly, is to be built, where.

The form of the contract may vary slightly, depending on whether it is for new build or rehabilitation, and whether there are to be *nominated sub-contractors*. These are specialist firms, which the client may want for some specialised activities (e.g. for wood treatment in rehabilitation work). In addition, the organisation itself, or its funders, may have particular requirements for adjustments to the standard JCT form. Once the contract is signed, the contractor can commence work on site.

Monitoring the progress of construction

There are many possible approaches to constructing dwellings, which are beyond the scope of this text. However, the majority of new, low-rise dwellings built today use traditional methods, with cavity walls (a double wall of brick and block, with a space or *cavity* between to improve insulation and deter damp penetration) and tiles fixed to sloping roofs. These schemes might be expected to progress roughly as indicated below. It is, of course, the duty of the consultant to oversee the quality and progress of this work, with day-to-day monitoring by the clerk of works.

Progression of traditional approaches to new build house construction

- Clear the site (of existing buildings, unwanted vegetation, and top-soil).
- Dig and lay the foundations (on which the walls are constructed).
- Build the walls.
- Construct the roof.
- Fix the external joinery (such as windows and doors); this provides a relatively secure shell for the next stages.
- Fix some internal joinery such as floors and stairs, and internal wall-partitions.
- Fix internal utilities, such as electricity cables, gas pipes, water and heating supplies.
- Complete internal finishes – plastering walls, skirtings and door casings.

- Install fixtures, such as fitted kitchen units.
- Paint internal walls and complete final finishes.

The stages in a rehabilitation project are much more variable, since the exact nature of the refurbishment will vary greatly from one scheme to another.

Variations to the contract: architect's instructions (AIs)

Unless the development is being constructed under some sort of 'package' arrangement, the consultant may make changes to the design details as work progresses. The commonest causes of changes by the consultant are last-minute economies due to unforeseen financial constraints, or changes to design details, perhaps caused by supply problems or by details that do not work in practice.

Additionally, external factors may force changes. The likelihood of unforeseen problems arising on site is reduced, but not eliminated by, a site survey. However, such problems are more likely in rehabilitation schemes, when many problems may become apparent only after demolition work.

All variations to the contract details must be specified in *architect's instructions*, also known as *variation orders*. These are instructions issued by the consultant, which specify the alteration required (or agreed to) and, most importantly, identify the *cost* of the change. If the instruction is simply intended to clarify something, there may be no financial implication. But, where there is an added cost, the client should insist on strict limits to the amounts that can be agreed by the consultant, without *prior* approval. This is an important method by which the client can exercise tight control over costs.

An example of an architect's instruction is given in Fig. 4.15.

Extending the contract period

If the effect of an instruction is to extend the construction period, then an *extension of time certificate* will need to be issued. The cost implications of this depend on the cause of the delay:

- Extensions due to consultant's changes or errors will have to be paid for by the client. Clearly, if the contractor has to spend longer on site, it will increase the firm's costs, for labour, plant hire, insurance, etc.
- Extensions may be allowed for factors outside the contractor's control, for which no extra payment is made. These include bad weather, delays caused by the contractor's own sub-contractors, or strikes.

If the contractor is at fault for a delay then no extensions to the contract are granted. If the contract runs over the contract completion date the client can seek compensation. This is normally in the form of *liquidated and ascertained damages*, and are deducted from any payments due to the contractor.

The client will wish to monitor the development, to ensure that it is progressing satisfactorily, and that excessive numbers of expensive or delaying variation orders

Issued by:	Edwin Trotter Associates	
address:	21 High Street, Stokesley	

Architect's Instruction

Employer:	
address:	Phoenix Housing Associations Ltd
	27 Yarm Road, Stockton on Tees

Contractor:	Ideal Homes (Northern) Ltd
address:	Ideal house, Allensway
	Thornaby on Tees

Job reference: 0122-L

Instruction no: 2

Issue date: 8th July 1993

Works:	
situated at:	25 New Dwellings
	Turnbull street, Hartlepool

Sheet: 1 of 2

– 9 JUL 1993

MANAGER	*GD*
ACTION	
FILE	

Contract dated: 3rd June 1993

Under the terms of the above-mentioned Contract, I/we issue the following instructions:

	Office use: Approx costs	
	£ omit	£add

1. Arrange for the provisions of the Clause 21.2.1 insurance cover all as you letter and enclosure dated 22nd June 1993.

   Omit the provisional sum of £800.00 in the Bill of Quantities (item C page 7/3) for insurance cover.

	800
800	

2. Place an order and pay all all costs incurred with Northern Electric for the provision of the electricity supplies to the above dwellings (including landlord's supply) all as their letters and enclosures dated 3rd February 1993 and 4th February 1993. Please liaise with Northern Electric at all times and use the application forms enclosed as requested by them.

   Omit the provisional sum of £7,900.00 in the Bill of Quantities (item B page 7/1) for service connection charges.

7900	

To be signed by or for the issuer named above

Signed

8700	7300

Amount of Contract Sum	£	764925
± Approximate value of previous Instructions	£	+ 150
	£	765075
±Approximate value of the Instruction		–1400
Approximate adjusted total	£	763675

Distribution	☐ Original to:	☐ Copies to:		
	☐ Contractor	☐ Employer	☑ Quantity Surveyor	☐ Clerk of works
		☐ Nominated Sub-Contractors	☐ Consultants	☐ File

Fig. 4.15 An example of an architect's instruction relating to Turnbull Street

Issued by: Edwin Trotter Associates
address: 21 High Street,
Stokesley
North Yorkshire

Instruction
Continuation

Serial no: 2

Job reference: 0122-L

Issue date: 8th July 1993

	Office use: Approx costs	
	£ omit	£add
Brought forward:	8700	7300
3. Place an order and pay all costs incurred with Hartlepools Water Company for the provision of the water supplies to the above dwellings, all as their letter and enclosures dated 9th December 1992. Please liaise with Hartlepools Water Company at all times and use the application forms enclosed as requested by them.	–	21000
Omit the p.c. sum of £21,000.00 in the Bill of Quantities (item A page 7/1) for water service connection charges.	21000	
4. Liaise with British Telecom and arrange for the supply and laying of all duties and draw wires etc. in accordance with their proposals dated 16th February, 1993. Provision for this included within th Bills of Quantities.	–	–
5. Confirmation of drawing issue date 23/6/93 enclosing revised drainage layout drawing no. 0122-133A and manhole schedule drawing no. 0122-113A	–	–
	29700	
	28300	28300
	1400	

To be signed by or for
the issuer named   Signed _*M.U.F.*_____
above

Amount of Contract Sum   £

± Approximate value of previous instructions   £ _____

£

±Approximate value of the instruction   £

Approximate adjusted total   £ _____

Distribution	☐ Employer	☐ Contractor	☑ Quantity Surveyor	☐ Services Engineer
	☐	☐ Nominated Sub-Contractors	☐ Structural Engineer	☐ File

Fig. 4.15   Continued

are not being issued. The main sources of information about progress available to the client are indicated below.

Monitoring information available to the client

Site meetings
These provide a regular forum for the consultant, quantity surveyor and contractor to discuss progress. The client may attend, but should certainly receive copies of the *minutes* of site meetings, which record what was discussed and agreed, including any need for architect's instructions and extensions of time.

Progress reports
The consultants will make their own, regular reports to the client, identifying progress to date and any problems. They should cover the two key elements for control, costs and time, which will be the subject of architect's instructions and extensions of time certificates. These should be identified and explained. Quality issues should be resolved as the dwellings are being built.

Site inspections
The consultant will, of course, make regular site inspections, as part of the supervisory role, and there is normally a clerk of works to report to the client. However, it is also useful for the client to make occasional inspections, *not* to give instructions (which might overrule the architect), but to check generally on quality and progress. Any problems which are noted on inspection should be taken up with the consultant.

Ending the contract
This will occur only in extreme circumstances when, for example, the contractor is declared bankrupt or consistently fails to deliver the standards of work required. This is known as *determining* the contract. Another contractor will have to be found very quickly to finish the work, which is why the determination of contracts is comparatively rare! Since there are complex legal requirements to determining a contract, the organisation's solicitors have to be involved at an early stage.

Paying the contractor during construction

It is usual to make payments to the contractor in *stages* as work progresses, because the firm has to pay for all materials and labour as they are used. Workers will not wait until the end of the contract to be paid! If the contractor should cease work, the client will be left with the portion of the scheme which has already been completed – it cannot be taken away – so there is little risk in making *interim payments*.

Interim payment procedures

Interim certificates
The procedure for making interim payments to contractors involves the issue of *certificates* by the consultant. The quantity surveyor undertakes a valuation of the work

completed, which is *certified* by the consultant. Valuations are undertaken at specific stages in the progress of construction; for example, when foundations are completed, when the building has reached first floor level, etc. and *stage payments* are made. Alternatively, monthly interim payments are paid based on a valuation of all work done at that time. Since the valuation relates to *all* of the work completed, the value of *previous payments* is then deducted, to calculate the payment due.

Retention monies

Some percentage will normally be *retained*, so that the contractor is never paid *fully* for the work completed. This is intended to provide an incentive to complete the work; if *full* payments were always made, the contractor could leave the site without losing anything. The retention is also there to cover the cost of any work that may prove to be defective and which the contractor fails to remedy.

The contractor will be keen to receive as high a payment as possible, so may contest the quantity surveyors valuation of the work. The consultant must then take the final decision about the valuation, and, in effect, arbitrate between the quantity surveyor and the contractor.

If valuations include payments to *nominated sub-contractors*, the contractor will normally have to pass this payment on to the sub-contractor. For the contractor's own sub-contractors, it is the contractor's responsibility to agree their share of any payments.

Receipt of HAG

Housing associations receive their funding in pre-determined percentages (called *tranches*), at three *key* stages in the construction process. The tranche percentages depend on the type of scheme – new build or rehabilitation.

The key stages are:

(i)   site acquisition;
(ii) start on site of main works;
(iii) practical completion – when the work is largely finished.

Since these stages do not correspond with stage payments, which are made during the progress of construction, the client organisation must ensure that there are sufficient reserves, or access to borrowed funds (such as a bank overdraft) to make payments to the contractor prior to completion.

Agreeing completion

The consultant will need to ensure that the properties are substantially completed, ready for occupation, before formally accepting the work as complete. This is known as *practical completion*. The consultant is responsible for agreeing the date of practical completion, but it is important for the client to check personally, since the consultant's perspective is different to the client's. However, the consultant has the final contractual responsibility for deciding whether the scheme is practically complete and if so will issue a *certificate of practical completion*.

Snagging inspection

The '*snagging*' inspection is intended to identify any outstanding work for completion, and occurs about two weeks before the date for practical completion. It is undertaken by the client with the consultant and contractor. Other interested parties may also attend. When the client is a social housing provider, the important issue is whether the properties are ready for occupation, well built, and with everything operating properly. A systematic approach to the inspection must be adopted, if possible problems are not to be missed. The approach suggested by the National Federation of Housing Associations (now the NHF) appears below, and provides a useful indication of the sorts of details which must be carefully examined at the snagging inspection.

The snagging inspection

'It is important to have a system which can be used in a variety of circumstances rather than to wander around in an aimless fashion just saying that the colours look good: instead, the association needs a critical and systematic review of the building. Start at the top of the building, proceeding downwards; check the internal parts of the building first, then the external parts. Check each room carefully and systematically:

- Do the windows fit properly? Are they sticking?
- Do the doors fit properly?
- Have the floorboards been fitted properly and securely?
- Has all the painting and decoration been carried out to a reasonable standard?
- Check all the services to the building as applicable.
- Check bath, basin, toilet, to ensure they are not leaking.
- Make sure the heating system is working.
- Ensure all manholes are lifted to check that the drainage system seems to be working properly.
- Check there is a separate water stopcock for each house.
- Check that all stopcocks are properly labelled.
- Check that the interior and exterior of the building are clean.
- Check that the builders rubbish, tools, etc. have been cleared away.'

(*Source:* National Federation of Housing Associations, 1988, pp. 36–7.)

Work to be completed

Following the snagging inspection, the client and consultant will need to agree a list of work which remains to be completed satisfactorily. This is then given to the contractor, who must ensure that this is undertaken prior to the date for practical completion.

Practical completion inspection

The official 'handover' of the scheme occurs at practical completion, which does not have to mean perfection. A few minor items may still need to be completed by the contractor, but the social housing organisation must be certain that the property is fit to be *occupied*. Outstanding items would not have to affect tenants in any significant way. For this reason, it is usual for there to be a final inspection of the properties, to ensure the consultant and client are satisfied that the work is substantially finished.

Handover of the development

The consultant issues a *certificate of practical completion*, and the contractor hands over all items relating to the completed properties, such as keys and operating instructions for electrical and heating equipment.

Management issues

Arrangements for letting or selling the completed properties must begin well in advance of completion. Rents or prices must to be determined, and the properties assessed by the valuation officer for *council tax*.

Social housing organisations will normally have a *waiting list*, or a *transfer list*, from which prospective tenants may be selected. If the waiting list is not relevant to the type of development under construction – perhaps because the need being met is not usual for the organisation, such as shared ownership – then the organisation will need to place advertisements in the local press, to invite applications from eligible persons. Interviews will have to be arranged, and time allowed for offers to be accepted or rejected, and replacement tenants or buyers found. If the local authority has *nomination rights* to a housing association development, there must be close liaison to ensure that tenants have been selected and informed.

For rehabilitation schemes, where existing tenants will be returning, they should receive regular reports of the progress of the development, and be informed of the date when they will be able to return.

Depending on the nature of the scheme, there may be other requirements prior to completion. For example, the appointment of wardens, project workers or caretakers; or the selection and ordering of communal furnishings and equipment.

It is important that all of these management issues are resolved in sufficient time for the new tenants to move into their dwellings at practical completion, otherwise the organisation will lose valuable rental income, or incur higher interest charges on outstanding debts in the case of properties for sale. There will also be a substantial risk in some areas of vandalism and theft from the empty properties. Figures 4.16 to 4.18 show Commercial Buildings and Turnball Street after completion.

4.7 After completion: what then?

Defects liability period

No further outstanding payments are made until the expiry of a *defects liability period*. Normally, the contractor remains responsible for any defects which are the result of

Fig. 4.16 Part of the completed Commercial Buildings after letting

poor materials or workmanship for a period of six months after practical completion. The consultant determines which defects are the builder's responsibility, so they should learn of all reported defects. While serious defects should be dealt with promptly by the contractor, most trivial ones can wait until the end of the defects period, so that they can all be completed together. It is expensive for a contractor to keep sending workers to rectify small problems.

The contractor has an incentive to rectify defects, because the final monies have not yet been paid. Once the defects have been rectified, the consultant issues a *certificate of completion of making good defects*. Only then is the *final account* settled.

Final account

The contractor will usually have prepared the final account shortly after the date of practical completion. This sets out the total sums payable, less any monies already paid. It is generally prepared in conjunction with the quantity surveyor, and then checked by the consultant. This can take many months. Even with a fixed price contract, variation orders may have resulted in changes to the total contract sum, so the preparation of the final account is not always a simple matter.

Final certificate

Once the client approves the final account, the consultant issues the *final certificate*, releasing all remaining retention monies to the contractor. This will, of course,

Fig. 4.17 The completed development at Turnbull Street

Fig. 4.18 Close-up of Turnbull Street after completion

have been adjusted for any *liquidated and ascertained* damages, which may be due to the client in the event of late completion caused by the contractor.

Latent defects

Some defects may not be apparent at the end of the defects liability period. The contractor, nevertheless, remains responsible for *latent* defects, usually for a period of six years from practical completion. However, the contractor may well prove reluctant to accept responsibility, and it is expensive to pursue this through the legal system, so the client should take advice about whether this is likely to prove worthwhile.

Evaluating the development process

This vital step is sometimes overlooked by the client, but it is essential if lessons are to be learned for future projects.

The performance of all of the parties in the development process, including the client, should be evaluated. These assessments should enable the organisation to decide whether the same people should be engaged in future, as well as whether to adapt their own procedures – including the briefing – where necessary.

The design should be evaluated, both by the tenants and by the housing managers responsible for the scheme. This will have to be undertaken at a later stage than the evaluation of the roles of the main parties, because it may take some time for design problems to become apparent. Particular attention should be paid to elements which may have significant maintenance and repair implications, with a view to ensuring that these are not replicated in future schemes.

Further reading

Bell, M. and Lowe, R. (1996) *Directory of Energy Efficient Housing*.

Cadman, D. and Austin-Crowe, L. (1991) *Property Development*, 3rd edn, Spon, London.

Crime Prevention on Council Estates (1993) HMSO.

Dunmore, K. (1992) *Planning for Affordable Housing: A Practical Guide*, Charted Institute of Housing/Royal Institute of British Architects, Coventry.

Fordham, G. (1995) *Made to Last: Creating Sustainable Neighbourhood and Estate Regeneration*, Joseph Rowntree Foundation, York.

Karn, V. and Sheridan, L. (1994) *New Homes in the 1990s: A Study of Design, Space and Amenity in Housing Association and Private Sector Production*, Joseph Rowntree Foundation, York.

Metropolitan Police (1995) *Secured by Design* Metropolitan Police, London.

Roberts, M. (1991) *Living in a Man Made World*, Routledge, London.

Sim, D. (1995) *British Housing Design*, Longman/Chartered Institute of Housing, Harlow and Coventry.

Tenant Participation in Housing Design (undated) Chartered Institute of Housing/Royal Institute of British Architects, Coventry and London.

Woodhead, A. (1984) *House Construction: A Basic Guide*, Institute of Housing, London.

Chapter 5

MANAGING SOCIAL HOUSING

The previous two chapters have looked at the financing and development of social housing. This chapter now moves on to examine the key tasks involved in managing social housing in Britain. It starts by attempting to define what is meant by housing management before looking in more detail at those key tasks which housing managers perform, such as letting houses, collecting the rent, dealing with empty properties and carrying out repairs and maintenance to the housing stock.

5.1 Defining housing management

Introduction

In 1994 local authorities in the United Kingdom owned over 4,758,000 homes with a further 957,000 properties owned by housing associations, all of which have to be managed. So what are the key tasks which have to be undertaken by housing professionals in managing these properties? In their White Paper of 1992 (*Competing for Quality in Housing*) the Department of the Environment wrote that:

'There is no standard accepted definition of housing management.' (Department of the Environment, 1992.)

However although this is often repeated by researchers (York, 1993) there is a surprising level of agreement as to what housing management involves:

'the central tasks of housing management...letting houses, repairing them and collecting rent – are the core of a rather wider range of functions normally constituting "housing management", and this is characteristically only one element – albeit by far the largest element – in the operations of both housing authorities and housing associations'. (Department of the Environment, 1990, p. 16.)

'letting houses, organising repairs, collecting rents, etc.'. (Centre for Housing Research, University of Glasgow, 1989, p. 5.)

'For the purpose of this study, "housing management" has been defined to encompass the core landlord activities of letting houses, collecting rents and carrying out repairs. These functions are clearly integral to the management of housing.' (Centre for Housing Policy, University of York, 1993, p.13.)

Housing management as defined by the compulsory competitive tendering rules

In June 1992 the government decided that it wanted to introduce compulsory competitive tendering into housing management. This involves local authorities placing their housing management activities out to competitive tender with the possibility that an external contractor might win a tender (this is dealt with more fully in Chapter 6). As part of this process the Department of the Environment has had to specify those housing management tasks which it wishes to see placed out to competitive tender. In *Competing for Quality in Housing*, the 1992 Consultation Paper on competition in the provision of housing management, the government set out what it considered to be the key housing management activities, which included all of the following:

- waiting lists and selection
- transfers and exchanges
- void property management
- rent collection and arrears recovery
- estate management
- repairs inspection and ordering
- neighbourhood disputes and harassment
- tenancy enforcement
- tenant consultation and participation
- tenants welfare
- benefit advice

(*Source*: Department of the Environment, 1992.)

These can easily be grouped together into more general areas as below.

Lettings of properties
- waiting lists and selection
- transfers and exchanges
- void property management

Rent collection and arrears control
- rent collection and arrears recovery
- benefit advice
- tenants welfare

Repairs and maintenance
- estate management
- repairs inspection and ordering

Tenancy management
- neighbourhood disputes and harassment
- tenancy enforcement
- tenant consultation and participation

Housing management then is essentially about four key tasks;

- letting houses
- collecting the rent
- maintaining the properties in good condition
- managing tenancies

The rest of this chapter will look at these key tasks in greater detail.

5.2 Letting properties

Introduction

One of the key tasks of housing management is the letting of homes. Every year local authorities and housing associations have to let many thousands of homes. Some of these are newly built or refurbished homes which are being let for the first time (new lets) but the overwhelming majority will be lettings of existing homes where the previous tenant has moved or died, creating a vacancy to be let (relets).

Tables 5.1 and 5.2 show the numbers of lettings carried out by social housing landlords.

Table 5.1 Lettings by local authorities 1993/94

	Total lets	To existing tenants (transfers)	New lettings
England	404 900	170 500	234 300
Wales	23 400	10 800	12 500
Scotland	65 300	25 500	39 900

Source: adapted from Table 9.8 in Housing and Construction Statistics 1984–1994 (1996)

Table 5.2 Housing association lettings in England

Year	Total lets	To existing tenants	New lettings
1993/94	134 000	21 000	113 000

Source: adapted from Housing Corporation/Audit Commission (1995), Table 4

Who are homes let to?

As discussed in Chapter 2 there is generally a greater demand from households for rented housing than that which is available. This means that when there is a vacancy to be let the social landlord is often faced with a number of people who wish to be considered for that vacancy. In these circumstances the social landlord needs to decide to whom of the competing applicants it should let the available housing. Of course if it faces a situation where there is little demand it will have the problem of identifying suitable applicants to minimise its rental loss and to prevent vandalism. In some parts of the country and for particular properties this problem of the 'difficult-to-let property' is a real one and poses significant challenges for housing managers. However, in most cases social landlords are faced with the situation where they have more than one person wanting a particular home and they need to decide to whom the property should be allocated. This is often a complex issue because of the number of potential applicants who may need to be considered including:

- people whose homes have been demolished through slum clearance programmes;
- homeless applicants;
- existing tenants who wish to transfer to this type of property;
- applicants who are not already tenants who are on a waiting list held by the landlord for rented housing;
- applicants on a national register of people wanting to obtain rented housing in another area through the *national mobility scheme* (called HOMES).

Figure 5.1 depicts the groups competing for housing.

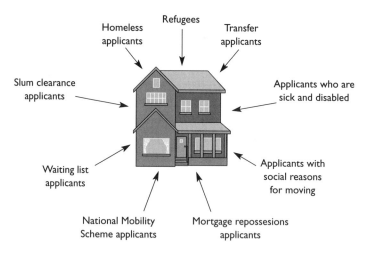

Fig. 5.1 Groups competing for housing

Table 5.3 (opposite) shows what percentage of new lettings went to people in various categories in 1993/94.

All of the people in these categories will have pressing needs; so how does the social landlord decide to whom they should let their homes?

Table 5.3 Lettings to new tenants 1993/94 by category of letting, percentage

	Slum clearance	Homeless	Waiting list	Other
England	1	31	54	4
Wales	1	20	74	6
Scotland	0	23	75	2

Source: adapted from Table 9.8 in Housing and Construction Statistics, 1984–1994 (1996)

What the law says

All social landlords have to take account of the legislation about their policies and procedures for letting their houses and this is now contained in a number of different pieces of legislation, which do not always apply equally to housing associations or local authorities. In 1995 the government, in its White Paper entitled 'Our Future Homes', announced its decision to radically change the way in which local authorities allocated their housing and the way in which they dealt with homelessness applications. The main objective of this change was to stop the alleged queue jumping of homeless applicants into council housing above other applicants.

Many of the proposals put forward in the White Paper were implemented in the Housing Act 1996 which has repealed many of the earlier provisions relating to the allocation of homes as set out in the 1985 Housing Act.

Housing Act 1995 (Housing Scotland Act 1987)

All local housing authorities have a duty to consider the housing needs of their area and the need that might exist for additional accommodation.

1996 Housing Act

The 1996 Act sets out for the first time clear procedures for local authorities in England and Wales to follow in relation to the allocation of housing. Section 159 of the Act now requires local authorities to allocate their housing in accordance with the Act, including nominations to housing associations.

Section 161 of the Act requires local authorities to maintain a register of those persons seeking housing. Local authorities are now only allowed to allocate housing to a 'qualifying person'. Such a 'qualifying person' can be defined by the local authority, although the Secretary of State has reserved for himself the powers to lay down particular categories of applicants who must or must not be included in the definition of a 'qualifying person'.

Section 167 of the 1996 Act requires every local authority in England and Wales to establish and publish an allocation scheme which sets out clearly how they will allocate their housing. The allocation scheme must give 'reasonable preference' to the following groups:

- people occupying insanitary or overcrowded housing or otherwise living in unsatisfactory housing conditions;
- people occupying housing accommodation which is temporary or occupied on insecure terms;

- families with dependent children;
- households consisting of or including someone who is expecting a child;
- households consisting of or including someone with a particular need for settled accommodation on medical or welfare grounds;
- households whose social or economic circumstances are such that they have difficulty in securing settled accommodation.

It should be noted that homeless applicants did not initially come within the groups who should be given reasonable preference although in June 1997 the government ammended the regulations allowing local authorities to give reasonable preference to homeless applicants.

These categories are broadly similar to the provisions set out in the 1985 Housing Act as to the groups which previously had to receive reasonable preference:

- people living in unsanitary or overcrowded accommodation;
- people with large families;
- the statutory homeless;
- persons living in unsatisfactory conditions;
- (Scotland only) people living in housing below the tolerable standard.

1988 Housing Act

Under the Tenants' Guarantee introduced under the 1988 Housing Act housing associations (in England and Wales) must supply a copy of their allocations policy for assured tenants to the local authority and the Housing Corporation (or Tai Cymru).

Under the Tenants' Guarantee housing associations are required to ensure that housing is provided for those who:

> 'are inadequately housed or homeless and for whom suitable housing is not available at prices within their means or at all elsewhere in the local market...Associations should pay special attention to the specific housing difficulties experienced by particular groups. These will vary from time to time and from place to place. They may include – subject to the Associations' specific objects – elderly people, single people, families with young children, single parent families, people from ethnic minorities, young people without any family support, women suffering from domestic violence, disabled people, refugees and those who care for people who would otherwise be unable to remain in their own home.'
> (*Source*: Housing Corporation, 1994a.)

Housing Act 1996 (Part VII)

Homelessness provisions

The 1996 Housing Act effectively repeals the homelessness provisions as set out in Part 3 of the 1985 Housing Act, which required local authorities to secure permanent accommodation for those applicants who were unintentionally homeless and in priority need. In assessing whether an applicant was entitled to permanent housing the applicant had to jump over a number of hurdles:

- Is the applicant homeless or threatened with homelessness?
- Is the applicant in priority need?
- Is the applicant homeless unintentionally?
- Does the applicant have a local connection with the area?

Although the definitions of a *homeless applicant, intentionality, local connection* and *priority need* are largely unchanged from the 1985 Act, the key difference in the 1996 Housing Act is that local authorities are now required only to provide *temporary* accommodation for a *two-year period* to applicants who are unintentionally homeless and in priority need. This means that homeless applicants can no longer obtain secure tenancies following acceptance of their homelessness application. They can obtain a temporary two-year non-secure tenancy from the local authority but can only obtain permanent accommodation if they qualify for housing under the local authority's normal allocation scheme. This change was made by the government in an effort to prevent the alleged abuse where homeless applicants could obtain permanent housing above other applicants who were on the local authority's housing list. Another important aspect of the 1996 Act provisions is that local authorities cannot provide accommodation in their own stock for more than two out of every three years for homeless applicants.

Land Compensation Act 1973
This requires local authorities to either provide or ensure that accommodation is available for persons who are made homeless because of slum clearance or redevelopment schemes.

Rent (Agriculture) Act 1976
Under this Act local authorities in England and Wales must *'use their best endeavours'* to ensure that accommodation is available to rehouse former agricultural workers from their tied accommodation, if the employer requires that accommodation for another agricultural worker and cannot provide accommodation for the displaced worker.

Race Relations Act 1976
The selection of tenants and the subsequent allocation of properties to successful applicants is governed by the laws on discrimination. In their *Code of Practice in Rented Housing* (published in 1991) the Commission for Racial Equality (CRE) indicate that a number of research studies over recent years have clearly demonstrated that ethnic minorities have suffered severe discrimination in housing. This has occurred in two main ways: the first in access to housing registers where people from minority ethnic groups may not be able to get on to the waiting lists; the second in the type and quality of accommodation offered to minority ethnic groups. In a number of research studies these groups have been shown to have been offered poorer accommodation than whites.

The Commission for Racial Equality has launched a number of investigations into the selection and allocation policies of local authorities and found discrimination to be a significant problem. For example, the Commission for Racial Equality's report into Liverpool City Council found that white people were twice as likely to get a nomination to a housing association home compared to a black applicant, four times as likely to get a new home, four times as likely to get a garden and twice as likely to get a property with central heating. The CRE have published a detailed Code of Guidance (1991) for all the housing organisations managing rented housing which sets out what the housing organisations should do to avoid discrimination in their allocations and selection policies and procedures.

Sex Discrimination Act 1975

This requires that landlords should not discriminate on the grounds of sex in the allocation of their property.

Types of allocations systems

All landlords need to have established a procedural system to decide who should be offered the housing that they have available to let. Under the 1996 Housing Act these procedures must be published and made available to anyone who asks for them. The scheme must give reasonable preference to those applicants set down in Section 167 of the Act.

Date order system

Under this system landlords will house applicants in strict date order making offers to those who have been registered longest on the list. Even where other systems are used date order can still be important. For example homeless applicants in the past usually had priority for rehousing but it was often the case that local authorities would aim to house first those who had been registered as homeless the longest.

Merit systems

With this system the decision as to who is allocated a particular property is based on the merits of each applicant's case. Usually the organisation will have a lettings policy and applicants are considered against the criteria set out in the policy to determine who is in the greatest need. A common problem with merit systems is that the decision to allocate a property is often based on a very subjective judgement as to which applicant is in the greatest need and therefore the most deserving to get the property.

Example of a merit system operated by a housing association.

'In considering nominations from local authorities and in selecting applicants from the Association's waiting list the following matters are taken into account:

1. Size, type and location of dwelling available for reletting and suitability to meet the applicant's housing need.
2. The applicant's housing conditions including:
   - threatened or actual homelessness
   - overcrowding or under occupation
   - sharing facilities
   - location in relation to work, relatives, friends and services
   - state of repair of the present property and ability to influence the state of repair

---

3. The applicant's ability to cope with their existing housing conditions including:
   - income
   - health
   - stress
   - previous housing history
   - the needs of dependants
4. The availability of alternative housing including:
   - potential access to home ownership
   - ability to meet local authority residential requirements
5. The length of time the applicant has had to tolerate unsatisfactory housing conditions.'

Individual applicants are considered against these criteria and the applicant with the 'greatest need' is offered the property. However, the key problem is which criteria is given the most weight in the decision-making process and in many cases the decision may be difficult to justify given the many subjective judgements that this type of allocation system entails.

Points schemes

These exist where the applicant's circumstances are considered against a scheme where points are awarded for various indicators of housing need. For example, 10 points may be awarded to someone living in rented accommodation but 20 points to someone living in tied accommodation.

The points are totalled and the applicant with the highest points is usually awarded priority. Such schemes are relatively easy to understand and it is relatively easy to query the points score awarded. They are of course subjective in terms of the factors considered and the weighting attached to individual points scores.

Below is an example if a point scheme used by a housing association.

The Housing Register

The Association operates a single Housing Register. In all cases applicants, if they are to be accepted onto the Housing Register, must demonstrate that they are in housing need – the factors which the Association considers are:

- Existing housing conditions.
- Ability to cope with these conditions.
- Other prospects for housing. Since our aim is to help those in greatest need, we consider the following as priority examples:

Homeless applicants

People in overcrowded, insanitary or insecure conditions.

People living in accommodation lacking in standard amenities.

People in shared housing who would benefit from moving to a self-contained property.

People living in under-occupied property.

People who would benefit from rehousing for social, emotional or medical reasons.

People fleeing violence.

People suffering harassment.

Points Scheme

The factors which the Association will consider and the weighting attached are set out in the points scheme:

1. Security of Tenure

The Association will not normally award points under this heading for applicants with secure or assured tenancies.

a) *Homeless applicant* **(30 points)**

b) *Applicants without their own home* **(20 points)**

People normally falling into this group are detailed below:

Assured Shorthold tenants/Licencees.
Residents of bed and breakfast accommodation.
Residents of hostels.
Residents of hospital, prison and other institutions.
Young people leaving care.
Applicants living in caravans.
Living with family/friends/carers.
Service tenancies and service licences, i.e. tied accommodation.
Sub-tenants and persons in rooms with a resident landlord.

c) *Households Living Separately* **(25 points)**

Applicants who could reasonably be expected to live together as a household including;

Couples with or without children
Families with dependent relatives

2. Size and Type of Property

(In assessing overcrowding the Association will take account of an unborn child where a mother is more than 6 months pregnant.)

a) *Overcrowding* (For each bedroom lacking.) **(20 points)**

We consider a separate bedroom necessary for:

Each couple living together.
A parent in a single parent family.
A single adult over 16 years.
Each child of 10 years or over who would otherwise have to share with a child of the opposite sex.
(A single bedroom in one bedspace, a double bedroom is two bedspaces.)

b) *Under-occupation* **(10 points)**

For each surplus bedroom.
(One bedroom is allowed above the household's needs.)

c) *People Living in Flats* **(10 points)**

Families with children under 10 years living above ground floor.
Elderly people living in flats above first floor without a lift.

3. Condition of Property

a) *Lack of Basic Facilities* (for any lack of amenity)　　　　　　*(40 points)*
　No kitchen facilities.
　No bathroom.
　No inside toilet.

b) *Property in need of major repair*　　　　　　　　　　　　*(50 points)*
　Property declared unfit to occupy.

4. Sharing any Facilities
　(except for applicants living with their family)　　　　　　*(10 points)*

　Living room.
　Kitchen facilities.
　Bathroom.
　Toilet.

5. Disability/Medical Circumstances　　　　　　　　*(30 points)*
　If anyone included in the application is in poor health or has a disability which could be assisted by rehousing.

6. Social Needs　　　　　　　　　　　　　　　　*(25 points)*
　These points may be awarded to take account of other housing related problems or needs including:

　To move to be nearer family.
　To move to be nearer work.
　To move to be nearer community support.
　To move to be nearer carers.
　To avoid harassment/nuisance or violence.
　To assist applicants with high rents/housing benefit restrictions.

Group systems

A group system operates where applicants are initially placed into different groups and the organisation then allocates homes to people from individual groups. It will normally have a quota which says that a specified proportion of allocations go to each group. The groups can be few or numerous but typical schemes will include groups for:

- homeless families
- medical cases
- elderly
- special needs

Within each group applicants can be ranked by a variety of means: merit, date order or points. If an organisation has adopted a group system it will need to decide which group should receive which proportion of lettings.

Combined systems

Most landlords will operate a variety of allocation schemes. For example, even where a landlord has a points scheme they may still use other systems within it.

Some applicants may be given priority over others on the list, so that homeless applicants may have priority over people with very high points on the waiting list. In addition, it may be difficult to compare people on the transfer list who want a move to more suitable accommodation with those living in unsuitable private accommodation. It is the case that many local authorities will say that they will let a certain percentage of their properties to applicants off the transfer list, and the choice of the transfer applicant will go to the person with the most points.

Nominations to housing associations

Housing associations are normally expected to offer local authorities *nominations*. This means that the housing association agrees to rehouse people referred (nominated) by the local authority. The precise arrangements for nominations differ from local authority to authority. In some cases the local authority will give the association a number of possible applicants to consider and the association will make its choice. In other cases perhaps only one applicant will be put forward for each vacancy. The association must retain the right to refuse a nomination if it feels that the applicant does not meet the association's own lettings criteria. Where local authorities give free land or other financial support to associations they will often require 100 per cent nominations to be given.

Transfers of existing tenants

Any allocations policy also has to consider the needs of existing tenants who may wish to move to a different home. This can be for a variety of reasons:

- Medical; where the current home is unsuitable (e.g. a two-storey house with someone with a heart problem who has difficulty climbing stairs).
- Social; where someone may wish to move home to be nearer family, friends, school or work.
- Increased family size; where the property is no longer large enough to meet the household's requirements.
- Others; such as a wish to move away from an undesirable area.

In designing its allocations policies and procedures it is essential that the landlord considers the needs of those who wish to transfer. If it does not then these people may end up trapped in housing which is unsuitable for them. Most landlords will therefore devise a transfer policy which sets out the rules by which people may transfer and usually indicates the preference which will be given to transfer applicants above others on the waiting list. For example, if a council has a bungalow available it may consider allocating it first to an elderly tenant living alone in a three-bedroom house. This means that the elderly tenant's housing needs are met and the resulting vacancy of the three-bedroom house can then be let to someone off the council waiting list, such as a homeless family. (All landlords will have different views as to the preference which they give to transfer applicants but they are required to make clear in their published policies and procedures how they deal with transfer applicants.)

Mutual Exchanges

A mutual exchange is where one tenant swops their tenancy with another tenant, usually of the same landlord but not necessarily so. The rules on such transfers are complex but normally such transfers have to be approved, unless the tenant has rent arrears. It is important to recognise that a mutual exchange is technically an *assignment* of the tenancy. In other words there is not a new tenancy created but the outgoing tenant passes on (*assigns*) their existing tenancy to the incoming tenant. This is important because it means that if a secure tenant exchanges with an assured tenant the person who was the secure tenant now takes over an assured tenancy. The assured tenancy has fewer rights than a secure tenancy, for example the right to buy does not apply to assured tenants, and an exchange can lead to changes in the rights of the tenants involved.

Social housing landlords will wish to encourage such exchanges as they are a means by which tenants can move to more suitable accommodation, and they may assist the process by means of computerised exchange lists or simply by means of a display board in the housing office.

Nationally local authority and housing association tenants can swap tenancies by means of the HOMES national mobility scheme or the tenants exchange scheme. Under the national mobility scheme participating organisations agree to allow a certain number of lettings to go to the national mobility scheme. This enables a person who wishes to move to a different part of the country, usually for work or employment reasons, to do so. The tenants exchange scheme is effectively a computerised list of tenants who wish to be considered for a mutual exchange to another part of the country.

Common waiting lists

One of the current issues under debate in housing is whether local authorities and housing associations working in the same area should attempt to develop common waiting lists. This is to deal with the all too frequent problem of a person seeking housing having to register on the waiting list of the local authority and all local housing associations to maximise their chance of rehousing. This can mean in some cases completing up to ten application forms for housing, all of which ask for very similar information.

In order to resolve this problem a number of local authorities have taken the initiative of developing common approaches to allocations. In some cases this amounts to the local authorities and housing associations devising a common application form which is logged centrally and then made available to all housing providers. This saves the applicant having to complete numerous forms.

In other cases the landlords have gone further by not only having a common waiting list but by developing a common allocations system in which all social housing landlords agree about the priority to be attached to every applicant so that when a vacancy arises in any of the participant's stock the highest priority applicant for that vacancy is selected no matter who is the landlord. This is much more difficult to achieve as many landlords have different allocations policies and it may be difficult for a number of associations and the local authority to agree on a system.

However Bristol City Council and Lichfield District Council, among others, have successfully developed such common registers in recent years (Chartered Institute of Housing, 1995).

Restrictions on access to waiting lists

Most landlords impose restrictions as to who can register on their housing lists, with 92 per cent of local authorities and 77 per cent of housing associations having some restrictions on access to their lists (York, 1993). Partly this is because some organisations do not have particular types of property and therefore there is no sense in being registered. For example, a housing association which only provides sheltered housing would not accept young single people onto its lists.

But other restrictions may be imposed to reduce the demand for the available housing. The most common of these restrictions is the need to have a local connection with the area before a person can register on the waiting list. The Centre for Housing Policy at York University found that 90 per cent of local authorities and 44 per cent of housing associations placed such a restriction on access to the waiting list. This practice could be seen as potentially discriminatory in that it excludes people who have not been resident in an area from access to rented housing. The Commission for Racial Equality in their *Code of Practice in Rented Housing* (1991) suggest that a lengthy residence requirement 'which persons of one racial group are less able to comply with than others' is 'indirectly discriminatory unless it can be justified'. This is because if people from an minority ethnic group move into an area they may be unable to gain access to the list because of the lack of a residential connection. Table 5.4 sets out the main restrictions which are applied to access to the waiting lists.

Table 5.4 Main types of restriction placed on access to waiting lists by those organisations who operated some restrictions

Restriction	Local authorities, %	Housing associations, %
Applicants below age limit	70	68
Owner occupiers: non-pensioners	44	44
Owner occupiers: pensioners	30	29
No local connection	90	44
Applicants with high income/capital	15	57
Applicants adequately housed	35	85
Applicants with other alternatives	78	77
Former tenants with arrears	67	100

Source: adapted from York (1993) Tables A9.7 and A9.8

Size of waiting and transfer lists

As all housing organisations have a different approach to dealing with allocations issues it is difficult to make an accurate estimate of the numbers of people on housing lists who are seeking accommodation. In 1993 the Office of Population Census and Surveys did a major survey of housing and calculated that the numbers seeking local authority and housing association accommodation in England was over 1,260,000 (Green and Hansbro, 1995); see Table 5.5. Of course there will be a significant amount of duplication in these figures as people in housing association lists are also likely to be on local authority lists.

Table 5.5 Numbers of people on waiting and transfer lists for local authority and housing association accommodation in England

	Total
Waiting list	685 000
Transfer list	576 000
Total	1 261 000

Source: adapted from Green and Hansbro (1995)

What allocation schemes do housing organisations actually use?

In 1993 the Centre for Housing Policy at the University of York published for the Department of the Environment a major piece of research which looked at housing management in England. The survey made use of existing sources of data such as local authority housing investment programme returns and housing association statistical returns to the Housing Corporation but was mainly based on a postal survey of local authorities and housing associations in England. This was supplemented by in-depth interviews of seven local authorities and seven housing associations.

In examining the allocation systems used the study found that the majority of local authorities used a points scheme for the waiting list, although a smaller number used a points system for the transfer list. Within the housing association sector the York study found that the merit system was marginally more prevalent than the points system. The greater use of merit systems by housing associations may well reflect the fact that compared to local authorities they tend to deal with fewer lettings and may therefore be able to operate a merit system more effectively. It is undoubtedly the case that a merit system is a more time-consuming allocations system because of the need to carefully assess each application on its merits. However, there is evidence to suggest that in recent years more housing organisations have been adopting a points system as a fairer and more transparent means of allocating housing. (See Table 5.6; the figures in the table do not add up to 100 because some authorities will have used more than one allocation scheme.)

Table 5.6 Allocation schemes used by local authorities and housing associations in England

Scheme	Waiting list, %		Transfer list, %	
	LA	HA	LA	HA
Points	73	46	55	35
Date order	19	16	22	18
Merit	15	48	21	51
Group with points	13	6	11	4
Group with date order	17	7	18	7
Group with merit	7	14	11	16
Other	9	11	8	9

Source: adapted from York (1993) Tables 9.4 and 9.5

In 1994 a survey of waiting lists published by the Department of the Environment reported that nearly;

> '... three quarters of (*local*) authorities divide their (*waiting*) lists into distinctive groups or queues and half treat certain groups independently of the waiting list–most commonly homeless acceptances, but also transfers, nominees on medical grounds and applicants for mobility schemes.' (Prescott-Clarke *et al.*, 1994.)

The priority between groups was most commonly set on the basis of either ranking groups by urgency (e.g. homeless applicants having greater priority than transfers on social grounds) or by setting quotas. The 1994 report showed that where the list was divided into groups the ranking was done in 58 per cent of local authorities by urgency and in 13 per cent by a quota system.

Within each group the research found that the most common way of assessing the priority of individuals was to use a points scheme (in 80 per cent of cases) with date order being used in 26 per cent of authorities surveyed. This is similar to the findings in the York study.

5.3 Collecting the rents and arrears management

For all landlords the setting and collection of rents, and the recovery of rent arrears, are core housing management functions and this section considers the different approaches which housing organisations adopt.

Setting the rents

All landlords need to establish a mechanism for setting their rents. For social housing organisations a number of factors need to be taken into account in deciding the system they intend to use:

- the system needs to ensure that the landlord is able to recover enough money from its tenants to meet its costs of providing and managing its homes;
- the system needs to be easily understood by tenants and staff;
- the system needs to generate affordable rents;
- the system needs to be seen as fair and equitable;
- the system needs to comply with the law and guidance from regulatory authorities (such as the Housing Corporation).

The law and rent setting

Local authorities

Under the 1985 Housing Act (Section 24) and the Local Government and Housing Act 1989 housing authorities in England and Wales have to make a reasonable charge for the properties which they manage and also to ensure that their rents have regard to a general principle that the rents of their properties should bear the same relationship to each other as rents in the private sector. Thus if a flat in the private sector is charged less than a house then the council should have a similar relationship in its rent setting structures. They are further required to review their rents from time to time. Similar requirements exist in Scotland under the Housing (Scotland) Act 1987.

Housing authorities also have an obligation to balance their housing revenue account and the impact of the housing subsidy system will influence the levels of rents which are charged (this is covered in more detail in the Chapter 3 on Financing Social Housing). However, the legislation does *not* require social housing landlords to charge rents which are affordable, which is usually taken to mean rents within the reach of those in low paid employment.

Housing authorities will normally 'pool' all of their costs of managing and maintaining their housing and will have established a system to ensure that they recover these costs through their charges. Pooling means that rents for individual properties are no longer linked directly to the costs of providing that individual property.

Housing associations

Housing associations have two main types of tenancies: secure tenancies and assured tenancies. Tenants of housing associations whose tenancies commenced before 15 January 1989 will normally have secure tenancies as defined by the Housing Act 1985. These tenancies are almost identical to those enjoyed by local authority tenants, except in relation to rent setting. After 15 January 1989 all new housing association tenancies have been assured tenancies under the 1988 Housing Act. Assured tenancies have fewer statutory rights under the legislation (for example, they do not have the right to buy).

The way in which housing associations set their rents will differ according to the type of tenancy they are dealing with.

Secure tenancies

Housing association secure tenancies have their rents set not by the housing association but by the rent officer. The rent officer is an independent government officer who is charged with determining, among other things, a fair rent for housing association secure tenants. Fair rents are reviewed every two years and in determining fair rents the rent officer has to set a rent which reflects the 'age, character, location and state of repair of the property', with the aim of setting a rent which is fair to both the landlord and the tenant. In coming to a decision on the level of rent to set the rent officer is not allowed to take into account the personal circumstances of tenant or landlord. As rents are not set by the housing association the landlord here has no direct say over the rents which are charged for secure tenants, although landlords have to suggest what they feel the rent should be in their application to the rent officer to set the rent.

Assured tenancies

Since 1989 all new housing association lettings (both relets of previously secure tenancies or brand new lettings) have been let under assured tenancies and these properties are no longer subject to fair rents. Housing associations have therefore been free to determine their own rents. In some housing association tenancies a formula may be stipulated (for example, that rents are increased annually by the increase in the retail prices index for the previous 12 months). If the tenancy agreement does not specify the formula by which rents will be increased then the landlord is able to set a new rent each year but must allow the tenant to have the right to refer the proposed increase to the rent assessment committee for the determination of a market rent. A rent assessment committee composed of property professionals will then independently decide what a *market* rent should be for this type of property. Of course most housing associations rents are below the average market rent in an area and if housing association tenants refer their rents to the rent assessment committee for a determination they may find that their rent is increased further than that originally proposed by the housing association.

In determining their assured rents housing associations have to pay attention to the *Tenants' Guarantee* published by the Housing Corporation. This requires associations to ensure that the rents they charge for assured tenancies are affordable for people in low paid employment, and not to discriminate in their rents between people on housing benefit and those who are not in receipt of benefit. The Guarantee further indicates that this will normally mean setting rents below market levels although they are also required to ensure that the rents they charge cover the costs of providing the housing.

Housing associations therefore may well have three rent setting regimes:

- fair rents for secure tenancies;
- assured rents for relets of previously secure tenancies;
- assured rents on new schemes built since 1989 and let on assured tenancies.

Some associations will attempt to link their assured rents very closely to the equivalent fair rents so that if a fair rent on a three-bedroom house is £45 per week they may well charge the same rent on a similar three-bedroom house on the same estate which is let on an assured tenancy. However, most associations will charge significantly higher rents for their newly built schemes because of the need to raise income to pay for the substantial mortgages which are required to fund these developments. This is covered in more detail in Chapter 3 on Financing Social Housing.

Types of rent setting systems

All landlords need to raise income from rents to meet their costs of providing the dwelling, managing that dwelling and carrying out repairs and maintenance. However, if a landlord owns a number of dwellings it will need to establish a system for deciding what rents it will charge for what properties. For example, if a landlord owns 1,000 homes and needs to recover income of £45,000 each week to cover its costs it will need to work out what rent to charge on each property. Of course it could simply charge all properties the same rent (£45 per week in this example) but this may not be seen as reasonable if someone living in a bedsit in a tower block ends up paying exactly the same rent as someone living in a brand new four-bedroom house on a new estate.

Cost rents

Perhaps the simplest approach is for a landlord to charge what it costs to provide the individual dwelling. At its simplest this will involve the landlord calculating what is pays out for each property in terms of:

- loan repayments;
- management and maintenance costs;
- provisions for voids and bad debts.

and then charging sufficient rent to cover all of its costs.

Although this appears a straightforward system it does lead to a number of problems, not least that for many landlords it may be difficult to calculate exactly what an individual property has cost. It would also lead to a number of anomalies such as rents being reduced when loans were eventually paid off. Properties built at times of lower interest rates would have a lower rent than those built when interest rates were higher. Properties which face higher maintenance costs, such as system built properties, would have higher repair costs and so higher rents. It would also mean that similar properties in the same area built a few years apart may have very different rents because of interest rate changes and this can be very difficult for landlords to explain to their tenants.

In the early days of local authority housing this cost rent system was used by councils to set their rents but they soon found that the disadvantages of the system outweighed its benefits. They began to *pool* all of their costs to seek to recover the costs from all of their tenants in a different way, not linked to the costs involved in providing individual properties.

However, cost rents are still quite common in the housing association sector, particularly for developments that have been funded since the 1988 Housing Act with the help of a private mortgage. With these developments the association will know what it has cost to provide the properties and will seek to recover the costs on a scheme-by-scheme basis.

If rents are not to be linked to the costs of providing an individual property then it is necessary to devise a system for charging rents on individual properties and four main systems have traditionally been used.

Values

Many landlords have used the value of their stock as the basis of charging rents with properties of greater values paying higher rents. Two main variants on this theme have been adopted:

- gross values
- capital values

Gross values

Prior to the introduction of the community charge (then later the council tax) all properties were given a gross value by the district valuer for rating purposes. Rates were a property tax levied by local authorities on properties as a means of paying for local government services.

This gross value was assessed by the district valuer on the basis of the rental income a property might generate if the landlord was responsible for the cost of repairs, insurance and maintenance and was influenced by factors such as the size of a property, its age, location and state of repair. These valuations were supposed to be undertaken every five years by the District Valuer but in England the last revaluation took place in 1973 and in Scotland in 1985. However, following the introduction of the community charge gross values were no longer required for rating purposes. This has meant that new properties have not been valued and existing valuations are now out of date.

However, when the values were available how did landlords use them to calculate their rents? The landlord simply added up all the gross values of its properties and then worked out the proportion of the total rent to be collected which each individual property should pay on the basis of its individual valuation using the formula:

$$\text{Rent paid for an individual property} = \frac{\text{Gross value of property}}{\text{Total gross values of stock}} \times \text{Total rent required}$$

Consider the following example of rent setting using gross values. A local authority needs to collect £18,000,000 from its 10,000 homes. The gross value of its homes amounts to £3,500,000 as assessed by the district valuer. An individual property has a gross value of £450 and its rent is calculated using the formula:

$$= \frac{\text{Gross value of property}}{\text{Total gross values of stock}} \times \text{Total rent required}$$

$$= \frac{450}{3,500,000} \times 18,000,000$$

$$= £2,313 \text{ p.a.}$$

$$= £44.48 \text{ p.w.}$$

The key benefit of this system is that all properties were given a gross rateable value which was assessed by the district valuer, who was independent of the local authority. Valuations would tend to reflect size, amenities, location and state of repair and as such would be easily understood by tenants.

However, valuation is an inexact science and although location and size are important factors in valuations this does tend to lead to tenants who happen to live in more desirable areas paying significantly higher rents. But perhaps the biggest problem with using the gross valuation system was that values quickly became out of date (particularly when revaluations did not take place) and with the introduction of the community charge the district valuer stopped undertaking valuations and as such an alternative system was required.

Capital values

A similar system to the gross valuation one was to use capital values. This is where every property is given a capital valuation as if it were to be sold and the rent is related to this. In this system a property worth £80,000 would require twice as much rent as a property with a value of £40,000.

This method obviously requires all properties to be valued and given a capital value and this is then used to calculate the rent payable on an individual property using a similar formula:

$$\text{Rent paid for an individual property} = \frac{\text{Value of property} \times \text{Total rent required}}{\text{Total valuation of stock}}$$

A main advantage of the capital value system is that valuations will normally be done by an independent valuer and most people can understand the basis on which the rent is calculated, particularly as values will reflect property attributes such as size, location and state of repair.

But obtaining valuations may be costly as landlords will often need to commission a surveyor to carry them out and they need to be updated on a regular basis. A further problem is that the system leads to larger properties in more desirable areas attracting higher capital values and therefore rents. This may penalise those tenants who live in those areas or property types. Indeed, it may make large properties or properties in desirable areas unaffordable to people on low incomes and this will have implications for a landlord's policies on both affordability and equal opportunities.

Points system

A number of landlords have set up a points system where properties are given points for individual attributes. Factors which may be relevant include:

- number of bedrooms
- purpose built or modernised
- flat, house or bungalow
- heating systems
- garden
- amenities

- location
- age of property
- condition

Once a list of attributes is produced it is then necessary to assign points to each of these attributes to generate an overall points score for a property. Again the system involves the landlord totalling up all of the points in its stock and using the formula to decide individual rents as follows;

$$\text{Rent paid for an individual property} = \frac{\text{Points of property} \times \text{Total rent required}}{\text{Total points of stock}}$$

Using a points system enables differences in stock characteristics to be reflected in different points awards and the system does not require experts from outside the organisation to value the stock and much of the work on identifying stock characteristics can be done in-house. It also enables those characteristics which should lead to lower rents being reflected through the scores (for example, properties in less desirable areas could be given a negative points score for the location characteristic). The system is a flexible one and can be adjusted over time, both in terms of amending the property attributes and the points attached to each one.

But if too many attributes are used the system can be complicated to operate and the weighting attached to individual characteristics is inevitably a subjective decision. Each property needs to be assessed to decide the points score to be awarded and of course the points score may not reflect the actual costs or value of a property

Formula systems

A variation on the points system is a formula system. Here an average rent is determined by dividing the rent to be collected by the number of properties. This average rent is then adjusted by percentages depending on the characteristics of a property. For example, if the average rent of a landlord owing 10,000 properties and collecting £18,200,000 a year is £35 per week then the formula system can be used to determine the rent of a three-bedroom house. For example, the formula for a three-bedroom house might mean that the average rent had to be adjusted by these percentages:

Three-bedroom house	+2.00%
Downstairs WC	+0.25%
No garden	−0.05%
Full central heating	+0.75%
Refurbished property	−1.00%
No car parking	−0.05%
Unpopular location	−1.00%
Total change required	+0.90%

Average rent £35 + (0.90% × 35) = £35.51 p.w.

All landlords need to have a system for determining the rents that they charge. For housing association secure tenancies these rents are determined by the rent officer but in all other cases the landlord has the right to set the rent and a number of systems are available to determine the rents set for individual properties in individual locations. Whatever system is used the resulting rents which are generated must lead to sufficient rent being collected to ensure that the landlord meets the costs of providing their housing service, and each system which is used has its own particular advantages and disadvantages.

Collecting the rent

For both local authorities and housing associations rents are by far the most important source of revenue. The importance of rents for the financing of social housing organisations is examined in more detail in Chapter 3 on Financing Social Housing). Unless landlords collect the rent due to them then they will not be able to fund their repairs service, service their mortgage loans or pay for their housing management staff.

The amount of rent which social housing landlords collect is an important indicator of their financial health, and is monitored closely by the Department of the Environment (Scottish Homes and the Welsh Office) in relation to local authorities. Similarly, in the housing association sector, rent collection and the level of arrears is monitored closely by the Housing Corporation (Tai Cymru and Scottish Homes). Under legislation contained in the Local Government and Housing Act 1989 and the Tenant's Guarantee for housing associations social housing landlords are required to tell their tenants in their annual report how much rent they have collected each year.

But it is not only tenants and regulatory bodies which look closely at rent collection performance. Committees of both housing associations and local authorities will normally wish to see regular reports from their officers about how well the organisation is doing in these areas. Auditors of local authorities and housing associations will also comment on the amount of rent which their clients collect and particularly in the housing association sector banks and building societies, who have lent money to housing associations, will want to receive regular reports on rent collection rates. This is because a housing association which is struggling to collect its rents may find itself in difficulty in relation to the payment of mortgages.

Recent legislative changes within the housing association and local authority sectors have also increased the pressure on social housing landlords to improve their performance in collecting rents from tenants. The Local Government and Housing Act 1989 'ring fenced' the housing revenue account which meant that if a local authority did not collect sufficient amounts of rent it could not make up this shortfall from a transfer from the council tax payers. The only way a shortfall could be made up therefore was by reducing expenditure on council house services. This is examined in more detail in Chapter 3 on Financing Social Housing.

Within the housing association sector the Housing Act of 1988 introduced private finance into housing associations' new development. Housing Corporation

(Scottish Homes/Tai Cymru) funding to associations through housing association grant was reduced significantly and housing associations were encouraged to borrow money from banks and building societies to pay for their new housing development. This has meant that most new housing association developments now carry substantial mortgages which must be repaid each year from rental income. Any shortfall in rental income may make it more difficult for the housing association to meet the loan repayments on their mortgages and because of this housing association committees (and their regulators) now pay much closer attention to levels of rent arrears than was previously the case.

The extent of rent arrears

The level of rent arrears has always been of concern to government and other agencies involved in the regulation of local authorities and housing associations.

> 'Any but the most limited and temporary arrears are damaging to the interests of all concerned: to the tenants involved, who have to manage a mounting burden of debt; to the landlord authorities which are deprived of resources in their Housing Revenue Account; to the other tenants who thereby suffer higher rents or an inferior service; and to ratepayers who in many cases have to bear the costs attached to meeting a larger deficit on the Housing Revenue Account. This inefficiency in the use of resources also damages the case for allocation of resources to local authorities for housing.' (*Source*: DoE Circular 18/87 quoted in Gray, *et al.*, 1994.)

Over the last twenty years there have been a number of influential reports on the extent of rent arrears. These are as follows.

Audit Commission 1994 – Bringing Council Tenant Arrears Under Control
This report looked at rent arrears in London, the English metropolitan district councils and 28 of the largest shire districts where the arrears problem was thought to be the worst. This report highlighted the extent of the problem of rent arrears and made a number of recommendations to local authorities as to how they should combat the increase in rent arrears which the report identified.

Audit Commission 1986 – Managing the Crisis in Council Housing
This report indicated that many local authorities had taken on board the recommendations of the earlier report but that in a minority of councils rent arrears were still increasing.

Audit Commission 1989 – Survey of Local Authority Rent Arrears.
This report showed an increase in rent arrears in 1988/89 with arrears at the 31 March 1989 standing at £450 million in English and Welsh local authorities. The main reason for the increase in arrears was attributed by the Audit Commission to the housing benefit changes introduced in 1988. These changes had led to a reduction in housing benefit payable to some households together with changes in the rates

at which benefit was withdrawn as incomes rose (the so-called tapers). These issues are discussed in more detail in Chapter 3 on Financing Social Housing.

Rent Arrears in Local Authorities and Housing Associations in England

This last major piece of research for the Department of the Environment on rent arrears (Gray *et al.*, 1994) showed that arrears had increased from 1982/83 to 1991/92 from £161 million to £458 million. Arrears expressed as a percentage of the debit (the annual amount of rent collectable) rose from 4.8 per cent to 8 per cent of the debit. Table 5.7 shows the increase in arrears over the period.

Table 5.7 Gross rent arrears statistics (local authorities in England)

Year	Arrears, £ million	Percentage of rent roll
1982/83	161	4.8
1983/84	178	5.2
1984/85	199	5.7
1985/86	211	5.7
1986/87	195	5.1
1987/88	227	5.7
1988/89	321	7.6
1989/90	361	8.1
1990/91	434	8.6
1991/92	458	8.0

Source: adapted from Gray *et al.* (1994) Table 4.1

Table 5.7 shows quite clearly that there had been an increase in rent arrears over the period with a significant jump in 1988/89. This is the same increase in arrears which was identified by the Audit Commission in the 1989 report.

The 1994 research indicated that the highest arrears were still to be found in the London local authorities and the metropolitan districts. This finding is consistent with those of the Audit Commission in their earlier reports. Indeed in 1994 the research showed that 75 per cent of all arrears were to be found in these local authority areas (and ten local authorities, mainly in London, owed two thirds of the total arrears in England). This pattern is also reflected in the statistics produced by CIPFA from local authority statistical returns, see Table 5.8.

Table 5.8 Rent arrears in England and Wales at 31 March 1994

	Total arrears, £
London boroughs	221 079 000
Metropolitan districts 1	141 532 000
Districts (England)	119 534 000
Districts (Wales)	13 761 000
Total	495 906 000

Source: adapted from CIPFA, (1995)

In 1995/96 the Audit Commission reported that local authorities in England and Wales owed £446 million (6.2 per cent of the rent roll). In 1994/95 arrears had been 6.4 per cent and the result for 1995/96 for the fifth successive year that arrears have fallen as a percentage of the rent roll (Audit Commission, 1997).

Collection methods

A number of methods are used by local authorities and housing associations to collect the rent owed by tenants. Research carried out by the Centre for Housing Policy at University of York in 1993 entitled *Managing Social Housing* looked at the different ways in which tenants paid their rent to their landlords and this showed some significant differences between local authorities and housing associations. The findings are set out in Table 5.9 which shows the percentage of tenants of local authorities and housing associations who pay their rent by a particular method.

Table 5.9 Summary of rent payment methods used by local authority and housing association tenants, percentage

	Local authority	Housing association
Door-to-door	24	5
Office	44	15
PO giro/voucher	24	18
Bank giro/standing order/direct debit	8	27
Rent direct (HB)	n/a	24
Other	2	11

Source: York (1993) adapted from Tables A8.1 and A8.2

Door-to-door collection

Twenty-four percent of local authority tenants compared to only five percent of housing association tenants pay their rent to a door-to-door rent collector. A number of research studies have shown that in the past door-to-door collection was the most common way in which rent was paid. The rent collector often carried out other roles in addition to receiving rent payments; such as taking repair requests or receiving transfer application forms. Door-to-door collection is usually associated with lower levels of rent arrears. This is because the collector calls on a regular (usually weekly or fortnightly) basis and it is more difficult for tenants to miss a rent payment. In addition, if a payment was missed it would be picked up very quickly and the arrears recovery staff could begin to take appropriate action to recover the missing payment.

In recent years the popularity of door-to-door collection has declined for a number of reasons. Door-to-door collection is labour intensive and as more and more landlords have had to review the cost of their service it has often been door-to-door collection which has been cut. As more tenants have been in receipt of full housing benefit the number of tenants paying rent themselves out of their own income has declined, which has meant that the amount of rent to be collected by a door-to-door service has fallen. And of course one of the most significant reasons for the decline in popularity of door-to-door collection has been the threat of robbery and assaults on rent collectors.

Door-to-door collection is most cost effective on estates where there are a large number of tenants from whom to collect the rent. This may well explain the significant difference in door-to-door collection rates between local authorities and housing associations. Housing association properties on the whole are scattered and there are very few housing association estates with a large number of properties.

Office collection

Almost half of all council tenants and fifteen percent of housing association tenants pay their rent at a local office. This may be the main office of the landlord or in some cases will be a decentralised local housing office. In most of these offices the landlord may well have installed secure cash receiving facilities where tenants can pay their rent, usually through a computerised till which issues the tenant with a receipt for the rent paid and automatically updates the tenant's computerised rent account.

For landlords there are significant benefits in having office rent collection. It can be more cost effective to have a cashier based in the office than rent collectors out on their patch doing rounds, cash tills can be made more secure and the use of computerised tills means that tenants' accounts can be updated immediately.

For the tenant coming in to the office to pay their rent they will usually have the opportunity to raise other tenancy matters with the staff in the office. However, the main problem with office collection in terms of arrears levels is that payment of rent is at the discretion of the tenant. There is no door-to-door collector knocking on the door requesting that the rent be paid. This means that tenants may find it easier to miss a rent payment and the research evidence suggests that levels of rent arrears are higher with office collection than they are with door-to-door. If landlords use an office collection system it is essential that the arrears recovery procedure can quickly identify a missed payment so that appropriate action to recover the missing payment can be instigated.

The lower level of office collection for housing association tenants as compared to their local authority counterparts may be explained again by the fact that housing association tenancies may be spread over a large area. Many housing associations will only have one office and this may not be accessible to a majority of the association tenants. In these circumstances housing associations need to offer alternative methods of rent payment to their tenants.

Post office giro and voucher payment

A significant number of tenants pay their rent through the Post Office where the Post Office staff will issue a receipt for the rent paid and send the rent and data collected to the landlord. In other cases tenants may be able to pay their rent through the Post Office giro system, where rents are processed by the Post Office Girobank and payments credited to the landlord's account. As the 1993 York research shows

24 per cent of council tenants and 18 per cent of housing association tenants pay their rents through this system. Again the evidence suggests that payment by these methods is associated with higher levels of arrears and this can largely be explained by the fact that there is no external pressure on the tenant to pay the rent and it takes longer for missing payments to be identified.

Bank payment systems

Tenants can also pay their rents through a bank standing order or direct debit, transferring money from their own bank account into a landlord's account. In addition some landlords have issued tenants with bank giro books where tenants can use these paying-in books to pay their rent into a bank nominated by the landlord. The 1993 research indicated that this type of system was more popular within the housing association sector than with local authority tenants.

Rent direct

A majority of social housing tenants are now in receipt of housing benefit to assist them with their rent payments. For local authority tenants the housing benefit is rebated from their rent (in other words, it is deducted at source by their landlord). For housing association tenants a rent allowance is paid to the tenant to assist them with meeting their rent payments. These tenants can opt to have their housing benefit payments transferred directly to their housing association landlord. The 1993 research showed that over 24 per cent of housing association tenants had their benefit paid in this way. Most housing associations will prefer their tenants who are in receipt of housing benefit to opt for their benefit to be paid directly to the landlord. This means that the landlord can be certain of receiving housing benefit which is due to the tenant. However, unless the tenant is in serious arrears such arrangements cannot be made compulsory.

The link between collection methods and rent arrears

Research carried out by Sue Duncan and Keith Kirby in 1983, entitled *Preventing Rent Arrears,* and by the York University Centre for Housing Policy in 1993, entitled *Managing Social Housing,* indicated a clear link between the collection method used and the level of rent arrears. All of the research shows very clearly that when rents were collected by a rent collector these organisations had much lower arrears compared to other methods of collection. The research also showed that while door-to-door collection was associated with the lowest arrears, the Post Office giro was linked to the highest proportion of tenants in serious arrears.

In 1994 the Department of the Environment commissioned a housing research report on *Rent Arrears in Local Authorities and Housing Associations in England* by Becky Gray *et al.* The study similarly found that a higher percentage of tenants who paid their rent via the Post Office were in serious rent arrears. By contrast, payment to a door-to-door rent collector was associated with a below average incidence of rent arrears. This is a significant finding for those organisations which are reviewing their door-to-door collection service. Although door-to-door collection may appear to be a labour intensive and therefore expensive service the effect of reducing the service may be to lead to higher arrears and the costs and benefits of door-to-door collection need to be considered carefully when reviewing options for rent collection.

Causes of rent arrears

Although it is clear that the type of payment method used by social housing land-lords is linked to the level of arrears it is also important to determine the other causes of rent arrears. In recent years there have been a number of research reports looking at the reasons why tenants get into rent arrears.

*   *Preventing Rent Arrears*, Sue Duncan and Keith Kirby, 1983.
*   *Tenants in Serious Rent Arrears; Some Recent Research Findings*, Susan Wainwright, 1987.
*   *Rent Arrears in Local Authorities and Housing Associations in England*, Becky Gray *et al.*, 1994.

Households in arrears

The 1983 research *Preventing Rent Arrears* found that serious arrears tended to be concentrated in certain types of households. These were:

*   single parent families
*   families with dependent children, particularly families with three or more dependent children

It was often the case that families in serious arrears had experienced a change in the household composition through either an increase in the number of dependent family members or a reduction in the number of income earners, both of which would lead to significant pressures on the family budget. The 1983 research noted that the elderly were much less likely to be in serious rent arrears.

These findings were confirmed by the 1994 research *Rent Arrears in Local Authorities and Housing Associations in England*, which showed that households with dependent children and single adults were most likely to be in arrears with their rent. They also confirmed that pensioner households were less likely to be in arrears and the report concluded that;

> 'statistical analysis confirms that age of the head of household and presence of children in households are among the most important predictive factors for rent arrears.' (Gray, B. 1994.)

Employment and unemployment

People who are unemployed or sick almost by definition have low income and may well have problems in meeting their rent and other financial obligations. The 1983 research showed that there was a link between unemployment and households in serious rent arrears. This was also confirmed by a report by the Scottish Accounts Commission *Tenants Rent Arrears – a Problem?* in 1991. This showed that tenants in arrears tended to be those whose financial circumstances were uncertain and changing because of unemployment, sickness or other changes in household composition. This led inevitably to fluctuating incomes and variations in housing benefit entitlement.

The study in 1994 reported that:

'Reduced income as a result of employment related reasons, such as unemployment, redundancy, reduced pay or retirement, is given as an explanation for rent debts by over one-fifth of tenants in rent arrears.' (Gray, 1994.)

Most social housing tenants have low incomes and the majority of tenants are now in receipt of some form of social security benefits. Around 60 per cent of all tenants now receive housing benefit to assist them with their rent obligations. Tenants in serious arrears tend to have larger households and thus lower disposable incomes. If income falls because of illness, unemployment, relationship breakdown or the birth of a baby it is likely to lead to higher levels of rent arrears.

The 1994 research showed that only a small proportion of tenants in serious arrears had any savings at all (11 per cent of local authority tenants and 18 per cent of housing association tenants) which they could use to cover their arrears.

Extravagance and rent arrears

Although it is often asserted that the tenants in rent arrears often live beyond their means and waste money on cars, video recorders and so on, the research evidence does not support this. *Preventing Rent Arrears* (1983) showed that tenants in serious arrears had fewer consumer goods such as televisions and washing machines than other tenants.

There are clearly a large number of factors associated with getting into rent arrears. Researchers in 1994 undertook a sophisticated statistical analysis to ascertain which factors had the strongest association with serious arrears and the list below (adapted from Gray, 1994, Table 8.2) shows the results of this analysis.

- young household (below 60 years old)
- existence of multiple debts
- living in an area of above average social/economic deprivation
- living in London
- dependent children
- receipt of housing benefit
- experience of problems related to housing benefit
- payment at a Post Office
- high rents

The receipt of housing benefit and its link to rent arrears may be surprising in that housing benefit is meant to assist tenants with their rent payment. This link is explained by the fact that tenants in receipt of housing benefit will by definition have low incomes and they may have accumulated arrears before making claims for benefit. It has also been noted that changes in household size or household circumstances are linked to rent arrears. These changes may also affect the ability of the household to claim housing benefit and delays in processing and renewing housing benefit claims are all given by tenants as reasons for arrears increasing.

A further report by the Department of the Environment published in 1995 looked at the characteristics of people in arrears. This survey *Housing in England 1993/94* (Green and Hansbro, 1995) was carried out by the Office of Population Census and Surveys (OPCS) by means of a survey of 20,000 people. The survey found that the council tenant most likely to be in arrears was:

- young
- living in London or the North West
- economically active
- on a low income
- in a household of a couple with children or several adults

This research concluded that age was the most important factor with the younger the tenant the more likely they were to be in arrears. A very similar picture emerged for housing association tenants in arrears. With the continuing restrictions in housing benefit for young people under 25 it is not surprising that this group of tenants is more likely to get into arrears.

Prevention of rent arrears

Social housing organisations need to give as much attention as possible to the prevention of rent arrears in the first place and there are a number of steps which social housing landlords can take to stop tenants getting into rent arrears.

At the commencement of a tenancy it is essential that tenants are given proper advice and counselling about all aspects of their tenancy. Housing staff should ensure that tenants claim any housing benefit which is due to them as well as giving them advice and assistance with claiming other welfare benefits. A number of research studies have shown that tenants who have rent arrears also have other debts and it is essential that tenants' income is maximised. In a number of housing organisations specialist officers have been employed to assist tenants in maximising their claims for the benefits which are available.

As part of this pre-tenancy counselling, it is essential also that housing officers stress to tenants the need to maintain regular rent payments and to advise tenants as to what action the landlord will take if the tenant falls into arrears. This is to generate what the 1994 report calls a *payment culture* (Gray *et al.*, 1994). From the organisational perspective it is also important that landlords ensure that sufficient staff are available to deal with their rent arrears. In some cases this may mean establishing a separate arrears team but, where arrears work is decentralised to more generic (all purpose) housing officers, it is important that the numbers of tenancies which they manage is small enough for them to effectively control rent arrears in their patch.

When arrears develop it is essential that these are spotted quickly by housing staff and attention should be given to the information technology which is available to enable arrears action to be started as soon as possible.

Tackling rent arrears

Rent arrears policy and procedure

If staff are to tackle rent arrears effectively it is essential that the organisation has thought about and written down the policy and procedure it wishes to adopt for rent arrears. These procedures should reflect the good practice which a number of organisations have developed over recent years.

1. Early Action

It is important when a rent payment is missed that the tenant is contacted by the organisation to remind them of the missing payment. As soon as the payment is missed it is advisable to contact the tenant, and certainly within two weeks of a missing payment a letter or a personal visit should have been arranged by the landlord. Clearly, an important issue here is for the housing organisation to have an information technology system available which can identify missing payments promptly.

2. Personal contact

If there has been no response to an arrears reminder letter then it is advisable that personal contact is made by a housing officer to ascertain the reasons for the non-payment of rent and to offer the tenant any assistance which may be required to reduce the rent arrears. In some cases this might mean helping complete a housing benefit claim or in other cases negotiating a suitable arrangement to reduce the arrears by instalments. It must be remembered that tenants in rent arrears may also have other debts and that they may not respond to a letter sent to them. In these circumstances a personal visit is likely to lead to greater chances of success.

3. Legal action

However, if letters and visits fail to achieve a reduction in arrears then the landlord will need to take legal action in the courts to recover the debt. For local authority and housing association tenants the first step is usually to serve a Notice of Intention to Seek Possession. This is a legal document which advises the tenant that if they fail to repay the arrears the landlord may take the matter to court to seek a possession order on the property.

4. Arrangements

When negotiating arrangements to repay arrears by instalments it is essential that these arrangements are satisfactory for both the landlord and the tenant. It might be possible for the landlord to arrange to reduce the arrears through the payment of housing benefit direct to the landlord or by the arrears direct method, through which deductions for arrears are made from income support and paid direct to the landlord.

5. Other measures

As an alternative to seeking possession of the properties through the courts it may be possible for landlords to investigate other measures by which they might recover the debt. This could include making claims in the small claims court or, if tenants are working, seeking an attachment of earnings order, where the court can order an employer to make deductions from earnings and pay the money direct to the landlord.

6. Former tenants arrears

A significant part of the total debt owing to housing associations and local authorities is not owed by current tenants but is arrears of rent owed by former tenants. In many cases the landlord will not know the whereabouts of the former tenant and it may be very difficult to recover the arrears in these circumstances. However, when the landlord does know the whereabouts of the former tenant then he needs to seek to recover the debt from them. Clearly, as the former tenant is no longer occupying a property owned by the landlord then the sanction of repossession is no longer available. In order to recover former tenants debts the landlord has to use all of the remedies available in the civil courts for the repayment of debt.

Key good practice points

The 1994 Department of the Environment report *Rent Arrears in Local Authorities and Housing Associations in England* recommended a number of good practice points in relation to arrears recovery as listed below.

Prevention of rent arrears
- Pre-tenancy counselling on the total financial obligations of taking up a tenancy.
- Maximising of tenant's income through appropriate advice.
- Creation of a payment culture with tenants being made fully aware of the landlord's policies on rent collection and that eviction is the ultimate consequence of non-payment.
- Ensuring housing officer's patch sizes are related to the task of collecting arrears.
- Developing a management organisation with suitable information technology support to enable a rapid response to the emerging problem of arrears.
- Providing tenants with up-to-date information on their rent account.

Management of rent arrears cases
- The development of a management information system which gives clear and unambiguous records of the state of a tenant's rent account to enable the landlord to take early action.
- Notification within two weeks of missing payments.
- Negotiation of a workable repayment arrangement with the tenant.
- Legal action should only be taken as a last resort, but is recommended where after around eight weeks, despite all of the landlord's efforts, there has been no payment by the tenant.
- Eviction should remain as a final sanction against a persistent minority of non-payers.
- Landlords should pursue former tenants for arrears where there is a realistic prospect of recovery. Specialist teams working on former tenant arrears are recommended.
- Monitoring of arrears recovery by committees and tenants.
- Establishing a specialist arrears team where the arrears situation of the organisation is serious.
- The consideration of alternative recovery methods such as through the small claims court, rent direct or the attachment of earnings.

(Adapted from Gray, 1994.)

Rent arrears are a key issue for all social housing landlords and with the increasing poverty of council and housing association tenants it is likely that the recovery of rent arrears is going to be an increasingly difficult task for housing managers. In this context it is essential that housing managers implement fair and effective recovery procedures.

5.4 Managing empty properties

Letting properties is not simply about identifying applicants and then offering them the properties. It is a much longer and more complex process. All social housing landlords need to ensure that they keep the time that their properties are empty (their void periods) to a minimum. This is because every week a property is left empty there is a lost week's rent with the added danger of crime and vandalism to the empty properties. Indeed in 1990/91 it has been estimated that the total rent lost on local authority stock in England was £92 million with housing associations losing some £14 million (York, 1993).

One of the key ways traditionally of measuring how well a housing organisation is performing is to look at the number of empty properties. This is usually expressed as the number of voids (empty properties) as a percentage of their stock, so if a social landlord has 10,000 properties and at any one time 200 are empty then it has 2 per cent of its stock empty (or a void rate of 2 per cent).

Table 5.10 Empty properties in England at 31 March 1993

	Total empty properties
Private (including owner occupied and private rented)	765 000
Local authority	79 000
Housing association	26 700
Government and other public sector[a]	12 400
Total	844 000

Source: adapted from CHAS (1994) Table 54.
[a]Great Britain

Table 5.10 shows that 5 per cent of the private housing was empty at 31 March 1993 compared with 1.9 per cent of the local authority stock, 3.8 per cent of housing association homes and 6.9 per cent of Government homes. However it is not enough to simply compare voids percentage and to decide that a landlord with a high void percentage is necessarily a worse performer This can be seen from the following list.

	West housing association	East housing association
Stock	5 000	10 000
Voids at 31 March	154	100
Voids percentage	3.08%	1.0%
Lettings in year	500	200
(Turnover percentage)	10%	2%

This list shows a somewhat confused picture. East housing association seems on the face of it to be performing better. It has fewer empty properties at the end of March and these voids represent a much smaller percentage of its total stock. However, although this is true it does not give a full picture as to the performance of each association in minimising voids.

The other piece of data which needs to be considered is the total number of dwellings becoming empty in the year which each association needs to deal with. West association has to deal with 500 relets each year (10 per cent of its stock). The East association has much less work to do; it only has to deal with 200 relets each year, representing just 2 per cent of its stock. In this context the ability of the West association to keep its voids at the year end down to 154 looks much more impressive and suggests that they are able to let each property that becomes vacant quite quickly.

The one piece of information which we now need to demonstrate that this is indeed the case is the *average relet interval* (or the time that each property on average is empty before being relet) of each property that is let. In terms of performance this is the most important indicator as it shows how quickly empty properties are brought back into use. The relationship between the three variables can be expressed crudely as;

$$\text{Voids rate} = \text{Average relet time} \times \text{turnover rate}$$

Assume a landlord has a stock of 120 dwellings and each year 12 become vacant (at an average of one a month). If it takes on average just over 26 weeks to let each one then at the year end it will have let 6 of the homes that become vacant in the year but will have 6 more still to be let. So it will have a voids rate of 5 per cent. Using the equation above we can demonstrate this is the case.

$$\text{Voids} = 5\% \text{ of the stock (i.e. 6 out of 120)}$$
$$\text{Turnover} = 10\% \text{ of the stock (i.e. 12 out of 120)}$$

Using the formula we can demonstrate that the average relet interval will be 26 weeks if the voids rate is 5 per cent and the turnover 10 per cent;

$$
\begin{aligned}
\text{Average relet interval} \ &= \ \text{Voids rate/turnover} \\
&= \ 5 \text{ per cent/10 per cent} \\
&= \ 0.5 \text{ year or 26 weeks}
\end{aligned}
$$

This may seem a strange calculation at first but it can best be seen more clearly by working back with our example of West association. It has a turnover of 10 per cent of the stock and a voids rate of 3.08 per cent. Using the formula we can calculate that it will have an average vacancy interval of 16 weeks.

$$
\begin{aligned}
\text{Average relet interval} \ &= \ \text{Voids per cent/turnover} \\
&= \ 3.08 \text{ per cent/10 per cent} \\
&= \ 0.308 \text{ year} \\
&= \ 16.06 \text{ weeks}
\end{aligned}
$$

For the East housing association there is a voids rate of 1 per cent (0.01). The turnover is 2 per cent (0.002) so the average vacancy interval is 26 weeks.

$$\begin{aligned} \text{Average relet interval} &= \text{Voids per cent/turnover} \\ &= 1 \text{ per cent}/2 \text{ per cent} \\ &= 26 \text{ weeks} \end{aligned}$$

Clearly, East housing association is the worst performer in that it is taking significantly longer on average to relet each empty property. But on the crude statistics we might have thought that it was performing well. Of course it is not always this simple as there may be reasons to do with poor performance to explain the high turnover rate of West housing association. Nonetheless, it does seem to be able to deal more quickly with more voids than its neighbouring association. We can also look at this in the context of rent loss as a result of voids. In West association there are 500 voids a year on which it loses 16 weeks rent on each, so its rent loss is 8,000 rent weeks. If the average rent is £40 p.w. this amounts to £320,000. If it performed as badly as East housing association it would take on average 26 weeks to let each void and so its rent loss would be £520,000, a significant difference.

The Audit Commission (1986b) in their influential report on housing management *Managing the Crisis in Council Housing* argued strongly against focusing on the voids rate as a key performance indicator and they suggested that the turnover rate and the time taken to relet each property were more significant as performance indicators.

In their publication *The Challenge of Empty Housing*, Smith and Merrett (1988) have produced a matrix which enables the vacancy interval to be calculated using the void rate and the turnover rate. In this matrix the following terms are used:

- *vacancy generation rate* – the turnover rate;
- *average vacancy duration* – the average relet interval.
- *vacancy quotient* – the voids rate

Figure 5.2 shows the voids rate associated with each vacancy generation rate and average vacancy duration.

Reasons for void properties

There are many reasons why properties are empty at any one point in time. They may be empty while a new tenant is being found and in some cases they may be awaiting minor repairs. In fact these two categories account for the overwhelming majority of empty properties. In other cases, however, properties are empty often for long periods because they are in need of major repair or refurbishment. Indeed some may be awaiting demolition because they are no longer in a fit state to be lived in or because they are to be included in a major redevelopment scheme. Table 5.11 sets out the reasons for vacant local authority dwellings in England in 1993. The duration of voids is shown in Table 5.12.

THE VACANCY MATRIX: WHAT IT IS AND HOW TO USE IT.*

Vacancy generation rate per annum (%)	Average vacancy duration (in weeks)																								
	2	4	6	8	10	12	14	16	18	20	22	24	26	28	30	32	34	36	38	40	42	44	46	48	50
1	0.04	0.08	0.12	0.15	0.19	0.23	0.27	0.31	0.35	0.38	0.42	0.46	0.50	0.54	0.58	0.62	0.65	0.69	0.73	0.77	0.81	0.85	0.88	0.92	0.96
2	0.08	0.15	0.23	0.31	0.38	0.46	0.54	0.62	0.69	0.77	0.85	0.92	1.00	1.08	1.15	1.23	1.31	1.38	1.46	1.54	1.62	1.69	1.77	1.85	1.92
3	0.12	0.23	0.35	0.46	0.58	0.69	0.81	0.92	1.04	1.15	1.27	1.38	1.50	1.62	1.73	1.85	1.96	2.08	2.19	2.31	2.42	2.54	2.65	2.77	2.88
4	0.15	0.31	0.46	0.62	0.77	0.92	1.08	1.23	1.38	1.54	1.69	1.85	2.00	2.15	2.31	2.46	2.62	2.77	2.92	3.08	3.23	3.38	3.54	3.69	3.85
5	0.19	0.38	0.58	0.77	0.96	1.15	1.35	1.54	1.73	1.92	2.12	2.31	2.50	2.69	2.88	3.08	3.27	3.46	3.65	3.85	4.04	4.23	4.42	4.62	4.81
6	0.23	0.46	0.69	0.92	1.15	1.38	1.62	1.85	2.08	2.31	2.54	2.77	3.00	3.23	3.46	3.69	3.92	4.15	4.38	4.62	4.85	5.08	5.31	5.54	5.77
7	0.27	0.54	0.81	1.08	1.35	1.62	1.88	2.15	2.42	2.69	2.96	3.23	3.50	3.77	4.04	4.31	4.58	4.85	5.12	5.38	5.65	5.92	6.19	6.46	6.73
8	0.31	0.62	0.92	1.23	1.54	1.85	2.15	2.46	2.77	3.08	3.38	3.69	4.00	4.31	4.62	4.92	5.23	5.54	5.85	6.15	6.46	6.77	7.08	7.38	7.69
9	0.35	0.69	1.04	1.38	1.73	2.08	2.42	2.77	3.12	3.46	3.81	4.15	4.50	4.85	5.19	5.54	5.88	6.23	6.58	6.92	7.27	7.62	7.96	8.31	8.65
10	0.38	0.77	1.15	1.54	1.92	2.31	2.69	3.08	3.46	3.85	4.23	4.62	5.00	5.38	5.77	6.15	6.54	6.92	7.31	7.69	8.08	8.46	8.85	9.23	9.62
11	0.42	0.85	1.27	1.69	2.12	2.54	2.96	3.38	3.81	4.23	4.65	5.08	5.50	5.92	6.35	6.77	7.19	7.62	8.04	8.46	8.88	9.31	9.73	10.15	10.58
12	0.46	0.92	1.38	1.85	2.31	2.77	3.23	3.69	4.15	4.62	5.08	5.54	6.00	6.46	6.92	7.38	7.85	8.31	8.77	9.23	9.69	10.15	10.62	11.08	11.54
13	0.50	1.00	1.50	2.00	2.50	3.00	3.50	4.00	4.50	5.00	5.50	6.00	6.50	7.00	7.50	8.00	8.50	9.00	9.50	10.00	10.50	11.00	11.50	12.00	12.50
14	0.54	1.08	1.62	2.15	2.69	3.23	3.77	4.31	4.85	5.38	5.92	6.46	7.00	7.54	8.08	8.62	9.15	9.69	10.23	10.77	11.31	11.85	12.38	12.92	13.46
15	0.58	1.15	1.73	2.31	2.88	3.46	4.04	4.62	5.19	5.77	6.35	6.92	7.50	8.08	8.65	9.23	9.81	10.38	10.96	11.54	12.12	12.69	13.27	13.85	14.42
16	0.62	1.23	1.85	2.46	3.08	3.69	4.31	4.92	5.54	6.15	6.77	7.38	8.00	8.62	9.23	9.85	10.46	11.08	11.69	12.31	12.92	13.54	14.15	14.77	15.38
17	0.65	1.31	1.96	2.62	3.27	3.92	4.58	5.23	5.88	6.54	7.19	7.85	8.50	9.15	9.81	10.46	11.12	11.77	12.42	13.08	13.73	14.38	15.04	15.69	16.35
18	0.69	1.38	2.08	2.77	3.46	4.15	4.85	5.54	6.23	6.92	7.62	8.31	9.00	9.69	10.38	11.08	11.77	12.46	13.15	13.85	14.54	15.23	15.92	16.62	17.31
19	0.73	1.46	2.19	2.92	3.65	4.38	5.12	5.85	6.58	7.31	8.04	8.77	9.50	10.23	10.96	11.69	12.42	13.15	13.88	14.62	15.35	16.08	16.81	17.54	18.27
20	0.77	1.54	2.31	3.08	3.85	4.62	5.38	6.15	6.92	7.69	8.46	9.23	10.00	10.77	11.54	12.31	13.08	13.85	14.62	15.38	16.15	16.92	17.69	18.46	19.23
21	0.81	1.62	2.42	3.23	4.04	4.85	5.65	6.46	7.27	8.08	8.88	9.69	10.50	11.31	12.12	12.92	13.73	14.54	15.35	16.15	16.96	17.77	18.58	19.38	20.19
22	0.85	1.69	2.54	3.38	4.23	5.08	5.92	6.77	7.62	8.46	9.31	10.15	11.00	11.85	12.69	13.54	14.38	15.23	16.08	16.92	17.77	18.62	19.46	20.31	21.15
23	0.88	1.77	2.65	3.54	4.42	5.31	6.19	7.08	7.96	8.85	9.73	10.62	11.50	12.38	13.27	14.15	15.04	15.92	16.81	17.69	18.58	19.46	20.35	21.23	22.12
24	0.92	1.85	2.77	3.69	4.62	5.54	6.46	7.38	8.31	9.23	10.15	11.08	12.00	12.92	13.85	14.77	15.69	16.62	17.54	18.46	19.38	20.31	21.23	22.15	23.08
25	0.96	1.92	2.88	3.85	4.81	5.77	6.73	7.69	8.65	9.62	10.58	11.54	12.50	13.46	14.42	15.38	16.35	17.31	18.27	19.23	20.19	21.15	22.12	23.08	24.04

Notes: *The vacancy quotient is expressed as a percentage, e.g. the figure in the second row, thirteenth column means a one per cent vacancy quotient. Similarly the vacancy generation rate indicates the number of vacancies which appear in a stock of dwellings in any given year divided by that stock and expressed as a percentage. The vacancy generation rate is written per year and the void duration in weeks for ease of comprehension.

What it is.
The matrix uses three statistics: vacancy duration, vacancy generation rate and vacancy quotient.
Vacancy duration (D): the columns refer to how long dwellings are empty on average from when they first become vacant to when they cease to be vacant and it is measured in weeks.
Vacancy generation rate (G): the rows refer to the ratio between the number of dwellings becoming void in any given year (eg through newbuild and turnover) as a percentage of the total stock at the start of the year.
Vacancy quotient (Q): the ratio of all vacancies to the total stock at the end of the year. This is the mass of figures appearing in the main body of the table.
As a general guide Q is equal to G multiplied by D divided by 52.

How to use it.
Two examples.
First, you know Q and G are respectively 5% and 10%. You want to know D. Read along the row G equals 10% until you reach 5%, then read up the column to see D equals 26 weeks.
Second, you know Q and G and D are respectively 8% and 8 weeks. So Q equals 1.23%. How will the vacancy quotient increase if transfers policy raises G to 12% but leaves D unchanged in its average value? Read along the 12% row to the 8 weeks column to see that Q will rise to 1.85%. If your total stock is 10,000 units, voids will rise as a result of the policy change from 123 up to 185.

This matrix is published by the School for Advanced Urban Studies, University of Bristol and is the creation of Stephen Merrett and Robert Smith.

Fig. 5.2 Vacancy matrix
(Source: Smith and Merrett, 1988)

Table 5.11 Vacant local authority dwellings by duration and cause in England

	1992/93	1994/95
Available for letting	17 500	
Awaiting minor works	22 200	
Awaiting major works	14 300	
Awaiting sale	6 600	
Awaiting demolition	5 900	
Other	4 300	
Total	70 900	72,000

Source: CHAS (1994) adapted from Table 116, Wilcox (1997) adapted from Table 89

Table 5.12 Duration of voids in England at 31 March 1993

Time vacant	Number of voids
3 weeks or less	18 600
Over 3 weeks but less than 6 months	11 300
Over 6 months	18 000
Over 6 months but less than 1 year	7 300
Over 1 year	15 700
Total	70 900

Source CHAS (1994) adapted from Table 116

In its publication *Local Authority Performance Indicators 1995/96* the Audit Commission found that the average time taken to relet empty properties in England and Wales was 5.3 weeks, compared with 5.1 weeks in 1994/95. The report does show a number of councils had made significant improvements although in others the position has got worse. The Audit Commission also found that a minority of councils, especially in London, have performance which is unacceptably low. See Table 5.13.

Table 5.13 Average relet times of Council homes, 1995/96

	1995/96 average (weeks)	1994/95 average (weeks)
London Boroughs	9.1	8.9
Metropolitan Councils	5.5	5.6
District Councils	4.8	4.6
England and Wales	5.3	5.1

Source: adapted from Audit Commission (1997)

Of course it is never the case that having nil voids is a sensible or achievable option. There will always be people moving home or transferring or properties required to be empty for major repairs. However, what is important is that the period that they are left empty is minimised.

Improving the management of voids

Having empty properties can be an expensive business, both in terms of lost rent but also in terms of the costs of additional repairs if empty properties are vandalised. It is important then that all landlords have in place policies and procedures designed to minimise the time that properties are empty. The Audit Commission recommended that a benchmark for performance outside of London is that voids should be let within three weeks (Audit Commission, 1986b). A higher figure was suggested for London because of the difficulties of achieving the three-week target in some of the most deprived parts of the country.

Identifying a void and getting four weeks notice

Most tenancy agreements specify that a tenant should give four weeks notice of their intention to end the tenancy. In most cases, however, it is likely that the housing organisation will get much less notice. Often the first they know is when a house is broken into or when a neighbour reports that a house appears empty.

However, it makes sense to encourage tenants to give four weeks' notice so that a new letting can be arranged in the meantime and any essential repairs carried out. Some organisations will make an incentive payment to any tenant who gives four weeks notice to encourage this to happen. Other organisations will also continue to charge four weeks rent as if notice had been given.

Securing voids

One of the main causes of additional expenditure with empty properties is the vandalism which is caused to them. In many areas thousands of pounds worth of damage can be caused to an empty property within hours. It is essential that steps are taken to make secure those empty properties which are vulnerable to vandalism.

Many landlords will secure void properties by using plywood boards to cover the windows and doors but these are relatively easy to remove. An alternative approach is to fix steel screens to windows and steel doors. These are much more difficult to vandalise and have been shown to be successful in a number of locations. See Figs. 5.3 and 5.4.

Some housing organisations have experimented with putting alarm systems into empty properties, whilst others have employed security guards to protect individual properties or to patrol areas where there are voids.

Pre-inspection and arranging for minor repairs

If four weeks' notice is given it is possible for a housing officer to visit the property and carry out an inspection. This will:

- identify whether the property can be relet immediately the existing tenant moves out;
- identify whether a decoration allowance should be paid to an incoming tenant if the state of the decoration is poor (or if the property should be redecorated);
- enable essential repairs to be identified;
- ensure that any costs of repair or redecoration which are to be recharged to the current tenants are agreed.

Fig. 5.3 A void property boarded with Sitex security screens

Fig. 5.4 Close-up of property boarded with Sitex security screens

Identifying potential applicants

If the housing manager has received notice that a tenant is about to leave they can then identify in advance a new tenant for the property. The ideal situation would be for the new tenants to take up occupation on the day that the outgoing tenant leaves. In order for this to happen the organisation needs to identify who the potential tenant is in order to make an offer of the accommodation to that tenant and, if the offer is accepted, make arrangements to start a new tenancy.

Whenever a void property becomes available it is necessary to identify an applicant for it. This means that the landlord's waiting list must be accurate and up to date so that time is not wasted making offers of properties to people who may already have been housed, have moved or who do not want the type of property or the areas in which it is located. It will usually involve organisations seeking to confirm on at least an annual basis that the details held on their waiting list are indeed accurate.

Offering the property

To assist in maximising the chances of take-up it is helpful if a housing officer can accompany the prospective tenants around the property which they are being offered. This enables the housing officer to establish a personal relationship with the applicant and to allow the applicant to ask any necessary questions about the property.

Cleaning of properties and repairs

Empty properties will often need, at the very least, to be cleaned out before prospective tenants are shown around and most voids will need some repairs doing to them. It is usually good practice to carry out only the essential repairs required before the new tenant moves in. This will save time and therefore reduce the void period. However, although this is sensible it can sometimes mean that a prospective tenant may refuse the property because it does not appear to be in a fit state of repair. In these circumstances it may be necessary to do more than those repairs which are strictly necessary.

If, however, only the basic repairs are to be carried out before the tenancy commences then it is essential that all of the outstanding repairs are done to the property very quickly after the new tenant moves in.

Redecoration

Most landlords will not redecorate a property when it becomes empty, although they may make an exception for the elderly. However, in some cases it may be necessary for the landlord to offer an incentive to a tenant to accept a property if the decoration is poor. This may be in the form of a cash incentive, a decoration allowance, (or a rent-free period of occupation) or in other cases the landlord may provide decorating materials for the incoming tenant.

Furniture

Many tenants find it difficult to furnish their new home and this has been exacerbated by the abolition of single payments from the DSS and the introduction of the social fund, where tenants have to borrow money from the DSS to purchase furniture. In some cases tenants will accept a tenancy, move in and then very quickly give up the tenancy because they can not afford to furnish their home. There are a number of ways in which landlords have responded to this. Some have supported the establishment of furniture projects which make available a package of second-hand furniture to new tenants, whilst others have introduced furnished tenancies where the rent will include an element for furniture. This has been particularly successful for housing young single people in some areas.

Signing-up

The most important stage in a new tenancy is at the start where a new tenant signs their tenancy agreement. This should be done with the member of staff who will be managing the tenancy and is an opportunity for the terms and conditions of the new tenancy to be explained in detail and any questions which the new tenant might have answered. At this stage housing benefit claim forms can be completed so that the tenant claims whatever benefit is due to them. Arrangements should also be made for the member of staff to visit the new tenant a few weeks after they have moved in to make sure that they are settling into their new home and are not experiencing any difficulties.

Management of voids

Voids management inevitably involves a number of staff, working in different sections of the organisation. Housing management staff will be involved in receiving the terminations of tenancies, while technical staff may need to inspect the void and arrange any necessary repairs. At that stage contractors may need to be brought in and their work supervised. Allocations staff will also need to begin the process of identifying a new tenant and showing them around the property.

With so many staff involved in the management of voids there is a danger that things may slip and it is essential that someone has overall responsibility for void management who can chase people when a property is standing empty longer than it should. This will inevitably mean that there needs to be accurate and timely information produced about the progress of a void so that people know at what stage each void is. As the Audit Commission say:

> '...the key to minimising the relet period is effective co-ordination of effort, to bring together the several activities required for rapid relet of a vacated property.' (Audit Commission, 1986b.)

Void policies and practices

The 1993 study of housing management of local authorities and housing associations in England entitled *Managing Social Housing* looked at the policies and procedures relating to voids management, see Table 5.14. The study showed that:

> 'in general both local authorities and housing associations had adopted good practice guidelines in the management and control of empty dwellings.' (York, 1993.)

Table 5.14 Void policies and practices in England

	Local authorities, %	Housing associations, %
Pre-allocation during notice period	69	82
Inspections before tenant leaves	41	60
Inspections after tenant leaves	97	93
Charging outgoing tenants for damage	71	56
Cleaning prior to reletting	39	34
Additional security to voids usually required	12	10
Decoration incentives offered	96	86
Target periods for reletting voids	75	65

Source: York (1993) adapted from Table 10.1

Although the implementation of good practice guidelines is important in improving voids performance, the survey found that there was also a strong link between an organisation's voids performance and the relative level of deprivation in each area. Using a z score (which is a measure of relative social deprivation) the survey found a correlation between those organisations with a low voids rate and a low z score. Organisations with a higher z score (and therefore higher levels of social deprivation) tended to have higher voids rates.

5.5 Repairing the stock

Introduction

Repairs and maintenance are key issues for housing managers. For almost all housing organisations repairs to their stock represent a very significant element of their revenue expenditure (60 per cent for local authorities, according to the York University Centre for Housing Policy, 1993). For tenants, the repairs service has been shown in numerous studies to be the most important service that they receive from their landlord and outside of paying the rent it is the service with which tenants have most contact.

According to the English House Condition Survey of 1991, 5.5 per cent of owner occupiers, 6.9 per cent of local authority homes and 6.7 per cent of housing association homes were unfit for human habitation, although by far the worst problem exists in the private rented sector where a staggering 20.5 per cent of properties were considered to be unfit in the survey (CHAS, 1994). The same survey looked at the cost of the remedial repairs needed to the housing stock. In Table 5.15 urgent repairs are those which represent a serious and immediate threat to occupiers, general repairs are all those repairs (including the urgent) that need to be done within five years, while comprehensive repairs include all repairs needed to be done within a ten-year period.

Table 5.15 Repairs needed to the English housing stock 1991

	Total urgent repairs, £million	Total general repairs, £million	Total comprehensive repairs, £ million
Owner occupied	8 136	13 644	26 508
Local authority	2 463	3 694	6 872
Housing association	294	451	839
Private rented	2 146	3 171	5 805
All vacant	1 891	1 943	2 684

Source: adapted from CHAS (1994) Table 55, p. 72

The estimated cost of undertaking comprehensive repairs to the local authority and housing association sector alone is £7.7 billion, with £2.7 billion of urgent repairs needed. Given this enormous backlog of repairs required to the social housing stock it is essential that housing managers spend their repairs and maintenance budgets wisely and adopt coherent strategies to deal with the significant problem of disrepair within the existing housing stock.

Organising an effective repairs and maintenance service involves housing management staff working closely with their technical colleagues and external contractors to ensure that the repairs service is of the highest quality. This section considers some of the key elements of providing a high quality maintenance service in social housing organisations.

Types of maintenance work

Repairs and maintenance work involves ensuring that the housing stock is kept in good condition. Over recent years the rate of new house building has been falling which means that the current housing stock needs to last much longer than was originally intended. To ensure that properties remain habitable it is necessary to keep them in good state of repair and also to improve them over time to ensure that they continue to provide a good standard of accommodation.

Jobbing or responsive repairs

Most repairs will be of the *jobbing* or responsive nature. These will be the small, everyday repairs that most households face and include examples such as:

- leaking taps
- faulty electric sockets
- damaged roof tiles
- doors and windows which need easing
- faulty heating systems

Cyclical repairs

These are works which can be predicted on a fairly regular basis. A good example is the external painting of woodwork and any necessary pre-painting repairs to external joinery. Most housing organisations will have a policy of repainting the outside of their homes every four or five years and where this is done the woodwork is normally inspected and any necessary pre-painting repairs to joinery carried out. Another example would be the annual servicing of gas appliances, which under the gas safety regulations landlords now need to do every twelve months.

Planned maintenance

There is other maintenance work which, although not on a cyclical basis, needs to be carried out on a planned basis and landlords will normally schedule this work well in advance. Examples might include reroofing of properties, replacement of heating systems or replacement of windows. This type of work is usually organised in larger contracts and happens less frequently than cyclical repairs.

Major repairs/improvements

On occasions, landlords will want to undertake major repairs or modernisation programmes to their properties. For example, replacing electric wiring, providing new kitchens, new bathrooms and heating systems. Often these works are done when a property is not occupied and they are treated as a building contract with architects and surveyors appointed to undertake the work. These types of works are often funded by borrowing or grant and are capital rather than revenue projects. However, local authorities face restrictions in the amount of money which they can borrow to finance capital works and in some cases these works might be funded from rental income as *revenue contributions to capital outlays*. (This is covered in Chapter 3 on Financing Social Housing.)

Some landlords will often carry out some significant works around the tenant. This means that the tenant does not have to be moved out (*decanted*) but this will only be possible if the works are such that the tenant can safely remain in occupation. Often kitchens and bathroom windows, for example, can be replaced with the tenant *in situ* although other types of major repairs or improvements may be harder to organise in this way. With the introduction of the CDM regulations in 1995 and the increased emphasis on health and safety such an approach to major repairs may be more difficult to organise in the future.

Why are these definitions important?

Jobbing repairs tend to be an expensive way of undertaking essential maintenance. Indeed the Audit Commission (1986a) in their influential report *Improving Council House Maintenance* suggest that a one-off job can cost up to 50 per cent more than the same job done as part of a planned programme. This is because the works are not planned in advance, they can not be predicted and often they need to be done quickly. This usually means higher costs because the jobs are small, the contractor has to include travelling times to and from jobs and the landlord cannot benefit from economies by having a contractor deal with the same problems on a number of properties.

Landlords normally deal with cyclical and planned programmes in a different way to their jobbing repairs. Because they know in advance that the work needs to be done they will normally draw up a detailed specification of the works required, go out to competitive tender to a number of contractors and achieve a cheaper price by virtue of both competition and the fact that works are usually grouped together. For example, a social landlord might arrange for all of the houses on an estate to be painted as part of the same contract. This will allow a contractor to have a team of painters on one estate for a number weeks and will almost certainly mean that a more competitive price can be agreed.

The landlord will also be able to closely supervise the work with a clerk of works or a surveyor and this is likely to mean that a better job will be done. With responsive repairs it is unlikely that many jobs will be able to be supervised by the landlord while the works are underway. The roles of a surveyor and clerk of works are looked at in more detail in Chapter 4 on Developing Social Housing.

The law and repairs

Landlords have certain statutory obligations relating to the repairs and maintenance of their homes. These are mainly set out in the Housing Act 1985 and the Landlord and Tenant Act 1985. In addition to the statutory obligations most landlords will also have obligations for repairs and maintenance which are set down in their tenancy agreements and are contractually binding on the landlord.

Landlord and Tenant Act 1985

Under Section 11 of the Landlord and Tenant Act 1985 (Section 113 of the Housing (Scotland) Act 1987) all landlords are required to:

- keep in repair the structure and exterior of the dwelling (including drains, gutters, and external pipes);
- keep in repair and proper working order installations for the supply of water, gas, electricity and sanitation (including basins, sinks, baths and sanitary conveniences, but not other fixtures, fittings and appliances for making use of the supply of water, gas or electricity);
- keep in repair and proper working order the installations for space heating and heating water.

For tenancies let after 15 January 1989 there is also a repairing obligation in relation to the common parts of buildings and installations such as communal heating systems.

This means that all landlords have clear repairing obligations for the structural and external elements such as doors, windows and roofs. In addition, they have obligations in terms of electrical installations, water supply and sanitary equipment. However, while many repairs are encompassed within these statutory obligations other repairs are not. If an internal door is damaged and in need of repair this would not come within the statutory requirements. Similarly, if a kitchen unit needs replacing this is not one of the statutory obligations of the landlord.

Social housing landlords often carry out far more repair work than is statutorily required and in the tenancy agreement they will usually indicate the repairs for which the tenant is responsible. This will vary from landlord to landlord and in

1986 the Audit Commission (1986a) reported on the responsibilities which local authorities placed on tenants. They found that the majority of landlords required tenants to be responsible for items such as:

- chimney/flue sweeping
- door furniture
- drain/waste blockages
- electric fuses
- glass(door/windows)
- internal decoration
- plugs/chains

Defective Premises Act 1972
This Act places a duty of care on landlords (in England and Wales) in respect of any building works that they carry out. Under the Act landlords and those engaged in building works (such as contractors and consultants) have a statutory duty of care to carry out works in a professional manner, to use proper materials and to ensure that the property is left in a state fit for human habitation.

Occupiers' Liability Act 1957
This Act (applicable in England and Wales) places a duty of care on the occupier of a dwelling in relation to all visitors to a dwelling. Although this is applicable to an occupier it can apply to a landlord insofar as they occupy part of the stock, for example in relation to lifts, communal entrances and other common parts of an estate.

A similar provision exists in Scotland under the Occupiers' Liability (Scotland) Act 1960, although in Scotland a landlord is given a specific duty of care to *any person* on their premises.

Housing Act 1985 section 96: the right to repair
Following criticisms, particularly of local authorities' performance in dealing with repairs, the government introduced a right to repair for council tenants under Section 96 the 1985 Housing Act. The 1985 scheme, which was very complex and involved the tenant being able to call in a contractor to undertake repair works where the landlord had failed to respond, was replaced with a revised scheme under the 1993 Leasehold Reform, Housing and Urban Development Act.

Under the new procedure for local authority tenants (introduced in 1995) a landlord can be instructed to issue a further repair order if the original request is not completed within a prescribed timescale. If the repair is still not completed the tenant can claim compensation of £10 plus an additional £2 for each day the repair is outstanding up to a maximum of £50.

For housing association tenants the Housing Corporation has introduced a similar scheme, although in the housing association scheme each individual association itself can determine which repairs come within the scheme and the timescales for completion. The compensation levels (£10 plus £2 a day thereafter up to a maximum of £50) are the same as the local authority scheme. In Scotland, Scottish Homes has also introduced a scheme which offers a £10 compensation payment if an emergency or urgent repair is not carried out within a specified period of time.

Issues in repairs and maintenance for housing managers

Organising the repairs function

In the past the repair of homes was often seen as a technical issue and housing management staff may have had little to do with repairs other than pass repair requests from the tenant to a contractor. However, in recent years it has been recognised that housing managers, if they are to deliver an effective housing service, must have greater control over repairs. This will involve housing management staff setting timescales for work, passing orders to contractors, monitoring performance and paying the bills.

Because many repairs are undertaken either by contractors or another department then it is necessary for the housing department to act as a client: issuing repairs orders, monitoring the performance of contractors and checking the quality of work undertaken on its behalf by contractors. Local authority housing departments increasingly have taken over this client role, although the 1993 York study on managing social housing showed that 20 per cent of councils still did not place responsibility for the control of the repairs function within the housing department.

The York study also found that it is the repair reporting aspect of the repairs service that is most likely to be partly or fully decentralised to local offices. This is not surprising in that if there is a local office tenants are most likely to make repairs requests at that location. However, in the majority of local authorities and housing associations tasks such as pre- and post-inspections of repairs and the management of external repairs contracts are most likely to be fully centralised (based in a central office), reflecting the fact that these are normally handled by specialist technical staff rather than the more generic (all purpose) housing staff at local offices. (The distinction between specialist and generic staff is covered fully in Chapter 6 on Organising the Housing Service.)

Following the 1980 Local Government, Planning and Land Act local authorities have been required to place their housing repairs maintenance contracts out to competitive tender and in some cases local authority direct works departments now no longer carry out any council house repairs. To administer competitive tendering for housing repairs the housing department will usually have established a client section to set standards, prepare specifications, let contracts and to maintain appropriate liaison and monitoring mechanisms with contractors.

The 1993 study on managing social housing (York, 1993) found that of those authorities which maintained a direct labour organisation to undertake repairs 78 per cent had set this up as a department separate from housing. Thirty-six per cent of Councils in the York survey had contracted out their council house repairs to an external contractor. Because of the size of the council house repairs contracts many councils place their repairs service out to tender using a schedule of rates. This is a list of typical repairs jobs and volumes which is priced by a contractor and enables authorities to identify in advance what the repairs service will cost for a given volume of work.

Housing associations in contrast to local authorities have much greater flexibility about the way in which they organise their repairs service and most repairs will be carried out by contractors. Indeed in the 1993 York survey 53 per cent of housing associations did not employ any maintenance staff at all, preferring to place all of their maintenance work out to private contractors. The survey also found that the overwhelming majority of housing associations controlled all aspects of the repairs service from taking repair requests, to placing of orders and post-inspections of repairs.

Reporting of repairs and issuing repairs receipts

Most repairs are reported by tenants over the telephone or in person. Clearly, if there is a local office it is often housing management staff who receive repairs requests and it is essential that housing staff taking these repairs requests have some understanding of the technical issues involved. A number of training courses can be provided for non-technical staff. Some organisations have produced booklets for tenants about repairs which advise tenants of the technical terms that they should use to ensure that a repair is properly reported in the first place. In other cases tenants have access to a repairs manual in the office and can indicate exactly what their problem is.

Good practice also suggests that tenants should be issued with a repairs receipt which will confirm the repair requested, the date of the repair request, any appointment time and the target time for completion. Research has shown that 51 per cent of local authorities and 43 per cent of housing associations now regularly issue receipts for repairs (York, 1993). Figure 5.5 gives an example of a repair receipt.

Pre-inspection of repairs

For responsive repairs most landlords will receive a repair request from a tenant in person, in writing or over the telephone. If a job is straightforward, such as a leaking tap, it may be passed by the housing officer directly to the contractor. In other cases it may not be clear what the problem is and in those circumstances a technical officer may be sent to inspect the property and identify the problem.

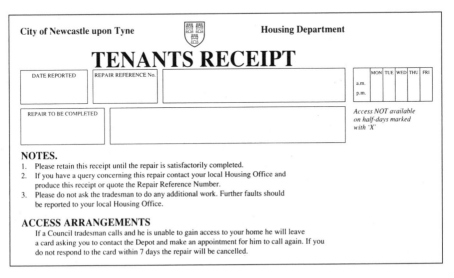

Fig. 5.5 Newcastle City Council repairs receipt

Clearly, if works are inspected before an order is placed it is more likely that clear instructions and specifications can be given to the contractor and greater control exercised over what is to be done. For example, if a tenant reports a leaking tap and the work is not pre-inspected an unscrupulous contractor may be able to go and replace the whole of the tap rather than the leaking washer.

Response times

Another key performance area which concerns both tenants and housing managers is the speed of response in dealing with repairs. All landlords should indicate target times for the completion of a repair from the time it was first reported and every organisation needs to establish systems to ensure that it can effectively monitor performance in meeting those response times. Many landlords have established response times such as:

Category of repair	Target
Dealing with emergencies	24 hours
Urgent repairs	5 days
Responsive repairs	28 days

Jobs which are outside the target time should be identified and checked to see why they are still outstanding and contractors who fail to perform can be penalised and eventually stopped from receiving any further work if they fail to improve their performance.

The government now expects both local authorities and housing associations to report annually to tenants on their performance in meeting repairs and the Housing Corporation has begun to publish league tables of performance in this key area.

Appointments for repairs

In recent years there has been an increasing trend to offer tenants appointment times for repairs to be done. In some organisations this is little more than agreeing that they will call on a particular morning or afternoon rather than a specific time. Many landlords argue that the volume of work they have makes it impossible to deal with appointments, although a number of organisations have now successfully introduced appointments systems. Indeed the York study found that 65 per cent of housing associations usually gave a specific appointment time compared to only 22 per cent of local authorities (York, 1993, p. 126).

Local repairs teams

Having a local repairs team is one of the ways in which a better repairs service can be delivered. A local team will know the estate and its problems and because they always work on the estate they will more likely want to do a good job the first time around. If they do not do so they will face criticism from tenants and will also be called back to the original job to put it right. Having a locally based team means that they can be called on more quickly to deal with problems and some costs such as travelling time can be reduced.

The Audit Commission have also supported the use of local multi trade repairs teams to deal with non-urgent repairs.

> 'the estate-based approach has distinct advantages in high-density areas, and minimises the risks of lost value through excess travel time, difficulty gaining access or problems with materials...' (Audit Commission, 1986a, p. 34.)

An alternative model would be a zoned maintenance system which does not rely on an estate-based team but is a system where a repairs team calls on an estate on a regular cycle and all non-urgent responsive repairs are packaged together for the team to deal with when they are next on the estate. This may well be appropriate where there are areas which do not have enough properties generating repair work to support an estate based team.

Post-inspections

Where works are not regularly inspected before an order is placed it is even more essential that landlords monitor the work that has been completed to ensure that a reasonable job has been done, that the work was carried out in a professional manner and that a reasonable price has been paid for the work. Many landlords will have a system of post-inspections where completed jobs will be inspected before an invoice is paid. This will rarely be all jobs because of the cost of inspections but often a sample of 10–15 per cent of jobs will be looked at. Many organisations will also have a policy that invoices over a certain level will always be post-inspected. The York study found that housing associations inspected a higher proportion of completed works than local authorities. This was because of their greater reliance on external contractors and the fact that they carried out fewer pre-inspections of repairs works.

Satisfaction surveys

It is increasingly common for social landlords to assess tenants' views about the repairs service by way of a satisfaction survey. These will usually be by a pre-paid questionnaire which asks tenants a number of questions about their repair, the results of which are then collated and analysed. This might be supplemented by satisfaction surveys carried out by technical staff when carrying out post-inspections of repairs. The York survey of housing management said:

> 'Many landlords have recognised the benefits of assessing tenants satisfaction with the repairs that have been carried out, as part of monitoring the effectiveness of their repair service. Seventy four per cent of local authorities and 66 per cent of housing associations *(in their survey)* did have a formal system for assessing tenants satisfaction with the repairs which had been carried out.' (York, 1993, p. 127.)

The report went on to say that this had been a significant improvement from the earlier Glasgow University study in the mid-1980s where only 35 per cent of housing associations and 15 per cent of local authorities were routinely carrying out satisfaction surveys. A typical repairs satisfaction survey card shown in Figure 5.6.

TEES VALLEY HOUSING ASSOCIATION				Job Number:	

Your views on our Repairs Service

When the repair you have requested has been completed please would you complete the questionnaire and return it to us. You do not need a stamp

Please tick one box for each question	**Excellent**	**Good**	**Satisfactory**	**Poor**
1. How do you rate the staff at Tees Valley who dealt with your repair request?	☐	☐	☐	☐
2. How do you rate the time taken to complete the repair?	☐	☐	☐	☐
3. How do you rate the quality of the completed repair work?	☐	☐	☐	☐
4. How do you rate the courtesy of the contractor who did your repair?	☐	☐	☐	☐

If you have any other comments please write them in the box below

Fig. 5.6 Repairs satisfaction survey card used by Tees Valley Housing Association

Customer charters for repairs

Many landlords recognise that repairs and maintenance is a very important service for tenants and often the biggest source of dissatisfaction for tenants about their landlord. A customer-orientated approach to repairs will include most of the following.

Information

Landlords should tell tenants very clearly what their rights and responsibilities are in relation to repairs and the standards which tenants can expect. For example, Dover District Council has published a customer charter which sets out clearly what tenants can expect. The York survey showed that 85 per cent of local authorities and 80 per cent of housing associations told tenants what repairs were their responsibility and 85 per cent of local authorities and 91 per cent of housing associations gave written information about repairs policies and procedures. Tenants need to be advised of response times for individual repairs and what to do if these response times are not met. They need to be advised of the availability for compensation and recourse to complaints mechanisms when things go wrong.

Appointments

Many landlords are now introducing appointments for repairs work. Although almost all social landlords ask tenants to specify access times (York, 1993) when they would be available for repairs far fewer have yet moved to specific appointment times.

Code of conduct

How contractors carry out the work in tenants' home is very important and a number of landlords now require their contractors to comply with a code of conduct which refers to issues such as equal opportunities, politeness and tidying-up of work.

Reports on performance

Local authorities and housing associations are required to report to tenants on their performance in dealing with repairs and these should be made available to tenants on a regular basis so that they can see the performance standard their organisation is meeting.

Reducing levels of responsive maintenance and increasing planned maintenance programmes

Given that it is more expensive to undertake responsive repairs many landlords have attempted to reduce the amount of responsive or jobbing repairs they do. This has been done by:

- Attempting to increase the amount of planned work to reduce costs and to minimise the number of responsive repairs. For example, a regular programme of roof maintenance may reduce the number of tiles that need to be replaced as one-off jobs.
- Grouping non-urgent repairs until a number of jobs have been collected to enable some economies to be gained. A contractor may be able to deal with a number of jobs in the same estate in the same day thus reducing the travelling times.
- Negotiating schedules or rates. These fix in advance the price for a particular job as long as an agreed volume of work is provided.

The Audit Commission (1986a) recommend that planned maintenance should increase to around 65-70 per cent of total expenditure on maintenance in order to maximise value for money. However, the York study found that there was still scope for housing organisations to improve their performance in this area but noted that resource constraints made it difficult for organisations to implement a more comprehensive planned maintenance system.

Stock condition surveys

One of the key approaches to reducing the amount of jobbing repairs has been to increase the size of planned maintenance programmes. The first step in developing a planned programme is to identify clearly what needs to be done and what the priorities are.

Many housing organisations have now undertaken stock condition surveys in an attempt to quantify more precisely the amount and type of maintenance work that needs to be done. These surveys will usually be on a sample basis taking a small proportion of the stock and carrying out a detailed survey of its condition. This is then used to build up a profile of the condition of the stock now, the remedial works needed immediately and a list of future maintenance works required. The data collected from the sample can then be aggregated to produce a profile for all of the organisation's stock.

Organisations may use their own staff to carry out a stock condition survey or may use external surveyors to undertake the work. In most cases the surveys indicate a significant backlog of repairs that will need to be tackled to bring the stock up to a reasonable condition and from the survey organisations will need to draw up a list of priorities for planned maintenance. The survey can also be used to plan future programmes of work over anything up to a 25-year cycle.

The development of this approach will also need to involve the finance staff who will need to be advised of the likely costs of the future planned and major maintenance programmes so that they can develop strategies to ensure that these can be funded. In local authorities this exercise will inform the housing strategy bids and their rent-setting strategies, as much of this work will need to be funded from a mixture of capital borrowing and revenue income (in the form of revenue contributions to capital outlay). Similarly in housing associations, stock condition surveys and the resulting planned maintenance programmes will be used to inform bids for major repairs grants, and the build-up of major repairs provisions and sinking funds for future programmes.

It is also essential that a stock condition survey is not seen as a one-off exercise. All organisations should undertake a rolling programme of surveys to ensure that programmes remain up to date and priorities can be adjusted in the light of developments in the condition of the stock.

5.6 Managing tenancies: away from the bricks and mortar approach

Introduction

In the previous sections of this chapter we have looked at the traditional tasks of housing managers; collecting the rent, dealing with voids, letting properties and carrying out repairs and maintenance. However, in recent years more and more time is being spent by housing managers on other tasks such as:

- dealing with neighbour disputes;
- dealing with the results of crime and vandalism on estates;
- ensuring that common parts of estates are properly managed and maintained;
- liaison with other agencies providing services to estates, such as police, health service, schools and community centres.

Indeed the increasing emphasis on these activities has led to a wide-ranging debate in the housing profession about the role of housing management and this is a subject which is discussed in greater detail in the last chapter of this book.

Dealing with neighbour disputes

In recent years one of the increasingly difficult problems which housing managers have faced has been the increasing incidence of nuisance and harassment on social housing estates.

This can take many forms from noisy and inconsiderate neighbours, to drug dealing from and around properties, to gangs of young people roaming the streets and terrorising whole communities, to serious public disorder. As the problem has grown and the expectations of tenants of the housing officer's ability to resolve the problem has increased then housing managers have had to learn new techniques to deal with anti-social behaviour and neighbour disputes.

Of course in may cases the problems complained of are criminal matters for the police but housing managers increasingly are called upon by tenants to take action themselves to deal more effectively with the problems. In the past the typical reaction of a housing manager to a neighbour dispute might have been to interview the alleged perpetrator and if the case was proven, to issue a warning letter. In some cases a notice to quit or notice of seeking possession might have been served but very few cases ever reached the county courts for possession.

However, more recently housing managers are developing a wider range of techniques to deal with this problem. For the typical neighbour dispute staff are often given training in interviewing and mediation skills. Indeed in some areas, such as Bolton Metropolitan Borough Council, independent mediation services have been employed in order to attempt to resolve disputes between neighbours. The Housing Association Tenants Ombudsman Service, now the Independent Housing Ombudsman, regularly makes use of mediation in an effort to resolve disputes between associations and tenants.

Social landlords are also making use of a wider range of legal powers to deal more effectively with the problems. As an alternative to seeking possession orders in the county court a number of landlords have pioneered the use of county court injunctions, requiring anti-social tenants to stop acting in a way which is contrary to the provisions of their tenancy agreement. In some cases these injunctions have been extended to visitors to the tenant's household and in a small number of cases have been obtained against individuals who are not tenants of the landlord but who are causing problems on the landlord's estate. The use of injunctions requiring tenants to comply with the terms of their tenancy agreements have now been used successfully in a number of areas to deal with persistent offenders and in other cases social housing landlords have obtained possession orders in the courts to evict people from their homes. Under the 1996 Housing Act the courts are now empowered to attach the power of arrest to injunctions if there is a threat of violence to victims. This enables the police to arrest someone immediately if there has been a breach of the injunction order.

In order to improve the chances of successful court action some landlords (such as Middlesbrough Borough Council, Hartlepool Borough Council and Dudley Borough Council) have taken the step of employing dedicated officers to investigate serious complaints of nuisance and harassment and to prepare the necessary statements and affidavits of Court. For example, Middlesbrough Borough Council's housing department has employed a specialist housing investigation officer since 1991 whose remit is to ensure that proper statements and investigation of cases are taken prior to court action. As a result, the council has successfully obtained a number of injunction orders against tenants. Of course, one of the benefits of an injunction is that if the tenants breach the terms of the injunction they can be committed to prison. This is often a very powerful deterrent to people who are causing a problem on estates.

In some areas social housing landlords, such as Sunderland City Council, have also employed professional witnesses. These are paid staff whose job is to witness anti-social behaviour and to provide signed statements to that effect. This initiative has been developed to overcome the reluctance of witnesses to give evidence in court proceedings because of their fears (often justified) of retaliation or intimidation.

Increasingly in particularly problematical areas social landlords are developing initiatives with the police to reduce the problems of anti-social behaviour. The types of initiatives which have been developed include the establishment of police stations or offices on estates, often based in the local housing office. This gives the police a direct presence on estates and also allows much closer liaison between the police and housing officers. In other areas protocols have been agreed between the police and housing organisations about the sharing of information and the assistance which police and housing officers will give each other. Newydd Housing Association has set up a formal agreement with social services, environmental health and the police on the management of neighbour complaints and in Redcar and Cleveland a safer estates initiative has established close links between the police and social housing landlords.

With the development of closed circuit television surveillance systems, these are increasingly being placed on housing estates to increase the levels of security. Similar surveillance systems utilising alarms or miniature cameras have also been developed to put into empty properties to enable the police to deal more effectively with those causing vandalism to empty properties.

At an operational level the police crime prevention officers work very closely with housing managers on identifying ways in which the security of existing homes can be improved through the installation of alarms, door locks and security lighting, so-called target hardening initiatives, and through advice on crime prevention features to be incorporated into new housing developments. Indeed many new housing developments which incorporate particular crime prevention features are awarded the police 'secure by design' certificate.

The use of probationary or introductory tenancies, where tenants are not given security of tenure for a period of twelve months, had been tried in a number of areas on a pilot basis in the mid-1990s and their wider use was trailed in the 1995 Housing White Paper. In the 1996 Housing Act local authorities have been given powers to use such introductory probationary tenancies where thought necessary. Although these types of tenancies have been criticised by some landlords because they only deal with new tenants and only last for twelve months a number of landlords will undoubtedly make use of them as an additional weapon in their armoury to deal with anti-social behaviour. The Housing Corporation is also looking carefully at proposals by individual housing associations to offer assured shorthold tenancies to new tenants, which offer less security and can be ended in the event of anti-social behaviour.

Intensive housing management

One of the responses to the problem of increasing anti-social behaviour has been to reinforce the need for more intensive local housing management. By having a local presence on estates housing officers may be better able to tackle problems of neighbour disputes and anti-social behaviour. This may often be in partnership with residents and residents groups and the links between local housing management and tenant involvement are well documented.

In addition to local housing management a further response has been to look at the physical redesign of estates to *design out* crime. This attention to physical causes of crime and anti-social behaviour is very much based on the work of Alice

Coleman, *Utopia on Trial: Vision and Reality in Planning Housing*, where she reported that there appeared to be a close correlation between high levels of crime and vandalism and poor design of estates (Coleman, 1990). Housing officers, often working with tenants, have been able to work effectively on some of the worst estates with architects to redesign the physical environment.

5.7 Performance monitoring

Introduction

In recent years there has been a growing interest in performance monitoring within most public sector organisations. There are a number of factors which are behind this increased concern for monitoring performances of housing organisations.

Financial constraints

The increasing financial constraints on local authorities and housing associations has led all housing organisations to review how they deliver their housing services in the face of declining resources. The concern to maximise value for money has inevitably led most organisations to establish systems for setting performance targets for key areas of work, such as rent arrears, voids and repairs and monitoring the performance of the organisation against these targets.

Influence of external bodies

The influence of external bodies has to be considered, such as the Audit Commission and the Housing Corporation (Scottish Homes/Tai Cymru) all of whom have been powerful advocates of performance monitoring and who have been able to influence the internal working of housing organisations.

Legislation

Legislation has set specific requirements on local authorities and housing associations to monitor and report on their performance.

1989 Local Government and Housing Act
Under this Act local housing authorities in England and Wales have a duty to provide their tenants with an annual report on their housing management performance. The government sets out the contents of such reports which are compiled at the end of the financial year, in March each year, and issued to tenants by the 30 September each year.

These annual reports to tenants include performance information on most of the key housing management activities such as rent arrears, voids, relet intervals and repairs response times and local housing authorities are encouraged to provide more detailed performance information to tenants in excess of that which is required by the legislation.

In Scotland the requirement to produce an annual report on housing management performance was introduced under the Leasehold Reform, Housing and Urban Development Act of 1993 with the first reports being required in September 1994, three years after the similar provisions were enacted for England and Wales.

The Citizens' Charter requirements

In 1992 the Government launched its Citizens Charter proposals which the government said was

> 'the most comprehensive programme ever to raise quality, increase choice, secure better value and extend accountability. It will ensure the quality of service to the public and the new pride it will give to those who work in the public service will be a central theme of Government policy for the 1990s. The Citizens Charter is about giving more power to the citizen and is a testament to our belief in peoples' rights to be informed and choose for themselves and emphasises that the citizen is also a tax payer and that public services must give value for money within a tax bill the nation can afford. The Citizens Charter will help raise the standard of the worst to the standard of the best.' (Press Notice 10 Downing Street July 1991.)

The thrust of the Citizens Charter programme was to require public bodies to set out clear service standards to their customers, to monitor their performance and to report to the public on how well they were doing. It was also the Citizens Charter initiative which first proposed that compulsory competitive tendering should be extended to housing management services.

In addition to the requirement to produce an annual report on housing management performance to tenants all local authorities are now required to publish detailed performance information on their services in accordance with the Citizens Charter provisions of the Local Government Act of 1992. This performance information has to be sent to the Audit Commission for England and Wales and the Scottish Accounts Commission and also has to be published in a local newspaper by December of each year. The performance information which is required under the Local Government Act includes some of the performance information included in the housing management reports to tenants but also includes information on other council services, such as education, social services and refuse collection.

Housing associations

Interestingly there is no statutory requirement on housing associations to publish performance information to their tenants. However, the Tenants' Guarantee does require housing associations to publish for their tenants annually information on their performance on a range of housing management issues such as rent arrears, repairs performance and voids.

In addition, the Housing Corporation and Tai Cymru also collect more details and statistical information from housing associations and some of this data is now being collated and published by the Housing Corporation.

Compulsory Competitive Tendering (CCT)

Compulsory competitive tendering has required councils to consider in detail both the services they provide and the means by which they are delivered, to draw up service specifications in contracts and to establish performance monitoring systems and performance targets to ensure that the service specifications are met by successful contractors.

The impact of performance monitoring on housing organisations

The development of a performance monitoring culture has been a relatively recent phenomenon for housing authorities and housing associations. Performance monitoring, the setting of performance targets and reporting on performance, are now common features of almost all housing organisations in Great Britain. All local housing authorities and most housing associations now publish annual reports to their tenants which include detailed performance monitoring information on their services and as a result of compulsory competitive tendering performance monitoring is now a key element in all CCT contracts.

The performance monitoring culture now permeates housing organisations at all levels. Housing committees and boards of housing associations regularly receive performance information at their committee meetings. Senior staff of housing organisations will review their key performance data on a regular basis and in most area housing offices staff will collect information on arrears performance, voids and repairs and compare how well they are doing to their colleagues in other offices.

In almost all of the housing management tasks discussed earlier in this chapter most housing organisations will have established performance monitoring systems to check how well the organisation is performing. For example, most housing organisations will collect information on arrears performance, the numbers of tenants in arrears and the amount of rent collected as a percentage of the rent debits. With empty properties again almost all housing organisations will collect performance data on the numbers of empty properties, the time they are empty and the rent lost as a result.

Further reading

City University Housing Research Group (1978) *Could Local Authorities be Better Landlords?*, City University, London.

Davies, C. (1992) *Housing for Life; a Guide to Housing Management Practices*, Spon, London.

Housing Corporation (1997) *Managing Voids and Difficult to Let Property*, Source 21, London.

National Federation of Housing Associations (1987) *Standards for Housing management*, National Federation of Housing Associations, London.

Power, A. (1987) *The PEP Guide to Local Housing Management 1,2 and 3*, DoE/Welsh Office, London.

Power, A. (1991) *Housing: A Guide to Quality and Creativity*, Longman, Harlow.

Spicker, P. (1983) *The Allocation of Council Housing*, Shelter, London.

Chapter 6

ORGANISING THE HOUSING SERVICE

6.1 Introduction

This chapter looks at how social housing landlords organise the delivery of their housing service. In the social housing world there are significant differences between landlords, from the large metropolitan district council managing over 100,000 properties with 2,000 plus staff to the small housing association owning ten properties with no paid staff. However, while there are significant differences between landlords it is the case that all social housing landlords have to undertake a number of common tasks.

In the local authority sector most councils in the past were organised on strict departmental lines and in some cases the work involved in managing a housing service was distributed among several different departments. In recent years, however, there has been a tendency to bring more of the work involved in the management of social housing within a single department, in order to provide a *comprehensive housing service*. This move to a comprehensive housing service has also been associated with a tendency to decentralise services, that is to deliver housing services from local estate based housing offices.

This chapter will explore the historical development of the housing service and the move towards a comprehensive housing service. It will also consider the reasons why social housing landlords have increasingly looked to decentralise the delivery of their housing services. Alongside this decentralisation of services there has also been a tendency for staff to become less specialised, with the development of *generic*, or multi-skilled, housing officers.

The chapter will also look at more recent influences on the way in which housing services are delivered. In particular the impact of compulsory competitive tendering, tenant participation and care in the community will all be explored.

6.2 The historical development of housing management

Looking back often gives us pointers to the future and many of the current debates about housing management have their roots in discussions which were taking place in Victorian England.

This section starts by examining the work of Octavia Hill, who is sometimes cited as the founder of modern housing management, and considers the principles which she adopted and discusses how applicable they are to contemporary housing managers.

Octavia Hill: the founder of housing management?

Housing management in itself is not intrinsically complex (although it is often demanding); the core tasks of lettings, rents and repairs are performed by all of those who manage housing. How then has housing management developed as a separate profession?

In the nineteenth century many landlords who owned a few properties would have carried out the housing management tasks themselves (as many private land-lords do today). Others would have employed agents to undertake this work. These would often have been other professionals who undertook these duties as a sideline, such as surveyors, land agents or factors.

In other situations the owner would have employed a middleman who would undertake repairs in exchange for a share in the rent. This system encouraged mid-dlemen to overcrowd properties to maximise their rental income and to minimise expenditure on repairs (Power, 1987).

However in the late nineteenth century a housing manager emerged who was to exert great influence on the way in which housing management was undertaken in the twentieth century and whose philosophy is still discussed by housing managers today. Octavia Hill was born in 1838 to a middle-class family and was persuaded between 1865 and 1866 to take on the management of a small number of dilapi-dated properties in the Marylebone area of London. Octavia Hill managed this housing herself and she took steps to improve what she saw were the poor housing management practices prevalent at the time. She considered that an essential ele-ment of good housing management was the necessity for close personal contact between landlord and tenants.

> 'In its early days, her management, operating on a small scale, was often intensely personal; Octavia Hill's principles that people and their homes could not be dealt with separately, and that a sound landlord/tenant relationship must be based on mutual recognition and discharging of responsibilities, were put into practice by her followers.' (Smith, 1989.)

Only by ensuring that there was close contact on a regular basis could landlords ensure that the investment in their property was safeguarded. Such visits were an opportunity to check on the condition of the property, to ensure that tenants were not abusing the property, to collect the rent and to deal with any necessary repairs. She took a firm line on arrears and would evict those who did not pay their rent and she took a similar line against those who were guilty of persistent anti-social behaviour. The visits were also seen as a means by which tenants, who inevitably were poor and of lower class, could be educated into a better standard of behav-iour. She was keen to encourage a sense of community and responsibility amongst her tenants and would also advise tenants on health and diet as a way of improving their standard of living (Power, 1987).

What echoes does this have for contemporary housing management? The emphasis on close contact between landlord and tenant is a key theme underlying local housing management. Those who argue for local offices suggest that one of the failings of centralised housing management has been that landlords have been too distant, both geographically and socially, from the tenants they house. The same idea underlies much of the support in recent years given to tenant participation and the need to work more closely with tenants.

However, it is important not to take Octavia Hill's influence too far. Octavia Hill, according to Spicker, was a *'moralistic and authoritarian'* landlord and this is something which most modern advocates of tenant participation and local management would want to avoid.

'...the legacy she left to housing managers has been baneful. She founded a tradition which is inconsistent with the rights of tenants and destructive of their welfare.' (Spicker, 1985.)

This criticism of Octavia Hill's approach is that she failed to treat tenants with respect. It suggests that her approach was based on a belief that the working classes were inclined to get into debt, to neglect their houses and to indulge in unacceptable behaviour. This tendency could only be overcome by strict housing management, which emphasised the need to pay the rent, to reduce the overcrowding which led to immoral behaviour and to encourage communal areas to be kept clean by tenants.

As Spicker goes on to say:

'...Octavia Hill's principles were misconceived at the time she formed them. Booth's research in the 1880s found that a third of the population of London did not have enough for the most basic sustenance – food, clothing, fuel and shelter. Landlords were "lax" about rent collection because tenants could not pay... Debt and bad housing were the result of poverty, not indolence.' (Spicker, 1995.)

Spicker suggests that her management practices were based on a misunderstanding of the circumstances in which tenants found themselves. She assumed that tenants would not pay; in fact tenants in many cases simply could not afford to pay. Of course one of the effects of Hill's management style was that she would weed out the poorest tenants and only house those who could afford to pay the rents she charged.

And the problem, according to Spicker, is that the practices which she advocated are still seen today as 'good' housing management; the heavy emphasis on rent payment as a priority, preventing transfers if there are any arrears on the account, the use of notices of seeking possession as a management tool, the emphasis on cleanliness and the treatment of problem tenants by transferring them to worse estates.

The relevance of Octavia Hill to contemporary housing management

It is fairly easy to suggest that many of Octavia Hill's practices were indeed paternalistic and many would no longer be seen as acceptable today. So why is it that her approach is still revered by many housing professionals? Perhaps it is because while the motivation behind some of her practices may no longer be acceptable the means are increasingly seen as positive housing management. In particular her emphasis on personal contact between landlord and tenant has become adopted as good practice by contemporary housing managers and has been linked to other initiatives such as decentralisation and tenant participation. However, supporters today of a personal approach, tenant participation and decentralisation would do so from a position which accorded tenants significant rights as consumers of a service.

She has also clearly influenced the thinking of those who now advocate the social/welfare role of housing management. Many contemporary housing managers would argue that although the key tasks of management remain rents, repairs and lettings they need increasingly to take on welfare roles with tenants, advising them on welfare benefits, working closely with social workers, the police and other agencies to overcome some of the problems faced by tenants living in housing estates. This issue is discussed in more detail in the last chapter.

However, some supporters of Octavia Hill also bemoan the passing of the traditional 'housing visitor' whose main role was to carry out regular inspections of tenants' properties and gardens and who would take strong action against tenants whose homes were not up to standard. They also regret the passing, in some places at least, of the housing application forms which asked housing visitors to grade the state of prospective tenants' homes as 'clean', 'satisfactory' or 'dirty'. This approach is very much in the Octavia Hill tradition but one which is increasingly viewed as unacceptable by today's housing managers.

6.3 Organising the delivery of housing services

Introduction

Chapter 1 describes in detail the development of local authorities as landlords since the First World War. As local authorities became landlords of significant numbers of homes very few of them had a coordinated approach to the management of their housing services. This was because the housing management function was relatively new and involved a number of local government disciplines and perhaps it was not surprising that the task of providing and managing social housing fell to a number of different departments. For example a typical local authority might have organised:

• the provision of new homes through the borough surveyor;
• the collection of rents and arrears recovery through the borough treasurer's department;
• the enforcement of tenancy conditions through the town clerk's department;
• the carrying out of repairs through the works department;
• grounds maintenance through the parks department.

In the inter-war years it was relatively rare to find a local authority housing department which carried out most of the key housing management functions itself. However, as the numbers of properties owned by local authorities increased then the need for a more coordinated approach to housing management led to more and more functions being brought together into a separate housing department. Of course, practice varied from local authority to local authority and even in the 1950s and 1960s it was still common to find a number of different departments undertaking housing responsibilities.

This fragmentation of service delivery was a cause for concern for the housing profession and in 1969 the Cullingworth Report, entitled *Council Housing: Purposes, Procedures and Priorities,* advocated the establishment of a separate housing department responsible for all housing functions of the local authority. This was echoed in 1972 by the Institute of Housing in their report *The Comprehensive Housing service: Organisation and Functions* and this influenced the way in which housing services were organised in the new local authorities which were established in the 1974 review of local government.

However, even in the 1980s a significant number of local authorities still had not set up a housing department with responsibility for the key housing management functions. The Audit Commission in 1986 was able therefore to write of local authorities:

> 'Some have all the housing functions under the direct control of a chief housing officer;
> others operate with the financial aspects outside the housing department, under the treasurer;
> yet others have no separate housing organisation at all, typically with the treasurer in control
> of the management of all council housing.' (Audit Commission, 1986b.)

In their report the Audit Commission had indicated that twelve small housing authorities had no separate housing department, while 108 authorities had the treasurer responsible for rent collection, rent accounting, arrears recovery and housing benefit.

The Audit Commission strongly advocated the creation of a single housing department and since the 1986 report local authorities have increasingly recognised the benefits to be obtained from having one department coordinating all housing activities. In 1993 the Centre for Housing Policy at the University of York found that a *truly* comprehensive housing department was still the exception rather than the norm. The research showed that only 29 per cent of local authorities had a separate housing department which carried out *all* housing management functions. On average 30 per cent of housing management work was carried out by departments other than housing.

The local authorities which were most likely to have a housing department carrying out most functions were those with the most properties. Indeed 85 per cent of local authorities with 30,000 properties carried out more than 70 per cent of housing management functions in the housing department alone compared to only 40 per cent of authorities with less than 5,000 units.

The Audit Commission in their 1986 report suggested that the department most likely to be involved in housing management activities outside of the housing department was that of the borough treasurer. Although the 1993 research reported that over 20 different types of local authority departments were involved with housing management it was clear that the treasurer's department was most likely to be undertaking some aspect of housing management work, being involved in 37 per cent of authorities in rent collection and in 17 per cent of authorities in arrears recovery. It was also the case that the treasurer's department was most likely to be involved in managing housing benefit for local authorities.

In most local authorities the key housing management functions of allocations, void control, rent collection and arrears recovery, are now carried out within a housing department. However, there is still a sizeable minority of local authorities where some of these key housing functions are not carried out by the housing department.

The organisation of housing association services

Most housing associations are very small compared to local authorities; a medium sized housing association will own between 1,000 and 2,500 homes, which of course would be considered small by local authority standards. There are significantly more housing associations than local authorities and within the housing association sector there is greater diversity in terms of the number of homes that associations manage, ranging from almshouses with perhaps a couple of homes to large national housing associations with over 30,000 homes in management. Many housing associations are not based in one geographical location, unlike local authorities, and associations may well operate in a number of local authority areas or even nationally, such as associations like Anchor Trust.

In contrast to local authorities some housing associations will specialise in meeting the housing needs of a particular client group rather than aiming to meet the housing needs of a general population, which is the normal remit for a local authority. For example, New Era housing association is a national housing association which concentrates on meeting the needs of people with learning difficulties.

Given these significant organisational differences between housing associations and local authorities it is not surprising that housing associations will deliver their housing service in a different way to local authorities. Perhaps the most significant difference is that housing associations are more likely to directly control all of their housing management services. Local authorities have a wide range of responsibilities to their local population and a number of different departments have been set up to meet these needs and some of these departments will carry out housing management responsibilities. A housing association, however, is established solely to provide housing services. It would be surprising therefore if key housing management functions were carried out by other organisations.

This was confirmed by the 1993 York research which showed that housing functions were unlikely to be outside of the direct administrative control of housing associations, with over 90 per cent of associations directly controlling rent collection and arrears recovery, void control, repairs and allocations. Some associations will of course have to contract out some of their work to outside agencies, while remaining in control of the work as the client. This may be because they do not have the staff or expertise within the association to carry out these functions. For example, the 1993 research showed that 47 per cent of associations employed an outside agency to administer at least one of their key functions, with services such as training, computer services and the management of special needs dwellings the most likely to have been contracted out to another body. The management of special needs dwellings is likely to have been contracted out by those associations which did not have the expertise in-house to manage such properties. The contracting out of training services may reflect the fact that many associations would not have the resources to employ their own training officers and would need to use outside agencies to undertake training. The contracting out of computer services may reflect the costs involved in maintaining a computer system and that it might be more appropriate for associations to purchase services from an outside agency.

The 1993 research suggested that this difference between local authority and housing associations reflects the different context in which they work:

> 'Housing departments exist within a relatively large bureaucracy with a great many functions, in which tasks outside the immediate expertise of the department may well be handled by specialists in another department. Housing associations are "housing only" organisations and may therefore be obliged to seek outside help with areas outside their main functions.' (York, 1993.)

6.4 Decentralisation of housing services

Introduction

One of the most important trends in housing management over recent years has been the decentralisation of housing services by both local authorities and housing associations. This trend towards the decentralisation of services has been encouraged by the housing profession, the Audit Commission, the Priority Estates Project among others, and this section will explore in more detail what is meant by decentralisation, the extent of decentralisation within local authorities and housing associations and the associated trend towards more generic working by housing managers where staff undertake a wider range of housing responsibilities.

The move to local housing management

In the 1980s there was an increasing recognition both within and outside of the profession, that housing management, particularly within local authorities, was in a crisis. Problems of rent arrears, difficult to let estates were all in the news. In the Audit Commission's influential report in 1986 the introduction started:

> '"Crisis" is a heavily over-worked word. Yet it is difficult to think of a more appropriate way to describe the state of much of the stock of ....council-owned dwellings in England and Wales.... . A combination of short-sighted national housing policies since the 1960s and shortcomings in local administration has produced a major management challenge in particular in many urban areas.' (Audit Commission, 1986b, p. 5.)

The crisis which the Audit Commission identified included problems such as:

- defective dwellings
- deteriorating stock

- shortages of housing for rent
- increases in homelessness
- low rents
- weak management control

In response to these problems a number of housing organisations had already taken positive steps to improve the way in which they managed their housing. Perhaps the most important of these was the move towards the decentralisation of housing management services. Although many housing professionals had long advocated the benefits of a more personal approach to housing management, not least of these being the Victorian housing reformer Octavia Hill, it was the case that the move towards more integrated housing departments tended to be accompanied by an increase in the number of staff based in town hall offices, rather than on estates.

Prior to the 1980s there had been a number of efforts to re-establish local housing management. In 1948 Leeds City Council decided to decentralise its housing management service through the establishment of a number of estate management offices (Cole *et al.*, 1991, pp. 147–148).

However it is widely acknowledged that the more recent trend towards the decentralisation of housing management began in the 1980s with decisions of some inner city local authorities, such as the London Borough of Islington and Walsall Metropolitan Council in the West Midlands, to set up local housing management offices. These initiatives were quickly emulated by a large number of other housing organisations and in particular the Priority Estates Project, originally a government-backed project established to look at best practice in managing difficult to let estates, advocated very strongly the establishment of local housing offices to deal with the worst estates.

Defining decentralised housing management

Whilst a large number of housing organisations have in recent years decentralised their housing services there is no agreed definition of a decentralised service. The following can all be features of a decentralised housing service.

A local management base

All decentralised housing management involves the delivery of some housing management services through a local, estate-based office, rather than through a central housing department based in the town hall or head office. In some cases almost all of the core housing management functions, such as rent collection, arrears recovery, lettings, void management and housing benefit administration are carried out from the local office. In other cases a much more limited service is offered, perhaps with the local office dealing with arrears and tenancy matters but with rent collection, housing benefit and lettings being carried out centrally.

Local decision making

Another common feature of decentralised housing management is the delegation of some decisions on housing management issues to housing managers based in local offices. For example, where allocations are devolved to a local housing office, the local housing manager will be able to decide who is allocated housing on the estate. This local control over decisions is also closely linked to control over resources. In some decentralised services local housing managers have control over some budgets, such as local repairs budgets, to enable them to provide a more responsive service to their customers.

Local political control and decision making

In a smaller number of housing organisations political or committee control over the housing service is decentralised. In some cases, for example, there may be an area housing committee which oversees work of the local housing office. This committee will often be given delegated powers by the main housing committee in respect of key housing management activities in their area.

This may also be linked to the greater involvement of tenants in the management of their estates at local level, which may take the form of residents associations which are consulted by the local housing manager or the direct representation of local residents on area housing committees.

Decentralisation can therefore include one or all of the following features:

- a local housing management base;
- local control of decisions and resources;
- local political control and tenant involvement.

In some cases decentralisation of housing services will amount to a local housing office being opened on an estate with responsibility for a very limited range of housing services. In other cases a local office will be established carrying out the full range of housing management services, with control over a sizeable budget and with an area committee which exercises political control over the housing service in the area.

The extent of decentralisation of services

Those who advocate the adoption of decentralised housing management believe that it leads to improvements to housing management services and performance. Staff who are working from a local office are more likely to be responsive to problems on their estates with the service being far more accessible to tenants.

In their 1993 research the Centre for Housing Policy at the University of York found that a large number of local authorities had decentralised some of their housing services to local offices. Indeed 59 per cent of local authorities had local offices with larger local authorities more likely to have decentralised their services. Ninety-one per cent of local authorities with a stock of between 10,000 and 20,000 and all of those with a stock of over 20,000 had established local offices. In smaller authorities with 5,000 or less properties only 26 per cent had decentralised some of their housing service. This difference is likely to reflect the fact that in smaller local authorities the problems of managing their stock may be less acute and also they may find it more difficult to provide the resources to deliver a local housing service.

The larger local authorities were more likely to have more severe problems and also access to the resources necessary to establish a network of local housing offices. The York study looked at the extent to which local offices carried out the key housing management functions, with an index being constructed for each authority on the extent of decentralisation of each of its housing management activities. They found that only 3 per cent of authorities had fully decentralised more than half of their key housing management activities to their local housing offices. Of the remainder, 25 per cent had decentralised between a third and half of their housing management and a further 26 per cent had decentralised up to a third of their functions.

Again there was a significant difference found between those local authorities with a large housing stock and those with a small housing stock. Only 8 per cent of those local authorities with less than 5,000 dwellings had a high level of decentralisation compared to 86 per cent of the larger authorities.

Decentralisation and housing associations

As was noted earlier most housing associations are small with only eleven housing associations in England with over 10,000 dwelling in 1994. It would not be surprising therefore if the pattern of decentralisation of services was significantly different for housing associations as compared to local authorities. Unlike local authorities which have all of their stock in one local authority district many of the larger housing associations will operate over a number of local authority areas and a key question for housing managers in these associations is how best to deliver the service. If an association has a substantial stock holding in a particular area or town it may be possible for the association to open a local office to provide the key housing services to their tenants in the area. However, if the stock is scattered or if there is insufficient stock in an area it will not be cost effective to establish a separate housing office.

For example, a small housing association with only 500 properties in a particular town is likely to have only one housing office. However, a larger national association like Anchor Trust will provide its services through a network of regional offices throughout the country. Although these large national associations may have a number of regional offices they are unlikely to provide local, estate-based offices, in the same way as local authorities. This is largely because most housing associations do not have large estates in one small area.

The York study found that 46 per cent of associations had only a central office. Like the local authorities it was the larger housing associations which were more likely to have decentralised services to local offices, with 88 per cent of housing associations with more than 3,000 homes having established a local office.

How successful has decentralised housing management been?

Many housing organisations have decentralised their housing management service in order to improve their performance in the key housing management tasks. The leading advocate of decentralised housing management has been the Priority Estates

Project (PEP). This was originally set up as a consultancy by the Department of the Environment in 1979 to advise on how to improve the management of difficult-to-let estates. The Priority Estates Project believes that the concept of local housing management is derived from the work of Octavia Hill in the nineteenth century, with a housing manager responsible for all aspects of the housing management service in a particular area. The Priority Estates Project advised a number of local authorities in the 1980s and 1990s on decentralised housing management and they indicated that there were ten key elements to successful local housing management:

- a local office
- local repairs service
- local lettings procedure
- local rent arrears control
- estate budgets
- resident caretakers for flatted estates
- tenant participation
- coordination and liaison with other services
- monitoring performance
- training

In 1987, PEP reported on the performance of nine estates where they had been working (Priority Estates Project, 1987). This report showed that in most of the nine projects there had been a significant improvement in performance in key areas such as:

- fewer empty dwellings
- improved repairs
- cleaner environment
- more tenant involvement
- reduced crime and vandalism
- rent arrears reduction
- quality of dwellings

In five of the projects there had also been a lower turnover of tenants.

This report showed quite clearly that there had been improvements in performance on these difficult-to-let estates and in addition PEP suggested there was much greater job satisfaction amongst staff which also manifested itself in reduced levels of staff turnover. With the improvement in performance and greater tenant involvement it was found that there were high levels of tenant satisfaction with the housing service.

In 1995 Anne Power of the Priority Estates Project together with Rebecca Tunstall published a further report which looked at 20 difficult-to-let estates over a period from 1978 to 1995. This research, entitled *Swimming against the Tide: Progress or Polarisation on 20 Unpopular Estates*, showed that local housing management had played a significant part in improving the conditions on the estates. Research showed that the physical conditions of the areas had improved as a result of both local management and the improved targeting of resources to estates by central and local government, together with the requirements of many of these funding regimes for local management and community involvement. Even though the process of residualisation (where council estates increasingly housed the very poorest in society) had accelerated, the report did confirm the earlier Priority Estates Project study that local management had led to an improvement in the performance of core housing management activities: voids had fallen on the whole, rent arrears had fallen generally, estates were now kept cleaner and local repairs budgets had improved the way in which repairs service operated.

The report concluded that the improvement in the popularity of estates was largely due to the efforts of local housing staff and residents and that the local management together with resident involvement had resulted in improvements in key housing management areas. However, in order to maintain conditions the estates needed a housing staff with the ability to control the management of their estates in permanent local offices.

6.5 Development of generic housing management

Introduction

One of the almost inevitable results of decentralising services to local housing offices is the requirement for housing staff based in these offices to take on a wider range of responsibilities. In centralised housing departments there may well be a separate lettings section, repairs section, housing benefits section and rent section, all of which will have staff who specialise in their particular activity. A small local office with perhaps six or seven staff providing services to 2,000-plus properties will be unable to specialise to the same extent and staff will be required to undertake a wider range of housing management functions.

One of the features therefore of local housing management has been the development of the housing officer with a range of skills and knowledge about all of the key housing management activities: the generic housing manager. In many respects this is a return to the estate management tradition advocated by Octavia Hill where a housing officer would be responsible for all of the housing management activities relating to an individual tenancy but it needs to be recognised that this development places additional pressures on housing staff.

If staff are to undertake a wider range of functions it is essential that the organisation has in place effective staff training and development programmes to equip staff to undertake this mode of working. Clear policies and procedures should be in place for all aspects of work to ensure that services are delivered in an effective and equitable manner. Given that staff may also be under significant pressure to deliver services in their local office the need for effective information technology systems and support from managers is also crucial.

The Department of Environment in their efficiency report on housing management training said that 'the pressures on staff were graphically evident from visits to estate offices...these impressions are given statistical support in the Glasgow study [on the efficiency and effectiveness of housing management in England] where – in an interesting and important finding– it emerged that some 44 per cent of staff in metropolitan authorities believed that they were expected to carry out too wide a range of functions' (Department of Environment, 1990). This finding was echoed by the Managing Social Housing report in 1993, where about half of the staff interviewed found themselves overstretched mentally and physically by their work (York, 1993).

If these problems are to be avoided and organisations are to maximise the benefits to be obtained from generic working it is essential that managers ensure that staff are properly trained and supported.

6.6 Compulsory competitive tendering of housing management

Introduction

In July 1991 the government published a White Paper on the Citizens' Charter in which it outlined some initial proposals to extend the compulsory competitive tendering (CCT) regime for local authorities to include housing management. A more detailed consultation paper *Competing for Quality in Housing* was issued in June 1992 which set out in greater detail the government's proposals for the introduction of compulsory competitive tendering into housing management (Department of Environment, 1992).

Under the CCT regulations, 95 per cent of certain housing management activities (defined activities) must be included in a housing management contract which should be let by means of a competitive tender, where the local authority's in-house bid must be considered alongside the bids of competing prospective landlords. The CCT contracts must cover 95 per cent of the defined activities, although other activities (non-defined) may be included if a local authority so chooses.

Defined activities

The defined activities as set out in the CCT regulations cover the following housing management tasks:

- rents and service charges
- collecting rent and service charges and dealing with arrears
- letting of properties
- dealing with applications after allocations have been made and exchanges
- vacant properties
- taking tenancy terminations
- inspection of voids and arranging repairs
- preventing vandalism of voids
- managing tenancies
- enforcing tenancy conditions
- dealing with illegal occupants

- dealing with neighbour disputes
- repairs and maintenance
- assessing repair requests and ensuring works are carried out
- carrying out stock condition surveys
- assessing the right to repair claims for compensation
- assessing claims for compensation under the right to improve
- caretaking and concierge services
- assessing the condition of common areas and arranging necessary works
- operating reception and security services

Non-defined activities

These include all housing related activities which are not defined under the regulations and could encompass all of the following:

- allocations of housing
- welfare benefits advice
- waiting list administration
- housing aid
- reporting and referring general non-housing enquiries to relevant agencies
- sheltered housing
- warden call alarm services
- homeless administration
- management of temporary accommodation
- client agency role in grounds maintenance contracts
- assessment of housing benefits

The first set of contracts were let from April 1996 in England with the bidding process taking place during the months leading up to it. A detailed timetable for letting of all housing management contracts has been set by the government depending on the size of the local authority and whether or not they are included in local government reorganisation.

The impact of housing management CCT on the organisation of housing services

Compulsory competitive tendering will inevitably affect the way in which local authorities deliver their housing service. As a result of the introduction of CCT three distinct roles have been required which will influence organisational structures and service delivery within local authorities. These three roles are:

- client role
- contractor role
- non-contractor role

The client and contractor roles are not unfamiliar to housing organisations. As was seen in Chapter 4 on Developing Social Housing all new development activity involves clients and contractors.

Client role

With CCT there is a need for local housing authority to have a client function. This function is responsible for drawing up the specification for the housing management contracts, supervising and administering the tendering process, awarding the contract and monitoring the performance of the successful contractor.

As a result of the introduction of CCT many local housing authorities have established a separate client unit in the housing department to undertake this role and even a cursory look at job advertisements in housing magazines will show that a significant number of new positions have been created in housing authorities to perform this client function.

The process of preparing housing management specifications requires all housing authorities to think carefully about the housing services that they provide and the way in which those services are delivered. For many authorities this has enabled a thorough review of housing management policies and practices to be undertaken and for consideration to have been given to different ways of carrying out the services.

Contractor role

Under CCT a contractor will be appointed following a competitive tender to undertake the defined activities as set out in the housing management contract. In many cases the local authority's in-house team will win the contract and will perform this role, but in other cases it will be undertaken by an external contractor who has won the contract.

Because of the importance of winning the contract many local authorities have restructured their housing services to establish a separate contractor section within the housing department which will bid for CCT contracts. This will act as a service delivery arm of the housing authority and will enable the authority to have a clear client/contractor split within its staffing structures. Contractor sections have been established to undertake all of the activities within the housing management contract. Staff who work in the contractor section need to acquire a range of new skills in:

- understanding contract conditions and specifications;
- writing method statements;
- performing to a detailed contract with penalty clauses;
- performing the contract to the agreed price;
- negotiating variations to the contract;
- budgeting and cash management.

This is in addition to the actual delivery of housing management services. These are new skills for many housing managers and the skills required reflect very much the skills which private sector contractors have acquired over a number of years. Indeed some local housing authorities, such as Sunderland City Council, have gone as far as referring to their housing managers as business unit managers.

The development of separate contractor units has had a significant impact on the way in which housing departments are structured as it is now fairly common to see housing authorities with:

- a separate client unit;
- a contractor unit;
- a unit undertaking activities which are not part of the main housing management CCT contract (such as homelessness or warden call services).

The desire for local authorities to win housing management contracts may also have an impact on local service delivery. Of course many local authorities who wish to maintain the benefits of local housing management have written contract specifications in such a way that the service continues to be provided through local decentralised offices. Others have taken the view that their current decentralised structures are too expensive and have sought to rationalise the service in order to ensure they can deliver a more cost-effective service. There is also a danger that the new business culture required of CCT may make the housing service less accessible to customers if contract managers refuse to undertake tasks which are not written specifically into the contract. Although this is unlikely to happen if the contract is won by the in-house team, because they still remain under the control of the local authority, there is a real risk of this happening if contracts are lost to external contractors.

Non-contract role

There still remain tasks which are not to be performed under the housing management contract and the authority will need to decide how these will be done. In some cases the work may be given to a separate non-contractor team within the authority. For example, a number of local authorities will not be including allocations and homelessness work within their CCT contract and this may be done by a separate allocations team within the authority and outside of the CCT contract.

Alternatively, the work may be given to the successful contractor after the main contract has been awarded. This of course is less likely to happen if the contract is won by an external contractor. In other cases local authorities have decided to include such non-defined activities within their housing management contract because they wish to obtain the benefits of a single contract providing for a range of housing services offered by the authority.

As can be seen the introduction of CCT may change significantly the way in which the housing service is delivered by a housing authority. At the very least it requires new roles to be performed and there are a variety of organisational responses possible to this. In the larger authorities where there may be a number of CCT contracts there is a possibility of different contractors providing the housing management service in the area and this will inevitably complicate the way in which the service is delivered. There are real concerns that this may lead to a fragmentation of service delivery in which the service to the customer is worsened. A further example of this problem is whether or not to include non-defined activities as part of the CCT contract.

Many authorities have attempted in the past to establish a comprehensive housing service, where most housing functions are organised in one department (including rent collection and arrears recovery, allocations, repairs and maintenance client roles, housing strategy, homelessness, housing benefits) and further that these services should be delivered through a network of local offices so that the customer coming in to one of the offices should be able to access the full range of housing services. However, if only the defined activities are included in the contract then there is a possibility for fragmentation of the services with some activities being carried out within the contract and the remainder by the client unit or possibly by the contractor (but outside of the formal housing management contract). This may lead to a confusion of roles and may mean that customers will be dealing with both the client and the contractor for their key housing services. However, the inclusion of non-defined activities in the housing management contract or adding such non-defined activities to the work undertaken by the successful contractor means that only one contractor is required to provide a fuller range of housing services and appears to be more compatible with the concept of a comprehensive approach to housing service delivery.

For elected members CCT also affects the way in which they are involved in the delivery of housing services. Under CCT they are very much involved in the decisions about the specification of the housing service to be provided and decisions about the way in which the organisation should structure itself to meet the challenges of CCT. They are also involved in the monitoring of the successful contract but elected members will be less involved in the day-to-day delivery of the housing services as this will now be left to the contractor, which in some cases may be a private sector firm external to the local authority. For those authorities where elected members have been more heavily involved in the day-to-day work of the housing service CCT may lead to significant changes in the way in which elected members are involved in the management of the housing service.

6.7 Involving tenants in the management of the housing service

Introduction

The extent to which tenants are involved in the management of housing services varies from landlord to landlord, from a situation where tenant involvement is at the legal minimum to housing cooperatives where tenants fully control and manage all aspects of their housing stock.

Statutory requirements

The legislation relating to the involvement of tenants in housing management is fairly weak as under the Housing Act 1985 local authorities and housing associations are only required to consult their secure tenants on a limited range of housing management matters.

Section 105 of the 1985 Housing Act requires landlords of secure tenants in England and Wales to consult them on changes to certain housing management practices or policies (with the significant exception of changes to rents and service charges).

Consultation is not defined in the legislation but will involve the landlord seeking the views of tenants affected by the change and the landlord considering the views of tenants before making any final decision on a matter subject to consultation. In addition, landlords of secure tenants have to publish details of their consultation arrangements and make these available to tenants on request.

For housing association assured tenants there is no statutory requirement for consultation. Under the *Tenants' Guarantee*, however, housing associations are required to consult with tenants before making a:

'decision about proposed changes in management and maintenance policy or practice which may affect a substantial proportion or number of tenants. Opportunities should be given to tenants to exercise genuine influence over the service that they receive.' (Housing Corporation, 1994a.)

The Tenants' Guarantee makes it clear that associations should consider the views of tenants expressed in the consultation process and that tenants should be subsequently informed about how their views were taken into account.

The Tenants' Guarantee also requires associations to help and encourage representative tenant organisations, including the provision of reasonable facilities for meetings and the provision of information about the association's performance. Associations are also required to provide opportunities to enable tenants to participate in the management of their association of the estate or group of dwellings of which they are tenants and the design of new developments.

The ladder of involvement

Although the legislation only requires housing organisations to consult tenants, tenants may be involved in the management of the housing at a variety of different levels. Indeed this involvement can work at a number of different levels ranging over:

- information giving
- tenant consultation
- tenant participation
- tenant control

Information giving

Working with tenants at this level involves providing them with more information about the housing service, the standards they can expect and the levels of services to be provided. This information might be given in the form of newsletters, leaflets and other publications or it might be in the form of resident meetings or one-to-one communication.

Tenant consultation

This involves housing officers actively seeking the views of tenants on housing issues. Tenants might be consulted, for example, about a change to allocations policy or rent-setting policy. Consultation involves a commitment to ask tenants what they think but involves no commitment to fully take account of their views. But it does enable tenants, usually through surveys, meetings or face-to-face communication, to influence the housing service which is provided.

Tenant participation

With tenant participation tenants are actively involved in the decision-making process. They may not have the ability to decide every issue but they will have a real voice in decision making. For example, a form of participation might include tenant representatives sitting on an area housing committee with a vote and a true voice in the proceedings, or it might be seen in an estate committee, where residents have control over a small improvements budget. Where tenant participation occurs tenants have a real influence over the decision-making process.

Tenant control

This involves tenants controlling most or all aspects of their housing service. There are a number of models of tenant control which can be seen in Britain today. In estate management boards residents control most aspects of the housing service on their estate and usually employ staff directly. In housing cooperatives tenants are shareholding members of their cooperative housing association and are fully responsible for the housing service which the cooperative, as landlord, provides. In some cases cooperative members may undertake the housing management work themselves or they may employ staff directly or indirectly, through a secondary housing cooperative to provide the housing service.

Tenant involvement is now a feature of most housing organisations, although the extent of that involvement does vary. However, involving tenants in the management of the housing services is a relatively recent phenomenon and as late as 1977 the Green Paper on Housing Policy proposed a new Tenants' Charter which would encourage tenant participation in housing. The ideas as set out in the 1977 Green Paper were eventually incorporated into the 1980 Housing Act in the Tenants' Charter but the extent of tenant involvement was limited to a requirement for consultation rather than participation or control.

Under the 1988 Housing Act (1988 Housing (Scotland) Act) council tenants were given the right under the Tenants' Choice legislation to transfer their homes to a new landlord. At the time this legislation was passed there was an expectation from government that large numbers of dissatisfied council tenants would vote to transfer to a new landlord. However, in practice very few such transfers have taken place but one of the interesting effects of the 1988 Act was to force many local authorities to consider more seriously ways of improving their communication with tenants and involving them more actively in the management of their homes. The 1996 Housing Act abolishes the tenants choice provisions which were originally included in the 1988 Housing Act.

Estate management boards and housing cooperatives

Whilst many tenants are happy simply to receive information from the landlord and to be consulted by the landlord on changes to housing management policy and practice there have been a number of models established through which tenants can exercise much greater control over their housing.

Where estate management boards are established, tenants control the housing management and maintenance of their estate by involvement in an estate management board which is a legally constituted organisation which undertakes the management of an estate from a local authority under the terms of a management agreement. Through the estate management board model residents control the management of their estate with much of the day-to-day management being undertaken by paid staff.

Housing Cooperatives

One of the more advanced forms of tenant participation and control is through the establishment of housing cooperatives. A housing cooperative consists of a group of tenants who come together to form a legal entity which manages and in some cases owns the houses in which the tenants live. Most cooperatives are registered as housing associations and subject to the scrutiny of the Housing Corporation (Scottish Homes, Tai Cymru). There are a number of different forms of housing cooperative including:

Par value cooperatives

This is a cooperative in which the shareholding members who are normally tenants or prospective tenants only hold a one pound financial stake in the cooperative. The homes in which they live are owned collectively by the cooperative of which they are shareholding members. As the cooperative is the landlord all housing management functions are undertaken by the cooperative and in many cases housing management tasks are delegated to individual cooperative members, such as collecting the rents and arranging repairs. However, as this poses an additional burden on tenant members many housing cooperatives have decided to employ paid staff themselves to carry out the day-to-day housing management work under the direction of cooperative members or have employed another housing association or secondary housing cooperative to provide such services under the terms of a management agreement.

Tenant management cooperatives

A tenant management cooperative is normally constituted in much the same way as a par value cooperative with the difference that the cooperative only manages and does not own the homes of the tenants. For example, the Langridge Crescent tenant management cooperative in Middlesbrough was initially established when the local authority agreed to transfer the management of a small estate to the tenant management cooperative. Under the terms of the management agreement between the local authority and the cooperative, the cooperative undertakes certain housing management and maintenance functions on behalf of the local authority and receives a fee from the authority for undertaking this work.

Although most tenant management cooperatives have been established on local authority estates there are a number of examples where housing associations have transferred the management of some of their estates to tenant management cooperatives under the terms of a managementıagreement.

The impact of tenant involvement on the delivery of housing services

There are many ways in which tenants have been involved in changing the ways in which organisation delivers their housing services and the organisational forms they have established to provide housing services. Some of this influence will come through the consultation process where tenants' views will affect the work of the organisation.

However, the more significant impact comes where tenants have a direct say in service delivery either through their participation in tenant forums, areas committees or through cooperatives. In these situations tenants can have a very real influence in the service which is delivered and the distribution of available resources amongst competing priorities.

The York study found that tenant participation was still *relatively undeveloped* among many social landlords, with the lowest levels of tenant participation occurring in the smaller non-urban organisations (York, 1993).

6.8 The impact of care in the community on the delivery of housing services

Introduction

In the 1980s there were a number of reports published about how best to meet the care needs of vulnerable persons, the most important of which was the Griffiths Report, *Community Care: Agenda for Action*, HMSO, 1988. This report showed how services for vulnerable people were fragmented with no single agency assuming full responsibility for the care needs of individuals and that there was often conflict and confusion between the various agencies involved in care services such as the health service, the local authority social services department and housing department and private or voluntary sector agencies. However, at the same time there was also a concern about the costs of residential care and nursing care, the bulk of which was being funded through the social security system and much of which was provided by private sector care homes. This generated worries that large numbers of dependent and vulnerable people were entering residential care and nursing care at high cost to the state when a more appropriate and cost effective solution might have been to provide domiciliary care services in their own home.

The government largely supported the conclusions of the Griffiths Report and in the White Paper of 1989 *Caring for People; Community Care in the next Decade and Beyond*, the government set a number of key objectives in relation to care in the community.

- Dependent people should be able to live as normal a life as possible in the community with the right amount of care and support to achieve independence.

- Dependent people should be able to stay in their own homes for as long as possible.
- Dependent people should have a greater say about the services they needed with more choice available to them.

The government also accepted that the local social services authority should be given the lead responsibility to provide community care services and these principles were included in the National Health Service and Community Care Act of 1990 which came into effect in 1993. Under this legislation social service authorities became the lead agency responsible for meeting social care needs in their areas and in addition had responsibilities to produce and publish community care plans after consultation with health authorities, housing authorities, community care service users and other interested parties.

The key feature of the 1990 Act was that social services were responsible for assessing the care needs of individuals and designing packages of care which met the users' assessed needs taking account of the need to ensure value for money.

'The concept of care in the community has been supported by all parties for 30 years, although with little clarity as to what this actually meant. In general terms, the concept reflects a move away from the provision of care from large institutional settings where people who were mentally ill, or who had learning disabilities, or physical disabilities or who were old were taken to receive care. This model of care took people with high dependency needs away from their own communities to isolated and segregated settings.' (Platt, 1995.)

A key thrust of the government's care in the community reforms has therefore been a switch in emphasis away from institutional care to the provision of more domiciliary, day care and respite care to enable individuals to live in their homes in the community. One of the more dramatic results of this policy change has been the closure of a large number of long-stay beds in hospitals which were previously occupied by people with mental health problems or learning disabilities in particular and the transfer of these individuals into the community to much smaller registered care homes or nursing homes.

Housing and community care

As more and more individuals no longer receive care services in large institutions then suitable alternative accommodation has to be provided for these individuals, often by local authorities or housing associations or the private/voluntary sector. Indeed in recent years a significant development has been the growth in small registered care homes providing housing and care services for perhaps 6–12 individuals who might previously have lived in a long-stay hospital.

In addition, with the emphasis on enabling individuals to remain in their own homes, it has been increasingly necessary to ensure that accommodation is made more suitable to the needs of individuals who might find it difficult to cope with their existing accommodation. For example, as the elderly become more infirm it may become necessary to provide a range of aids and adaptations to enable them to remain living at home, such as the provision of ramps, handrails and walk-in showers.

The impact of community care: how housing services are organised

Under the community care legislation the lead organisations for community care are the social services authorities. However, in any community care package the provision of suitable accommodation has to be a key component and as such housing authorities and housing associations both have important roles to play in the successful implementation of the community care programme.

A number of the larger local authorities have established separate community care sections within the housing department which have a responsibility for liaising with their social services colleagues on both the community care plan and the provision of accommodation to meet the needs as set out in the·community care planning process. Within housing associations there has also been a significant expansion in the provision of accommodation for people with special needs and associations have been required to establish much closer links with social services colleagues than was the case prior to the implementation of the 1990 Act.

At the operational level housing officers in both local authorities and housing associations have been required to develop a greater understanding of the workings of the community care legislation. They may be required to liaise with social workers who are seeking to find more appropriate accommodation for their clients moving from long-stay hospitals or housing officers may be required to investigate funding for possible adaptations to enable individuals to remain within their own homes. Indeed in some areas housing staff are now involved in the care assessment process undertaken by social workers.

Further reading

Department of the Environment (1989) *The Nature and Effectiveness of Housing Management in England*, HMSO, London.

Housing Services Advisory Group (1978) *Organising a Comprehensive Housing Service*, Department of the Environment, London.

Windle, K., Cole, I. and Arnold, P. (1988) *Research Working Papers 1–5, Housing Decentralisation Research Project*, Sheffield City Polytechnic, Sheffield.

Chapter 7

THE CHANGING FACE OF SOCIAL HOUSING

7.1 Introduction

The previous six chapters of this book have examined the evolution and role of social housing in the United Kingdom and analysed the work which housing managers do in relation to finance, development and housing management. Although these areas have been dealt with in separate chapters we have tried to highlight throughout the book that the task of managing social housing requires the integration of a wide range of skills and knowledge. For example, the successful development of a new housing scheme requires housing managers to have a thorough grasp of development, finance and management issues in order to address and answer all of the complex issues which have to be resolved.

As explored in the earlier chapters of the book, social housing has been affected by significant changes over the last decade and a half, with the result that the role of different providers has been changing substantially. This, in turn, has had an impact on the job of the housing manager. This final chapter integrates some of the issues raised in earlier chapters, to explore their combined effects and to consider their current and likely future impact on social housing providers and their tenants, creating new and emerging issues for housing managers. Our choice of issues is necessarily selective, but few commentators would disagree about their significance for social housing.

7.2 Increasing investment in the social housing stock: is tenure transfer the answer?

In Chapter 3 on housing finance we saw that social housing organisations are facing increasing restrictions on their ability to finance their activities. Local authorities have long been subject to restrictions on their capital expenditure and in recent years this has meant that new building by local authorities has ground to a halt and has prevented almost all local authorities themselves building homes to meet the needs of their communities. The housing association sector has not obtained sufficient

SHG/HAG to build all of the homes it would like. The result of these restrictions is that the volume of new house building for rent has fallen and has not been sufficient to compensate for the homes which have been lost from the social housing sector because of the right to buy. The restrictions on finance have also had an impact on the ability of social housing landlords to keep the stock they continue to hold in good repair, meaning that billions of pounds are still needed to bring the existing social housing stock up to acceptable standards. These problems have led local authorities to seek other ways of obtaining funding both to renovate existing stock and to build new housing and, recently, attention has focused increasingly on tenure transfer as an option to obtain additional resources. Tenure transfer policies are not new, and this section explores some of the different manifestations of tenure transfer in the United Kingdom since 1980 and their effects and implications for social housing.

Tenure transfer

Policies to encourage tenure transfer have probably had a greater impact on social housing provision than any other type of housing policy in recent years. As examined in earlier chapters, recent government policies have emphasised the *enabling* role of local authorities rather than their role as *providers* of social housing. There has been a continuing preference for private tenures, especially owner occupation. This resulted in new approaches to subsidising housing, conditional on a requirement to transfer tenure. In general, these initiatives were intended both to encourage the transfer of social housing tenants to owner occupation, and to encourage council tenants in particular to transfer to another rented tenure. There would simultaneously be more owner occupiers and fewer council tenants.

There are a number of quite different transfer policies, which vary by:

- the transfer tenure (the tenure to be transferred to);
- who and what transfers (only the *tenant*, or the tenant and the *property*);
- the target tenure (which tenure it is directed at).

However, over time, another significant distinction has emerged. This is whether the transfer is

- household initiated (the tenant, or prospective tenant, must initiate transfer);

or

- landlord initiated (generally, a local authority landlord, which encourages its tenants to agree to transfer).

This distinction has arisen, in part, because when the momentum of earlier government transfer policies seemed in danger of being lost – when, for example, sales through right to buy declined – the government was forced to consider new ways to encourage transfer.

It has also arisen as a result of local authorities' concerns about the detrimental impact of finance policies on the type and condition of their social housing stock, as well as on the type of households accommodated. They have been forced to consider a range of alternative approaches, which have resulted in the transfer of stock from local authority control.

The next section describes some of the main tenure transfer policies since 1980, and analyses their implications for social housing.

Tenure transfer policies

Household initiated

(i) Transfer to owner occupation by social sector property and tenant

The *right to buy* policy was the first and most significant attempt by the government to encourage council tenants to become owner occupiers. As examined in earlier chapters, it was introduced in the 1980 Housing Act (Housing Act (Scotland) 1980), offering substantial discounts on the market value of the property for existing council tenants. Over time, the discounts were increased (to a maximum of 70 per cent for flats) to encourage further purchases.

Right to buy sales to council tenants peaked in 1989 when, for example, there were sales of:

- 144,754 dwellings by English councils
- 12,753 by Welsh councils
- 38,713 by Scottish councils

By 1994, however, these were down to 43,992, 3,130 and 20,628 annually respectively (Wilcox, 1996).

Between 1980 and 1994, a total of 1,528,958 council homes in Britain had been sold through right to buy. In the United Kingdom as a whole, the stock of council housing diminished by 26.5 per cent between 1981 and 1993 (Wilcox, 1996). This means, of course, that fewer properties will become available for future as well as current council housing applicants, since a declining stock will usually cause a reduction in the annual supply of vacant properties.

An analysis by Forrest and Murie in 1988, *Selling the Welfare State*, identified that, in general, sales were highest:

- In localities where existing proportions of owner occupiers were high and council tenure low, so tenure differences between localities were being exaggerated by the policy.
- When tenants had higher than average incomes, so reducing the proportions of these households in council tenure.
- To households in work, predominantly skilled manual or higher paid occupations, leaving rising proportions of low paid or unemployed local authority tenants.
- Where houses were the main form of provision, because most purchases were of houses. This results in declining proportions of this more desired form of council housing.

Their analysis indicated that the right to buy transfer policy had accelerated the process of *residualisation* of council tenure, a process which:

> 'concentrates the least well off and least powerful sections of the population in the remaining, least desirable parts of the publicly rented stock.' (Malpass and Murie, 1994, p. 13.)

There is a view that the process of residualisation simply indicates that councils are, rightly, concentrating on housing those who most need their help. However, in response, Peter Malpass has argued:

> 'Residualisation matters because it is a threat to social cohesion. It promotes divisions in society and exacerbates social inequality. It reinforces the disadvantage that is generated elsewhere, in the education system and the labour market.' (Malpass, 1996, p. 14.)

A later *rent to mortgage* scheme was introduced by the 1993 Leasehold Reform, Housing and Urban Development Act to attract households unable to afford the full mortgage costs of a right to buy purchase, but this has stimulated little interest from council tenants.

Tenants of non-charitable housing associations were also given the right to buy by the 1980 Acts (with some exceptions, such as schemes for the elderly). However, with the introduction of *assured* tenancies for housing association tenants in the 1988 Housing Act, new association tenants lost this right (though old tenants, on housing association secure tenancies – subject to rent controls – retained it). This was because, as examined in Chapter 3, new association developments post-1988 were funded partly by private borrowing and private lenders would not wish to see their security, in the form of the dwellings, sold off cheaply.

However, under the Housing Act 1996, a *voluntary purchase grant* (VPG) scheme was introduced for association tenants, reinstating a right to buy similar to local authority tenants. Housing associations which take part in the VPG scheme will not have to refund any HAG paid on the property, so this will it is hoped reassure private lenders that their security remains intact. However, housing associations which develop in rural areas were concerned about the effects that this policy could have on their abilities to continue to offer provision in rural areas. It could also affect the availability of land for future developments, because, in some cases, they are able to obtain land cheaply from local landowners on the understanding that the properties will be made available only to local people in housing need. As a result, properties in small villages (with fewer than 3,000 inhabitants) have been exempted.

(ii) Transfer to owner occupation by social sector tenant (actual or potential)

Policies to permit tenants to move into a different property in owner-occupied tenure, or to occupy a property built by an association as part-owners, have become more important as right to buy sales have declined. For example, in 1995/6, the Housing Corporation – the funding body for English housing associations – allocated 31 per cent of capital funds to ownership initiatives. These are of the following two main types, full ownership schemes and part (or shared) ownership schemes.

Full ownership schemes These schemes offer a cash grant to tenants to permit them to move from housing association or council tenure and buy a private sector home.

The grant reduces the cost of purchase for the ex-tenant, so permitting them to take a smaller loan and have lower repayments. Housing association tenants have the *tenants' incentive scheme* (TIS), while council tenants may be offered a *cash incentive scheme* (CIS). These schemes are intended to 'free up' existing social sector homes for new, priority tenants. Since they provide properties for new tenants *which would not otherwise be available*, at a much lower price than the cost of building a new property, they are considered by the government to offer good value. However, they do not result in any *additional* homes being produced, and the stock of both public and private sector housing in the area remains the same.

Part (or shared) ownership schemes Part (or *shared*) ownership schemes apply only to housing association tenure. The new shared-owner can select the initial proportion to buy (from a choice of fixed proportions), and will then pay:

- a mortgage repayment, on the loan for the purchased share of the property;
- a rent payment to the housing association, for the rented share.

There are a number of different types of shared-ownership schemes. *Do it yourself shared ownership* (DIYSO) permits a tenant (or prospective tenant) to select a home on the private market, subject to cost limitations and requirements about the condition of the property. The property therefore shifts, at least temporarily, into part-social ownership, with a new shared owner who might otherwise be housed in housing association rented tenure.

With *conventional shared ownership* schemes (SO), the housing association generally builds new properties specifically for part-sale. There are also special schemes offering *shared ownership for the elderly* (formerly called leasehold schemes for the elderly).

All shared ownership schemes (except for shared ownership for the elderly) must permit *staircasing*, i.e. the part-owner can progressively buy a larger share of the property. However, the schemes do not permit staircasing in the opposite direction; part-owners cannot *reduce* their share. This has created problems for shared owners who find themselves in reduced financial circumstances, perhaps due to unemployment. Like full owners with mortgages, they face the risk of repossession by the private lender (usually a building society) and possible homelessness. Under the terms of their private mortgage, the financial institution has 'first call' on the property, leaving the housing association with little influence in these circumstances.

(iii) Transfer to other rented tenures by council tenant and property
These policies have been included as household initiated transfers, because they are not initiated by the landlord – the local authority. However, some transfers of this type may be initiated by another, third party, such as a housing association or the government, but they have to find favour with each individual tenant.

The possibility of council tenants transferring their properties to another landlord was introduced in the 1988 Housing Act. Under *Tenant's Choice*, tenants had to be balloted and agree the transfer, though there was some disquiet about the regulatory role of the housing associations' statutory funding bodies in this, because usually the proposed new landlord would be an association. In the event, the policy was largely unsuccessful, and it was abolished by the 1996 Housing Act.

At the same time, *housing action trusts* (HATs) were planned for a few run-down urban council estates, identified by the government in specific areas, such as in Lambeth, Sunderland and Leeds. With tenant agreement, it was proposed that a private sector trust would take over their council housing, and would receive very large amounts of public funding to rehabilitate the estates. The trusts were to be time limited, when the dwellings would pass to other private landlords. In the event, however, the policy generated significant hostility from tenants. Initially, it was proposed that a simple majority of *voting* tenants was sufficient to secure transfer – even if a majority had not voted. However, this was amended after many protests. The switch to the need for a majority of all tenants to vote in favour of a HAT resulted in universal rejection of the proposals. Generally, tenants seemed unwilling to leave the security of council tenure.

The lessons of these failed attempts to persuade tenants to transfer out of council ownership into another rented tenure were not lost on the government; it became clear that these policies were unlikely to meet with success without the support of the local authority landlord.

Landlord-initiated voluntary transfers

(i) Transfer to a HAT by council tenant and property

As a result of the defeat of the original HAT proposals, the policy was later amended to become, in effect, a landlord-initiated transfer policy. The local authority in Hull, attracted by the large sums of money offered to fund HATs, were able to persuade the Department of the Environment (DoE) that tenants should be able to choose to opt *back* into council tenure at the end of the trust's life. This promise helped Hull City council to persuade tenants on part of one estate that it was in their interests to vote to become a HAT. A number of other local authorities have since followed Hull's lead and persuaded tenants to agree to a HAT, with the next approvals including estates in Waltham Forest, Birmingham and Liverpool. By 1994/5, expenditure on these few HATs had risen to £89 million. However, HATs have recently been subjected to planned funding cutbacks by the DoE. At the time of writing (1997), no HAT had reached the end of its operational period, so the outcome remains, as yet, uncertain.

(ii) Transfer to a housing association by council tenant and property

In its efforts to expand tenure transfer in the 1988 Act, the government also provided funds to encourage the voluntary transfer of stock by local authorities themselves. Since 1988, there have been a number of large-scale, landlord-initiated transfers, known as *large-scale voluntary transfers* (LSVT). By April 1996, almost fifty English councils had (with the balloted consent of their tenants) transferred *all* their housing stock to housing associations. Usually, these have been newly created associations, funded in the same ways as existing associations. Thus, while the public sector pays some of the costs via housing association grant (HAG), the rest of the finance has to be raised from the private sector. This may partly explain why LSVTs to date have been largely in English shire districts, with relatively few stock condition or management problems. By April 1995, LSVT had involved the transfer of some 178,546 dwellings, at a transfer price of £1,618.6 million (Wilcox, 1996).

In contrast to the relative success of the LSVT scheme in England, in Scotland by the end of 1996 there had been only one LSVT (Berwickshire). However, smaller scale transfers have taken place, often to community-based housing associations (unique to Scotland, these are managed by a locally based committee). Scottish Homes has provided substantial HAG funding for transfers, and has itself transferred over 18,000 homes from its own (ex-Scottish Special Housing Association) stock.

The local authority must use the proceeds of LSVT to repay housing debt, with any remaining sums available for other purposes (but see more recent changes to Treasury rules, identified below). LSVT does not free councils of their statutory obligations to those in housing need, such as the homeless, but these obligations may be met by nomination rights to the new association, or the local authority may maintain its own accommodation for this purpose. Many have made large sums available to the new association via local authority HAG, to fund essential repairs and rehabilitation.

Why has LSVT proved attractive to some local authorities?

A key issue for debate in relation to housing finance is the restrictive role of the public sector borrowing requirement (PSBR), and the government's definitions of public spending (see Chapter 1). Most of local authorities' funds for capital spending on social housing are *borrowed*, predominantly from private sector sources. Only a small part comes from grants from central government or from rent (revenue) income. However, because of the way the PSBR is defined at present, local authority capital expenditure on housing counts as government borrowing and, as a result, has been subject to severe restrictions by a government committed to its reduction. In contrast, while the grants made to housing associations in the form of HAG/SHG count as part of public expenditure, any private finance which they borrow does not form part of the PSBR. If council stock is transferred to a housing association, as part of a *large-scale voluntary transfer*, for example, then the borrowed funds used to finance this lie beyond central government control. This has provided much of the impetus for councils which have already transferred some or all of their stock through LSVT.

Definitions of public spending

In the United Kingdom, definitions of public spending include spending by public corporations. These are organisations which are owned by the public sector but which operate independently, with their own management boards. They remain accountable to the government but are free, largely, to determine operational and strategic issues (under general, political direction). The most well-known public corporations were the nationalised industries of gas, water, telecommunications and electricity, prior to privatisation. A key incentive for their sale to private ownership was to free them of what was viewed as interfering, political control but also to free them to borrow and invest outside of government borrowing controls. These industries have since been able to expand investment significantly.

In much of the rest of Europe, public spending is defined as expenditure by central and local governments only. Instead of the PSBR, there is a *general government financial deficit* or GGFD. If the United Kingdom were to adopt this approach, public corporations would lie outside public sector borrowing controls. This would enable councils to set up some form of public corporations to run their social housing, freed from central government borrowing constraints, but with the advantage of remaining fully under the political control of the council. However, this seems unlikely to occur, at least in the near future, since neither the Conservative or Labour parties currently support it.

The costs of LSVT

Apart from the cost of the HAG/SHG subsidy, there are additional costs to the public sector of LSVT transfers. The DoE can no longer force LSVT councils, through reduced revenue subsidy, to subsidise housing benefit costs from their housing revenue accounts (see Chapter 3). As a result, LSVTs have resulted in rising housing benefit costs for the Treasury. In response to this, the government now imposes a 20 per cent levy on any LSVT receipts which remain after all housing debt has been cleared. This levy had raised £77.5 million by March 1995 (Wilcox, 1996). A limit to the size of the transfer has been imposed, which will force any large council housing providers to split their stock on transfer in future. This is an attempt to control the future magnitude of the costs to the Treasury of LSVT.

Estates renewal challenge fund

A more recent initiative to expand LSVT to more problematic, run-down estates in urban areas is the DoE's estates renewal challenge fund (ERCF). Under this scheme, launched in November 1995, local authorities may bid (competitively) for funding to transfer highly run-down estates to new social landlords. The ERCF can fund essential repairs, and will subsidise the new landlord if the estate has a negative *tenanted market value* (TMV). The TMV, the assumed 'market' value of the estate, takes account of the predicted net income (rents less essential management and maintenance costs), assuming that it stays in social ownership. The ERCF will also fund any set-up costs of the new landlord, but private finance must also be used. Over £300 million is planned to be available over three years. By June 1996, £174 million had been awarded to twelve schemes submitted by eleven local authorities. Of these, four or five plan to transfer the stock to a local housing company – a very new form of social landlord, part local authority controlled, which is examined next.

(iii) Transfer to a local housing company by council tenants and property

Despite the clear incentive to find ways around government constraints on capital spending, many councils are unwilling to consider LSVT because of the total loss of political control which it implies. One of the most recent and important ideas to emerge in response to this is the concept of *local housing companies* (LHCs).

This form of social housing, common in Sweden, has been promoted for some years by both the Chartered Institute of Housing and the Joseph Rowntree Foundation. Local housing companies are now permitted in the United Kingdom by the 1996 Housing Act, and will provide councils which wish to undertake capital spending on run-down stock with an alternative to LSVT, which (in contrast) permits them to retain some element of control.

What are local housing companies?

According to the Chartered Institute of Housing (1996, p. 35), a local housing company is an organisation which:

- has a constitution which makes it independent of the public sector;
- is accountable to the local authority, tenants and others;
- has a minority local authority interest;
- improves, manages and develops housing, usually transferred from the public sector.

Essentially, a new local housing company will buy stock from the local authority, and, like an LSVT association, this company can borrow private finance freed from the constraints of the PSBR. It is managed by a board, which no single group can control. The groups represented on the board will include the local authority, tenants, and business and professional groups, in roughly equal proportions. This is the essential difference to an LSVT – the local authority retains some interest and influence, albeit a minority one.

Local housing companies can be created only with the majority consent of both members (councillors) and tenants, the latter demonstrated in a formal ballot. This should ensure that LHCs are not forced upon tenants who wish to remain wholly in council tenure. Local housing companies are not-for-profit organisations, and maintaining rents at affordable levels will be a key objective. They must be approved by the Housing Corporation, Scottish Homes or Tai Cymru before they can purchase any properties or bid for SHG/HAG.

It is essential that local housing companies are able to attract not just HAG but also private finance if they are to achieve the goal of securing more funds for social housing. This seems to be entirely feasible: indeed, the Halifax Building Society has indicated (1996) that

'...many LHCs should prove to be very attractive propositions for lenders'

...and...

'the prospects are very good indeed for private finance for local housing companies'

However, they emphasise the importance of the quality of the LHC's business plan, to engender confidence in the private lender that the company can 'tackle the problems of the area'. (Business plans and their role are examined briefly in Chapter 3.)

As indicated above, some new LHCs are likely to emerge from the DoE's estates renewal challenge fund (ERCF) bids, awarded in 1996. One successful bidder was Sandwell MBC, which won over £40 million in ERCF funds for three LHCs, which (it is intended) will own, manage and refurbish 7,000 properties (out of a total stock of 45,000). This illustrates an important point in relation to LHCs – they need not include all of an authority's stock, so local authorities can retain their role as provider of some council housing if they wish.

However, there are undoubtedly some tenant concerns about LHCs. Some view them as simply another 'privatisation' initiative, designed merely to remove council housing from local authority management, within which, whatever its alleged faults, they feel largely secure. According to Marianne Hood, Director of TPAS (the Tenant Participation Advisory Service):

'the challenge to those thinking about LHCs is whether or not they are prepared to develop democratic, accountable bodies that really maintain a role for the local authority whilst giving real power and influence to tenants.' (Halifax Building Society, 1996.)

(iv) Transfer to housing association tenure by private tenure properties

An examination of the scope of tenure transfer policies would be incomplete without a recognition of policies intended both to retain private properties for renting and to expand their numbers. However, compared to efforts to persuade council tenants into other tenures, these have been very small scale.

The *housing associations as managing agents* (HAMA) scheme was intended to bring more properties into housing association management from the private sector, at least on a short-term basis, by persuading both existing and prospective private landlords that it was worth remaining in the sector if management were undertaken for them by a housing association. Essentially, the association lets and manages the property on behalf of the private landlord to homeless households which qualify for an association or local authority letting. It was hoped that the scheme would ensure an adequate supply of satisfactory short-term accommodation for this purpose. The private owner leases the property to the association and receives a negotiated sum for this. The association sets its own rent but management costs are subsidised by grant from the Housing Corporation and sometimes the local authority. However, take-up of this scheme has not been high.

As examined in Chapter 3, the *housing market package* provided once-only funding for housing associations to purchase private sector homes for rent in 1992/3, but this stemmed as much from a desire to boost private sector sales as to expand social renting. In Scotland, the *shared ownership off the shelf* (SOOTS) scheme similarly permitted associations to purchase properties from the private sector for sale to shared owners.

It could also be argued that the DIYSO scheme, examined above, transfers properties, at least temporarily, from the private sector to (partial) housing association tenure. Similarly, some conventional shared ownership properties, originally intended for owner occupation, were bought 'off the shelf' from private developers by associations in the early 1990s, when the collapse in property markets made their sale to outright purchasers difficult. It is likely to be some time before many of these transfer fully back to private tenure.

7.3 Can we ensure the affordability of social housing?

Prior to the 1980s, social housing in the United Kingdom, especially council housing, was offered at relatively low rents. In this way, the government attempted to ensure that households on lower than average incomes were able to afford decent housing. However, as examined in Chapter 4, the election of Margaret Thatcher in 1979 heralded a new era, in which public subsidy was to be targeted more accurately to those most in need. This spelt the end of the low rent policy for social housing, since low rents provided a general subsidy to all tenants, regardless of income. As a result, rents in both social tenures have been levered upwards throughout the 1980s and continuing into the 1990s, so that the affordability of social housing has now become a key issue for the providers of social housing. Successive government policies since 1979 have favoured owner occupation, so that the primary thrust of housing policy has been to increase the proportion of the population living within this tenure. As a result, there has been a concentration on tenure issues, with housing policy focusing heavily on tenure transfer initiatives (see above), to the detriment of concerns about the standard and affordability of accommodation available.

Indeed, the Conservative government's faith in the market as a mechanism for setting the price of housing resulted in the situation where no official government definition of affordability was been offered (Malpass and Murie, 1994). Instead, reliance was placed on the housing benefit system to support those households which could not afford the rising rents in social housing.

Defining affordability

The Chartered Institute of Housing has commented that there are a number of key variables affecting affordability. They point to four main items which will determine whether accommodation is affordable.

- *Rent levels* will clearly have an impact on the ability of a tenant to afford accommodation.
- However, as the level of rent cannot be considered in isolation, there also needs to be consideration of the *net household income*.
- The *type of household* will have an impact with certain family types usually having less essential requirements on which to spend, and therefore more disposable income than others (i.e. the family make-up, whether couple, single parent, elderly, etc.).
- Whether the household is *eligible for housing benefit*. The additional financial support afforded by housing benefit will have an obvious and direct impact on the ability of a household to afford particular accommodation at a particular price (Gibbs, 1992).

All of these factors will have an impact on whether particular accommodation is affordable.

Maclennan has offered the following definition of affordability:

'Affordability is concerned with securing some given standard of housing or different standards at a price or rent which does not impose...an unreasonable burden on household incomes....in broad terms affordability is assessed by the ratio of a chosen definition of household costs to a selected measure of household income in a given period.' (Maclennan and Williams, 1990.)

A number of suggestions have been made as to what this affordability ratio should be. The Association of Metropolitan Authorities has suggested that a rent level which cost 10 per cent of net household income is affordable, whilst the Housing Corporation has suggested that rents which cost as much as 35 per cent of net income are sustainable (Gibbs, 1992).

For his key research on the subject of assessing housing need, Bramley (1990) devised a technique for measuring affordability. He begins with a consideration of the price of new houses in a given geographical area, and compares this with income data to identify how many households can afford to sustain a mortgage necessary to buy at those prices. Bramley considered a mortgage of three times annual income for a single earner, and two and a half times joint income for households with two earners, to be a sustainable level of borrowing.

Bramley's research showed that, even allowing for low-cost home ownership and shared ownership schemes, there would still be nationally around a third of newly forming households who would be unable to afford owner occupation as an option, and would therefore be in need of some form of rented accommodation (Bramley, 1990).

The policy context

With the passing of the 1988 Housing Act the government set out to achieve a number of aims. Among these was the separation of the local authority and housing association sectors, allying associations with the private rented sector, creating a larger and growing 'independent rented sector'.

The Act expanded the range of landlords whose tenancies would be 'assured', and therefore subject to 'market rents' rather than 'fair rents'. As such, those private and housing association tenancies which commenced after the enactment of the 1988 Act (from 15 January 1989) do not enjoy the protection of the fair rents system.

Under the fair rents system a tenant would be entitled to a rent officer assessment of the rent due, which would be registered and would remain the maximum legally chargeable rent for the property until the property was due for reassessment after two years. The new system of market rents allowed rents to be set by landlords with tenants having a right of appeal to a local rent assessment committee to set a *market rent*.

In addition to the expansion of assured tenancies to new lets within this sector, the increasing privatisation of housing associations was further underlined by changes to the arrangement for funding new association developments.

The reduction in levels of housing association grant meant that those associations who wished to continue developing had to take on increased levels of borrowing from private financial markets, which has resulted in growing pressure to increase rents in order to meet the additional costs of private funding. One of the government's stated aims in introducing these changes was to give associations more freedom to borrow privately to enable them to increase levels of new development as they took over the role of main provider of new social rented accommodation from the local authorities.

As examined in Chapter 3, local authority rents were levered up by changes to the arrangements for subsidising their housing revenue accounts – though, in general, local authority rents still remain below rent levels for association properties. At the same time, the local authorities' development programmes were reduced to the point where in 1989 for the first time ever associations produced more new dwellings than the councils, and there was increasing pressure on associations to assist authorities in meeting their responsibilities for housing the homeless. Becoming the main provider of new social rented family housing meant a change in role for many associations who had previously been involved in the development of special needs accommodation, complementing council provision.

The impact of the changing role

Research carried out by Page (1993) has shown that the upshot of this combination of factors has been a situation in which many associations are building new estates of family housing with rents at such levels that they are not affordable to those working and in receipt of low incomes. Instead, Page found, many new association dwellings can only be afforded by those who are dependent on welfare benefits, with the higher rents being covered by housing benefit payments. These findings were echoed in the results of research carried out by Whitehead *et al.* (1995), which suggested that as grant rates fell associations were finding that new development at affordable rents was becoming increasingly an impossibility. They found that between 1990 and 1995 larger, diverse associations had managed to keep rent increases down to 4 per cent, but the rents of small, younger specialist associations had risen by around 12 per cent.

An associated issue is the impact of higher rents on tenants' willingness to seek and secure employment. As explored in the section on housing benefit in Chapter 3, for many households without a wage earner (or with low wages), most or all of the rent will be met by housing benefit. The higher the rent, the larger the contribution of housing benefit to the household income. The effect of rising rents has been, therefore, to significantly expand the breadth and depth of the unemployment trap created by dependency on housing benefit, in that as rent levels increase:

• many more households become eligible for housing benefit;

and

• it becomes necessary for each of these households to earn ever higher wages to escape benefit dependency.

Recent research by Ford and Kempson (1996) set out to explore the extent to which housing costs influence the wages that people seek and hence the employment that they are willing take. Whilst the research found that non-economic factors will often play a part in the decision to accept work – in some cases the commitment to work over-rode any consideration of likely income when deciding whether to take a job – in half of their respondents, people made an economic calculation and adhered to it when assessing employment opportunities. For some households, then, this research confirms the deepening of the unemployment trap, in that the higher the rent, the higher the wage needed to make it worthwhile for that tenant to take up employment.

Alongside this growing problem, research by Page (1993) found that the pressure to provide general needs accommodation linked to the changing financial regime has caused housing associations to try to achieve economies of scale, resulting in the production of larger housing estates than had been traditional within the tenure. Clearly, this is likely to have significant implications for the management of these larger estates, mainly populated by families who are trapped in unemployment by their dependency on benefits. The resources needed to collect rent and deal with arrears are likely to increase, as the associated poverty of many such families will mean more difficulty for them in meeting any payments which do not attract benefit. It might be expected that levels of turnover, and therefore void rates, could increase due both to the high cost of rents on such an estate and the stigmatisation that inevitably accrues to an area with a large proportion of unemployed tenants. Other costs in terms of estate management and environmental management are also likely to be higher than in traditional smaller association developments.

Recent restrictions on housing benefit for single households aged under 25 (who, for housing benefit purposes, are now assumed to be sharing) will create even greater problems of affordability for single people. Housing benefit is restricted to the average cost of a room in a shared house, so those with self-contained housing will find their benefit cut significantly, forced to move or to reduce expenditure on other items. This may have an impact also on the providers. Social landlords which provide self-contained accommodation for this group may be forced to consider offering shared lettings if the regulations are eventually applied to them – a type of provision previously supplied by social housing providers only for some special needs groups or as temporary, hostel-type accommodation. The problems of managing shared accommodation are vast, and as a result, social landlords may well be reluctant to be drawn into this area, or may have to withdraw from providing for young single households.

7.4 New Labour: new directions?

As this book was going to print, the general election in the United Kingdom on 1 May 1997 gave a landslide victory to a new Labour Government. This is likely to result in some changes in housing policy over the coming five years. This section briefly explores what these changes might be and considers their possible impact on social housing.

Housing did not gain much attention in the General Election campaign. However, the Labour Party Manifesto expressed the following views:

"Most families want to own their own homes. We will also support efficiently run social and private rented sectors offering quality and choice. The Conservatives' failure on housing has been twofold. The two-thirds of families who own their homes have suffered a massive increase in insecurity over the last decade, with record mortgage arrears, record negative equity and record repossessions. And the Conservatives' lack of a housing strategy has led to the virtual abandonment of social housing, the growth of homelessness, and a failure to address fully leaseholder reform. All these are the Tory legacy."

On the rented sector the Labour manifesto said;

"We support a three-way partnership between the public, private and housing association sectors to promote good social housing. With Labour, capital receipts from the sale of council houses, received but not spent by local councils, will be re-invested in building new houses and rehabilitating old ones. This will be phased to match the capacity of the building industry and to meet the requirements of prudent economic management.

We also support effective schemes to deploy private finance to improve the public housing stock and to introduce greater diversity and choice. Such schemes should only go ahead with the support of the tenants concerned: we oppose the government's threat to hand over council housing to private landlords without the consent of tenants and with no guarantees on rents or security of tenure.

We value a revived private rented sector. We will provide protection where most needed: for tenants in houses in multiple occupation. There will be a proper system of licensing by local authorities which will benefit tenants and responsible landlords alike.

On homelessness, the manifesto said;

"Homelessness has more than doubled under the Conservatives. Today more than 40, 000 families in England are in expensive temporary accommodation. The government, in the face of Labour opposition, has removed the duty on local authorities to find permanent housing for homeless families. We will impose a new duty on local authorities to protect those who are homeless through no fault of their own and are in priority need.

There is no more powerful symbol of Tory neglect in our society today than young people without homes living rough on the streets. Young people emerging from care without any family support are particularly vulnerable. We will attack the problem in two principal ways: the phased release of capital receipts from council house sales will increase the stock of housing for rent; and our welfare-to-work programme will lead the young unemployed into work and financial independence.

Source; Labour Party Manifesto 1997, Internet version at http://www.labourwin97.org.uk

In the light of these manifesto commitments, what changes might the new Labour Government make?

Capital receipts

The Labour Party gave a firm commitment to the phased release of capital receipts from council house sales, and the new government's Consultation Paper issued in June 1997 proposed to permit their release over the next 5 years. As we saw in Chapter 3 local authorities had been restricted to using only 25% of their capital receipts for new capital spending, but the new Labour policy suggests that over the next few years the estimated £5 billion in unspent capital receipts will be made available to spend on new housing and improvements to existing stock.

 . However, the areas with greatest housing need (particularly, run down, inner-city areas) are often those with fewest capital receipts. As a result, the Government intends to target resources on areas of greatest need by ensuring that two-thirds of the available capital receipts are allocated on the basis of need, with one-third allocated on the basis of the capital receipts held by the local authority. Rather than transferring receipts from one local authority to another, however, areas with greatest need and few capital receipts will be allocated resources in the form of additional supplementary credit approvals (see Chapter 3).

The release of capital receipts will be a welcome addition to local authorities' capital spending but it is unlikely to make a substantial contribution to meeting the housing needs. For example, the backlog of repairs alone is estimated at over £20 billion and the receipts could probably build up to 140,000 new homes over the 5 year period, compared to the 100,000 new homes each year estimated to be required. The use of capital receipts, whilst welcome, is not the panacea for all of the funding problems of local authorities and it is likely that tenure transfer policies, such as LSVT or Local Housing Companies, will remain popular options for local authorities in spite of greater flexibility on the use of receipts.

In a related move, the Labour Government has reversed the previous government's decision to allocate future Annual Capital Guidelines solely at the discretion of the relevant government office. From 1998/99, resources will be allocated 50% on need and 50% on discretion.

Homelessness

Chapter 5 examined the significant amendments made to the homelessness legislation by the 1996 Housing Act, effectively changing the obligations of local authorities to homeless people. From a situation where the local authority had to provide permanent accommodation for homeless persons, the 1996 Act amended this requirement to the provision of temporary accommodation for a two year period. In addition, the rules relating to the establishment of local authority waiting lists did not give any priority to homeless persons. During the passage of the Act the Labour opposition vehemently objected to these provisions, so it was not surprising that one of the first acts of the incoming Labour administration was to amend the regulations. These amendments enabled local authorities to give reasonable preference to homeless persons, thus enabling homeless people to have much quicker access to permanent accommodation.

The government is also promoting its 'welfare to work' policies in an attempt to encourage young people into work. It may also attempt further to reduce social housing rent increases in an effort to combat the poverty and unemployment traps which were described in Chapter 3.

CCT and Best Value

In the months prior to the general election the shadow Labour Housing Minister, Nick Raynsford, seemed to commit the Labour Party to an early abolition of the CCT rules (see Chapter 6). However the incoming Housing and Local Government Minister, Hilary Armstrong, has been less forthcoming and has said that CCT will remain for the time being, although she agreed to establish a number of pilot studies to examine alternative approaches to achieving 'best value' in housing management.

New Labour seems to be committed to the benefits of competition in housing and appears unwilling to replace CCT until it has an alternative regime in place which will demonstrate value for money. This has come as a grave disappointment for many housing professionals who had hoped that the new Labour Government would lead to the abolition of CCT rules.

Harold Wilson once said that a week is a long time in politics and over the coming years it is likely that Labour's housing policies will further develop. Readers should keep abreast of developments by reading the housing press, but the following are likely to be key features of the new Labour administration's future housing policies:

- a continuing commitment to the use of private finance in housing with support for housing associations and new registered social landlords
- a continuation of the LSVT route and the development of Local Housing Companies
- less emphasis on low cost home ownership initiatives
- greater emphasis on reducing rent levels in an effort to overcome the poverty and unemployment traps
- increasing emphasis on improving the quality of housing management in all sectors

---

7.5 In this changing context, what is the future role of housing managers?

Polarisation

Earlier sections have shown that as a result of residualisation, the least well-off and least powerful sections of the population can be found concentrated in the social housing sector. And, as new tenants for both council and housing association properties are increasingly the poorest, most vulnerable members of society, the more affluent tenants are leaving. The biggest exit route to date has been through the right to buy but in addition many relatively affluent council and housing association tenants have left their homes, attracted into owner occupation through other tenure transfer schemes as well as the effect of rising rents making social tenures less affordable. Together, these trends contribute to the process of *polarisation* whereby the poorest are consigned to social housing with the more affluent choosing to opt for owner occupation.

Housing stress

This process of residualisation and polarisation places enormous pressures on housing organisations in that they increasingly are having to provide services to the most disadvantaged groups in our society. And these groups are increasingly concentrated on large local authority estates and in new housing association developments, which can:

'become "benefit ghettos" where almost everyone is dependent on benefits, and economic and social deprivation combine to create problems such as vandalism, crime, racial harassment and drug abuse.' (Chartered Institute of Housing, 1993.)

Whilst it is accepted that these people are in acute housing need, this concentration of the most vulnerable in our society in social housing brings with it additional problems which housing managers have to face; such as how to deal with unemployment on housing estates, how to deal with the extreme poverty suffered by many households, how to handle the problems of crime, drugs and prostitution, how to deal with the chronic underachievement of many children living on social housing estates and how to deal with the despair which many households face.

Indeed as these issues have become more and more the bread and butter of housing managers a real debate has begun to open up about the nature of housing management. Perhaps the definition of housing management set out at the beginning of Chapter 5, that housing management was to do with rent collection, letting houses and repairing houses, is no longer as relevant as perhaps it once was. Indeed the Chartered Institute of Housing has written that:

'investment in social housing is too low, rents are rising fast and tenants and potential tenants are getting poorer – so that not only is demand for available homes higher, but social housing becomes increasingly the tenure for people with problems. This puts new pressures on housing managers to adopt a wider social role.' (Chartered Institute of Housing, 1993.)

In this context the Chartered Institute of Housing talks about two conflicting views of the way in which housing management should be undertaken.

The contractual role

The first is what David Clapham (1987) has called the contractual role. It refers to a model of housing management which focuses solely on the management of the property, where housing managers concentrate on the key property management tasks; collecting the rent, dealing with repairs and letting properties.

If tenants have additional welfare needs (which of course they do) then these are best dealt with by other agencies such as social services or primary health care services. Of course, in this model, housing officers need to understand how these caring agencies operate but they should not attempt to step into the breach and provide these services as part of their landlord role. The obvious attraction of this approach is that it delineates housing management quite neatly and does not attempt to cross over any real boundaries.

The social welfare role

The opposing view is what the Chartered Institute calls the 'social welfare' role which suggests that in contemporary housing management it is not possible for councils or housing associations to separate out the social aspects from the property management role. The social welfare role will include activities such as:

> '...advice on benefits, debt counselling, preventing racial harassment, care in the community, dealing with dogs, traffic or litter, welfare aspects of wardens' work and so on. In some areas these have become a major part of the workload.' (Chartered Institute of Housing, 1993.)

This view accepts the contemporary reality of housing management and suggests that if housing managers do not get involved in these types of areas then they will be unable to perform their core functions properly. For example, if social housing landlords want to maximise rent collection rates and reduce arrears they may find it cost effective to devote resources to debt counselling or welfare benefits advice to maximise the incomes of tenants who are in arrears.

However, the fact that such social welfare functions are not seen as core housing management activities is part of the problem. In some areas, particularly when there is pressure to reduce costs, it is tempting to say that housing staff should reduce their welfare role and return to their core housing management functions. Indeed one of the dilemmas for local authorities preparing for CCT is to decide how much of the social welfare role to include in contract specifications. Such work is often expensive and some would argue that it is the responsibility of other agencies and may therefore not be included in tender specifications. But the reality is that unless the work is done by housing managers it is unlikely to be done by anyone else and the failure to do it will have a very serious impact on the core functions. For example, as noted above, a failure of housing managers to deal with the problems of multiple debt and to offer assistance in debt counselling may lead to rent arrears getting worse and tenants prioritising, perhaps wrongly, other debts in preference to paying their housing debts. Trying to work with tenants, other agencies and the police to improve the image and security of an estate may have more impact on the number of empty properties than simply concentrating on improving the response times of contractors on repairs to empty properties.

This debate about the nature of housing management has also been exercising the minds of housing managers within housing associations. If anything the problems of affordability and residualisation with all of the associated problems are even greater for housing associations, with their high rents as a result of the reductions in HAG and the fact that increasingly the new lettings which associations make are to the most vulnerable and disadvantaged in our society. The National Federation of Housing Associations published a discussion paper in 1994 about housing management under the title '*Value Added*' where it indicated that housing associations would increasingly find that the competitive process faced by associations would inevitably bring the housing management service under closer scrutiny and that housing managers would face increasing pressures.

The discussion paper made reference to issues of rising rents and the associated problems of affordability discussed earlier, and the fact that housing associations increasingly were housing homeless and vulnerable households often in large concentrations on particular estates, that more tenants were facing long-term unemployment and poverty and that associations through care in the community were assisting even more vulnerable people with housing (National Federation of Housing Associations, 1994). However, even as these pressures were increasing on housing managers the Housing Corporation and government are concerned to reduce the costs of the housing management service in an attempt to keep rent increases down and rents to affordable levels. Of course these concerns are in conflict: housing management in the current context almost inevitably requires more resources than previously.

The NFHA also echoed the Chartered Institute of Housing in suggesting that housing management may well have additional objectives outside of its core property management role. It suggested that housing management might also be about:

- enabling the tenant to retain and maximise the benefits of the occupation of their homes;
- protecting against and providing support in the event of harassment;
- supporting and advising low-income households;
- providing affordable housing, particularly in relation to incentives to find and retain employment;
- coordinating care services to vulnerable tenants;
- being responsive to tenants' needs and expectations;
- helping to provide additional services that sustain communities under stress. (National Association of Housing Associations, 1994.)

This emphasis on the social role of housing management does not undermine the importance of traditional housing management. Indeed collecting the rents, letting the homes and repairing the properties remain key tasks for all housing managers. What it does mean, however, is that in the future the responsibilities of housing managers are increasingly going beyond these core tasks and that to be effective housing managers will need to adopt a wider social role in attempting to sustain the communities in which their tenants live. This will mean that housing managers will need a greater understanding of the context in which they are working. It will mean housing managers understanding the debates about costs of new schemes and rent levels. These are issues in which they must be involved and cannot be left solely to specialist finance or development staff. It will also bring additional pressures on housing managers as inevitably there will be a continued emphasis on cost effectiveness in service delivery which may mean for many organisations that as the housing managment task gets bigger and more demanding there may not be an increase in resources to deal with this. This will challenge housing managers to make the best use of their available resources to ensure that effective housing management will make a difference to the communities they serve – and either contribute to them prospering or declining.

Further reading

Donnison, D. and Maclennan, D. (eds) (1991) *The Housing Service of the Future*, Longman/CIH, Harlow.

Hawkworth, J. and Wlicox, S. (1995) *Challenging the Conventions*, Chartered Institute of Housing, Coventry.

Wilcox, S., Bramley, G., Ferguson, A., Perry, J. and Woods, C. (1993) *Local Housing Companies; New Opportunities for Council Housing*.

Zitron, J. (1996) *Housing Companies*, Chartered Institute of Housing, Coventry.

REFERENCES

Suggestions for further reading, in addition to the texts referred to here, are listed at the end of each chapter.

Audit Commission (1986a) *Improving Council House Maintenance*, HMSO, London.

Audit Commission (1986b) *Managing the Crisis in Council Housing*, HMSO, London.

Aughton, H. and Malpass, P. (1994) *Housing Finance: A Basic Guide*, Shelter, London.

Audit Commission (1997) *Local Authority Performed Indicators 1995/96*, HMSO, London.

Bramley, G. (1990) *Bridging the Affordability Gap*, BEC Publications, Bristol.

Centre for Housing Policy, University of York (1993) *Managing Social Housing*, HMSO, London. (Referred to as the York Report.)

Centre for Housing Research, University of Glasgow (1989) *The Nature and Effectiveness of Housing Management in England*, HMSO, London.

Central Housing Advisory Committee (1969) *Council Housing: Purposes, Procedures and Priorities*, HMSO, London. (Referred to as the Cullingworth Report.)

Chartered Institute of Housing (1992) *Rent Levels, Rent Structures and Affordability: A Guide for Local Authorities and Housing Associations*, Chartered Institute of Housing, Coventry.

Chartered Institute of Housing (1993) *More than Bricks and Mortar*, Chartered Institute of Housing, Coventry.

Chartered Institute of Housing (1995) *Housing Management Standards Manual*, Chartered Institute of Housing, Coventry.

Chartered Institute of Housing (1996) *Housing*, Sept, p.35.

CHAS (1994) *All in One Place – The British Housing Story 1976–1993*, 2nd edn, Catholic Housing Aid Society (CHAS) London.

CIPFA (1995) *Housing Rent Arrears and Benefit Statistics*, CIPFA, London.

Clapham, D. (1987) in Clapham, D. and English, J. (eds), *Public Housing – Current Trends and Future Developments*, Croom Helm, London.

Cole, I., Arnold, P. and Windle, K. (1991) in Donnison, D. and Maclennan, D. (eds) *The Housing Service of the Future*, Longman, Harlow.

Coleman, A. (1990) *Utopia on Trial: Vision and Reality in Planning Housing*, Hilary Shipman, 2nd edn, London.

Coles, A. (1991), The Future of the Housing Market, *Housing Review*, 43 (1).

Commission for Racial Equality (1991) *Code of Practice in Rented Housing*, CRE, London.

Cole, Arnold and Windle (1991) in Donnison, D. and Maclennan, D. (eds), *The Housing Service of the Future*, Longman, Harlow.

Cullingworth (1969) *see entry for* Central Housing Advisory Committee.

Department of the Environment (1990) *Efficiency Report and Action Plan: Training, Education and Performance in Housing Management*, Department of the Environment, London.

Department of the Environment (1992) *Competing for Quality in Housing*, Department of the Environment, London.

Duncan, S. and Kirby, K. (1983) *Preventing Rent Arrears*, HMSO, London.

English House Condition Survey 1991 (1993) HMSO, London.

Ford, J. and Kempson, E., (1996) *Into Work? The Impact of Housing Costs and the Benefit System on People's Decision to Work*, Joseph Rowntree Foundation, York.

Forrest, R. and Murie, A. (1988) *Selling the Welfare State*, Routledge, London.

Gibbs, J. (1992) *Rent Levels, Rent Structures and Affordability*, Institute of Housing: London.

Government Statistical Office (1995) *Social Trends*, 25th edn, HMSO, London.

Government White Paper (1987) Housing: the Government's Proposals, HMSO, London.

Government White Paper (1989) *Caring for People: Community Care in the Next Decade and Beyond*, HMSO, London.

Government White Paper (1995) *Our Future Homes: Opportunity, Choice, Responsibility – the Government Housing Policy for England and Wales*, HMSO, London.

Gray, B. (1994) *Housing Research Summary 24*, HMSO, London.

Gray, B. *et al.* (1994) *Rent Arrears in Local Authorities and Housing Associations in England*, HMSO, London.

Green, H. and Hansbro, J. (1995) *Housing in England 1993 to 1994*, HMSO, London.

Griffiths Report (1988) *Community Care: Agenda for Action*, HMSO, London.

Halifax Building Society (1996) Local Housing Companies: Have They Anything to Offer Tenants, *Local Housing Companies Newsletter*, Issue One, Autumn.

Holmans, A. *et al.* (1994) 'Trends in the Size of the Private Rented Sector in England', *Housing Finance*, No.2.

Housing and Construction Statistics 1984–1994 Great Britain (1996), HMSO, London.

Housing Corporation (1994a), *The Tenants' Guarantee*, Housing Corporation, London.

Housing Corporation (1994b) *Key Facts*, Housing Corporation, London.

Housing Corporation/Audit Commission (1995) *Homing in on Performance*, Housing Corporation, London.

Housing Corporation (1995) *Registry Statistics*, Housing Corporation, London.

Housing Review (1987), 36 (1), January to February.

Institute of Housing (1972) *The Comprehensive Housing Service; Organisation and Functions*, Institute of Housing, London.

Joseph Rowntree Foundation (1995a) *Rents and Risks; Investing in Housing Associations*, Joseph Rowntree Foundation, York.

Joseph Rowntree Foundation (1995b) *Search*, Autumn.

Kemp, P. (1995) *Private Tenants and Restrictions in Rents for Housing Benefit*, Housing Research Findings No. 144, Joseph Rowntree Foundation, York.

Maclennan, D. and Williams, R. (eds) (1990) *Affordable Housing in Britain and America*, Joseph Rowntree Foundation, York.

Maclennan, D., Gibb, K. and More, A. (1991) *Fairer Subsidies, Faster Growth,* Joseph Rowntree Foundation, York.

Malpass, P. (1996) The Poor Get Poorer, *Housing,* May.

Malpass, P. and Murie, A. (1994) *Housing Policy and Practice,* 4th edn, Macmillan, Basingstoke.

National Federation of Housing Associations (1988) *Development: A Guide for Housing Associations,* NFHA.

National Federation of Housing Associations (1994) *Value Added,* NFHA London.

Newman, O. (1972) *Defensible Space: Crime Prevention through Urban Design,* Macmillan, Basingstoke.

Netherlands Ministry of Housing, Physical Planning and the Environment (1992) *Statistics on Housing in the European Community.*

Office of Population Censuses and Surveys (1984) *Survey into Recently Moved Households,* HMSO, London.

Office of Population Censuses and Surveys (1993) *General Household Survey 1991,* HMSO, London.

Office of Population Censuses and Surveys (1994) *Census 1991,* HMSO, London.

Office of Population Censuses and Surveys (1995) *General Household Survey 1994,* HMSO, London.

Page, D. (1993) *Building for Communities,* Joseph Rowntree Foundation, York.

Platt, D. (1995) *Housing and Community Care in Housing – Today and Tomorrow,* 2nd suppl to the *Guide to Housing,* 3rd edn, Mary E H Smith (ed.), Housing Centre Trust, Cambridge.

Power, A. (1987) *Property Before People - The Management of Twentieth Century Council Housing,* Alan and Unwin, London.

Power, A. and Tunstall, R. (1995) *Swimming Against the Tide: Progress or Polarisation on 20 Unpopular Estates,* Joseph Rowntree Foundation, York.

Prescott-Clarke, P., Clemens, S., Park, A. (1994), *Routes into Local Authority Housing,* HMSO, London.

Priority Estates Project (1987), *PEP Guide to Local Housing Management,* Vol. 2, *The PEP Experience,* Department of the Environment, London.

Public Expenditure Survey report (1995/96), HMSO, London.

Public Services Yearbook (1995/96) Public Finance Foundation, Pitman Publishing, London.

Registrar General's Mid-Year Estimates and Projections (1995) HMSO, London.

Report of the Parker Morris Committee (1961) HMSO, London.

Scottish Accounts Commission (1991) *Tenants Rent Arrears – a Problem?,* Scottish Accounts Commission.

Scottish Homes (1994a) *Redefining Housing Association Business Plans,* Research Report 38, Scottish Homes, Edinburgh.

Scottish Homes (1994b) *Scottish Home's Future Relationship with Housing Associations and Cooperatives,* Scottish Homes, Edinburgh.

Scottish Homes (1995) *Scottish House Condition Survey,* Scottish Homes, Edinburgh.

Scottish Homes (1995/96), *Statistical Report,* Scottish Homes, Edinburgh.

Smith, M.E.H. (1989) *Guide to Housing,* 3rd edn, Housing Centre Trust, Cambridge.

Smith, R. and Merrett, S. (1988) *The Challenge of Empty Housing*, SAUS, Bristol.

Social Trends (1995), HMSO, London.

Spicker, P. (1985) Legacy of Octavia Hill, *Housing Magazine,* June 1985.

Tai Cymru (1996) *Welsh Housing Associations in 1996*, Tai Cymru, Cardiff.

Wainwright, S. (1987) *Tenants in Serious Rent Arrears; Some Recent Research Findings.*

Webster, D. (1994) Breaking the Mould, *Housing*, 30 (2) March 1994.

Whitehead, C., *et al.* (1995) *Rents and Risks: Investing in Housing Associations*, Joseph Rowntree Foundation, York.

Wilcox, S. (1995) *Housing Finance Review 1994/95,* Joseph Rowntree Foundation, York.

Wilcox, S. (1996) *Housing Finance Review 1995/96,* Joseph Rowntree Foundation, York.

Wilcox, S. (1997) *Housing Finance Review 1996/97,* Joseph Rowntree Foundation, York.

Willmot, P. (1963) *The Evolution of a Community: a study of Dagenham after 40 years*, Routledge and Kegan Paul, London.

Willmot, P. and Young, M. (1957) *Family and Kinship in East London,* Routledge and Kegan Paul, London.

York (1993) *see entry for* Centre for Housing Policy University of York.

INDEX